SEXUALLY ABUSED AND ABUSING CHILDREN IN SUBSTITUTE CARE

LIVING AWAY FROM HOME: STUDIES IN RESIDENTIAL CARE

Other titles in the series

SEXUALLY ABUSED AND ABUSING CHILDREN IN SUBSTITUTE CARE

Elaine Farmer
Sue Pollock

JOHN WILEY & SONS
Chichester · New York · Weinheim · Brisbane · Singapore · Toronto

Other Wiley Editorial Offices

John Wiley & Sons, Inc., 605 Third Avenue,
New York, NY 10158-0012, USA

WILEY-VCH Verlag GmbH, Pappelallee 3,
D-69469 Weinheim, Germany

Jacaranda Wiley Ltd, 33 Park Road, Milton,
Queensland 4064, Australia

John Wiley & Sons (Asia) Pte Ltd, 2 Clementi Loop #02-01,
Jin Xing Distripark, Singapore 129809

John Wiley & Sons (Canada) Ltd, 22 Worcester Road,
Rexdale, Ontario M9W 1L1, Canada

Library of Congress Cataloging-in-Publication Data

Farmer, Elaine.
    Sexually abused and abusing children in substitute care / Elaine
Farmer and Sue Pollock.
        p.   cm. — (Living away from home)
    Includes bibliographical references and index.
    ISBN 0-471-98478-7 (alk. paper)
    1. Sexually abused children—Institutional care.   2. Child
molesters—Institutional care.   3. Adolescent psychotherapy—
Residential treatment.   I. Pollock, Sue.   II. Title.   III. Series.
RJ504.5.F36   1998
618.92'85836—dc21   98–36241
                                                   CIP

British Library Cataloguing in Publication Data

A catalogue record for this book is available from the British Library

ISBN 0-471-98478-7

Typeset in 10/12pt Palatino by Dorwyn Ltd, Rowlands Castle, Hants
Printed and bound in Great Britain by Bookcraft (Bath) Ltd, Midsomer Norton, Somerset
This book is printed on acid-free paper responsibly manufactured from sustainable
forestation, in which at least two trees are planted for each one used for paper production.

CONTENTS

ABOUT THE AUTHORS

Dr Elaine Farmer is a Lecturer in the School for Policy Studies at Bristol University where she teaches on the courses in Social Work, Early Childhood Studies and the Masters Degree in Child Welfare. She spent several years as a social worker in the UK and Australia before moving into research and teaching. Her research interests include the reunification of separated children with their families, child protection and residential and foster care. She conducted studies in the Department of Health programme of research on Child Protection and the subsequent initiative on Residential Care. Her latest study is on the fostering task with behaviourally difficult adolescents and is part of a new research programme on Family Support. Her publications include *Trials and Tribulations: Returning Children from Local Authority Care to their Families* (HMSO, 1991), *Child Protection Practice: Private Risks and Public Remedies* (HMSO, 1995).

Sue Pollock is a Research Fellow in the School for Policy Studies at the University of Bristol where she combines teaching on the Diploma in Social Work and Early Childhood Studies Degree with research interests in parenting and child care. She also works as a social work practitioner, counsellor and independent trainer specialising in work with sexual abuse and is particularly committed to the development of links between research, teaching and practice. She has undertaken research in the recent Department of Health initiative on Residential Child Care and is currently working on a study of young men's transition to fatherhood as part of a new Economic and Social Research Council research programme on Youth, Citizenship and Social Change.

FOREWORD

We are pleased to have the opportunity to provide the foreword to this book, which is one of a series of publications which, we are sure, will prove to be a significant contribution to thinking in both the practice and management of the care of children who need to live away from home.

The group of studies about residential care was commissioned to address key concerns arising from public inquiries, such as the Utting (Children in the Public Care) and Pindown Inquiries, and to provide a balanced account of what life is like for children and staff in the majority of children's homes in the UK in the 1990s.

Twelve linked research studies were commissioned by the Department of Health in the period 1990–94: (a thirteenth – that of David Berridge and Isabelle Brodie – was not commissioned by the Department). These research studies came in the wake of the implementation of the Children Act 1989 and its Regulations and Guidance, which provided significant new safeguards for children living away from home. Additional government action to protect these children was taken following the publication of the reports "Children in the Public Care", "Accommodating Children", "Another Kind of Home" and "Choosing with Care", notably through the publications of the Support Force for Children's Residential Care and circulars issued by the relevant Departments of State. However, as Sir William Utting tells us in his second report "People Like Us", published in 1997, providing safe and caring settings for children looked after away from home remains a significant challenge for the 1990s.

This book, taken together with the overview publication, and the others in the series, contains lessons for all those concerned with children and young people living away from home, who are the responsibility of all of us.

Carolyn Davies, *Department of Health*
Lesley Archer, *University of York*
Leslie Hicks, *University of York*
Mike Little, *Dartington Social Research Unit*
—Editors

ACKNOWLEDGEMENTS

This research was funded by the Department of Health. We are very grateful for this assistance and for the help of our research liaison officer, Dr Carolyn Davies.

We are indebted to the two local authorities and their staff who enabled us to undertake this research. It is not easy to have one's work scrutinised, particularly on such a sensitive topic, but in spite of this we were given assistance wherever we went. We are also extremely grateful to the young people, residential workers, foster carers and social workers who talked to us at considerable length.

We were fortunate to have the assistance of Sue Rolfe from the School for Policy Studies at Bristol University who created the data base and entered the coded case file material as well as conducting some of the interviews. We are also grateful to Karen John and Carrie Hughes who analysed some of the measures and contributed two chapters in the original report. Lorraine Bush, Pam Freeman and Sarah Jackson gave us particular assistance with summarising the interviews and Jo Parker's early work on transcribing and summarising interviews was invaluable. Our thanks go to Taghi Doostgharin who patiently undertook the coding and some early analysis of the Achenbach Child Behaviour Checklist and Youth Self Report. We are grateful to colleagues who gave us useful advice during the course of the study, in particular Elizabeth Monck and Bryn Williams from the Institute of Child Health in London and to members of our Advisory Group, some of whom also commented on our drafts, that is Jane Aldgate, Ann Gross, Jean Packman, John Rowlands, Gerrilyn Smith, Kathleen Taylor and Dorothy Whitaker. Roy Parker deserves especial thanks for his full and helpful comments on our drafts. We are also indebted to Jane Gibbons who generously gave her time and skills to doing part of the editing of the original report to make it ready for publication.

Finally, we would like to thank two members of our own team. We are very grateful to our consultant David Quinton who gave us valuable advice and encouragement throughout the project. We are also greatly indebted to Patricia Lees, our research support officer, who helped to analyse the material, contributed substantially to two of the chapters and assisted throughout with the organisation of the study. To her our warmest thanks.

I

ABOUT THE STUDY

LOOKING AFTER SEXUALLY ABUSED AND ABUSING CHILDREN: THE RESEARCH AND PRACTICE LITERATURE

BACKGROUND: WHY WAS THE STUDY NEEDED?

The placement of sexually abused children in substitute care poses particular challenges for all those involved. Caring for an abused and emotionally troubled child can be a demanding task for residential workers, foster carers and their families, and at the same time caregivers have become increasingly aware that they themselves may be subject to allegations of abuse by the children in their care (see, for example, National Foster Care Association, 1988; Lowe and Verity, 1989; Nixon and Hicks, 1989; Levy and Kahan, 1991; Williams and McCreadie, 1992; Kirkwood, 1993; Utting, 1997). Local authorities, in their turn, are exercised by the task of trying to maintain a stock of foster carers and residential workers who have sufficient training, experience and resilience to cope with the demands of these children, and by the difficulty of trying to match the specific needs of individual children with the availability of suitable placements (Utting, 1991; Rickford, 1992). Substantial concerns have also emerged about children who sexually abuse others, and how they should be managed in substitute care (Utting, 1991; National Children's Home, 1992; Utting, 1997).

Use of Substitute Care

Since the Cleveland Inquiry (Secretary of State for Social Services, 1988) there has been widespread recognition that when sexual abuse is discovered it is preferable to exclude an alleged abuser from the family rather than remove the child. There is some evidence that local authorities have heeded the advice of the inquiry, since NSPCC statistics on child abuse trends in England and Wales show that for children on the child protection register there has been a decline in the proportion looked after amongst those registered for sexual abuse (Creighton, 1992). However, in Farmer and Owen's study (1995), of those children on the child protection register for reasons of sexual abuse, exclusion of the abuser was effected in just under half of the cases but in over a quarter it was the child who was placed away from home, whilst in 13% both the abuser and the child left the family. In some cases the abuser could not be ousted or an assessment was made that the child's protection could only be assured by placement out of the family. In other cases the sexual abuse was only one of a number of problems that steered the child into out-of-home care.

It is clear then that substitute care placements are still sought for a number of sexually abused children when the abuse is discovered. In addition, it is well recognised that some children, who have been removed for other reasons, disclose their experience of sexual abuse some time after a placement has been made (Devine and Tate, 1991; Hollows, 1991). Over and above this, there is an increasing awareness that children may be sexually abused by adults or by other children whilst in substitute care or when outside its ambit during periods of absconding (see for example Ryan, McFadden and Wiencek, 1986; Nunno and Rindfleisch, 1991; Westcott, 1991; Westcott and Clement, 1992). The number of sexually abused children and adolescents in out-of-home care is therefore likely to be considerably greater than the number of children looked after by local authorities as a consequence of the discovery of their victimisation.

Previous Research on the Placement of Sexually Abused Children in Substitute Care

In spite of the challenges which they pose, little research attention has been paid to the placement of sexually abused children in substitute care, particularly in residential or boarding school settings. Still less is known about the placement of children who are themselves abusers.

One American study compared the adoptive placements of 35 sexually abused children with those of 113 children with no identified history of abuse. The findings showed that the sexually abused children experienced more moves when in care, increased frequency of disrupted adoptive placements, greater behavioural difficulties and more attachment problems than the comparison group (Livingstone Smith and Howard, 1994). Another study (Lie and McMurtry, 1991) compared 110 children placed in foster care as a result of sexual abuse with a matched sample of children who were fostered for other reasons. The sexually abused children left foster care for planned alternative permanent living arrangements at a significantly faster rate than the non-abused children, which suggested that the abuse was seen as a reason for attempts at restoration to their families to be abandoned.

The Management of Sexually Abused and Abusing Children in Substitute Care

With the exception of Macaskill's study (1991) of foster and adoptive placements, which did not set out to be representative, there has been little research on the management of sexually abused children who are looked after. There is even less work on dealing with abusing children in placement, but Farmer and Owen (1995) showed that particular difficulties arise in relation to their management, with marked differences in the type and level of intervention by social workers. In cases of sibling abuse, for example, practice varied markedly as to whether the abusing and abused siblings were separated or not, and if they were, whether the victim or abuser was moved out. When the abusing child or young person was removed from the family there was difficulty in finding an appropriate placement and considerable uncertainty about what treatment or intervention to provide. In those cases where children had been placed in a foster home with little or no recognition of their potential to display inappropriately sexualised or sexually abusing behaviour, the resources of foster families were strained to the utmost. It is also worth noting that some studies of children in foster care have found an association between placement failure and the sexual acting out of the foster child (Walsh, 1981, Fanshel, Finch and Grundy, 1990).

In contrast, there is a much larger research literature on abuse in care, much of it from the USA. However, there is a *practice literature* on managing sexually abused children in out-of-home care, almost all of which concerns foster care and little of which deals explicitly with adolescents. One recent publication covers these issues in respect of residential care (Scottish Office, 1995).

Preparation of Caregivers

Much of the practice literature emphasises the importance of adequate preparation of the caregivers. A number of authors stress that foster carers should be given full details of the circumstances and type of sexual abuse suffered by the child (McFadden, 1986; Nobbs and Jones, 1989;

Davis *et al*, 1991; Fitzgerald, 1991) including information about the progression of events that were part of the grooming process (McFadden, 1987). However, Macaskill (1991) found that only 36% of the foster and adoptive carers in her study were satisfied with the background information about the abuse which they had been given and that the fact of the abuse was sometimes concealed or no details were given. The more scanty the information the more likely it was that carers would unintentionally recreate a situation which mimicked the original abuse.

Some writers advise that the preparation of caregivers should allow those who have themselves been abused to talk about the experience (Roberts, 1989; Devine and Tate, 1991, National Foster Care Association, 1993). Macaskill (1991) found that 14% of the foster and adoptive carers in her study had suffered sexual abuse in the past and that their understandable anger towards the child's abuser could be unhelpful. Burgess and Holmstrom (1978) consider that caregivers need to come to terms with their feelings about the child's sexuality and molestation and with their feelings about their own sexuality, whilst Roberts (1989) comments that caring for abused children raises questions about caregivers' attitudes to sex more generally.

Other points made about preparation are that other children should be asked to tell their carers if a foster child tries to involve them in sexual activities (Nobbs and Jones, 1989) and that children are quite likely to be recipients of a child's disclosure because often a fostered child has lost trust in adults (Macaskill, 1991; Martin, 1993). In addition, it has been found that caregivers wished to have details about any past therapy provided for the children, although frequently this information was not passed on (Macaskill, 1991).

The National Foster Care Association (1994), in its publication *Safe Caring,* suggests that children may feel more able to talk to foster carers about the abuse if they are told by them at the start that they know about what has happened in the past. In 67% of the placements in Macaskill's study the children did talk about the abuse to their caregivers although there was no pattern to the timing. Where foster carers were afraid of hearing about it the children said nothing. In 18 out of 55 cases the children would not have spoken without determined intervention by the caregivers. Talking brought the children relief, disturbed behaviour stopped and attachment became possible, but it was hard for caregivers if the child had gained some enjoyment from the abuse. Where the child did not speak of the abuse, the foster carers felt less satisfied with the progress of the placement (Macaskill, 1991).

Preparation should also alert caregivers to the possibility that an allegation will be made against them or one of their children (Martin, 1993). More than a third of the foster carers in Macaskill's study (1991) had not considered the possibility that an abused child might make an allegation of abuse against them and 4% of all the children did so. Allegations of abuse had a devastating effect on foster carers who had no independent source of help. A panic response was shown by social services departments and the carers felt stigmatised for life. McFadden's work in this area (1987) suggests that many substantiated allegations are from younger children whose sexualised behaviour was misinterpreted as giving sexual cues and that false allegations arise when children misinterpret the behaviour of foster carers in situations which are similar to those of their original abuse (McFadden and Stovall, 1984).

Sexual Behaviour in the Placement

The practice literature also emphasises that for many abused children sexualised behaviour has brought rewards and they may seek attention indiscriminately from others (Burch, 1991). Moreover, for abused children the intimacy of family life appears to involve what they interpret as a lot of sexual contact (McFadden, 1987) and caregivers need to help them to understand ordinary human sexuality and the role of sex in relationships (Hoorwitz, 1983). Smith (1989) suggests that for sexualised children to give up the sexual projections of the abuser means confronting the fear that they have no other value and Macaskill (1991) comments that abused children need help to survive without sex. Caregivers need to teach children non-sexualised ways to offer and receive affection (Devine and Tate, 1991) and assist them to change their behaviour so that they are not giving out sexual signals (Roberts, 1989). The children themselves need reassurance that they are not damaged and that people do not know by looking at them that they have been abused. They also need help with peer relationships and with developing a "cover story" about the move into care, as otherwise they may tell the whole story of the abuse hoping to be seen as special, and thus lose friends and privacy (Burch, 1991; Macaskill, 1991). However, although abused children have been prematurely sexualised they often lack the basics of sex education (McFadden, 1987; Smith, 1995a).

In placement, abused children may initiate sexual activities with other children and when abused siblings are placed together, sexual activity is likely to occur (Macaskill, 1991). It is therefore important that caregivers try to teach children how to play and interact normally with other children (Smith, 1989). However, not all abused children show sexualised behaviour. In the Macaskill study (1991), 20% showed none.

Sexually abused children may overeat or refuse food, especially any which resembles semen (Burch, 1991; Macaskill, 1991) and feelings that life is out of control can spill over into defiant behaviour. It has been suggested that some children do not want to accept the position of child after becoming used to being treated as an adult in relation to sex and that, as a result, battles for control may ensue. There are children who are preoccupied with bodily functions and their private parts, engage in excessive masturbation, use sexualised language, have nightmares, are afraid of bedtimes and are enuretic. Sexual overtures to the caregivers are not necessarily directed at the caregiver of the same gender as their abuser or alternatively children may strongly reject a caregiver. Adolescents may give out messages of sexual availability or occasionally make allegations against their peers at school (Macaskill, 1991).

Fitzgerald (1991) emphasises that sexual abuse is one of a range of damaging experiences that abused children have experienced and in placement they have to deal with the impact of separation and loss. In a similar vein, Macaskill (1991) states that the abuse is part of inadequate and neglectful parenting. The implications for management are that if children's sense of neglect is addressed so that they become more secure, difficult behaviours may diminish (McFadden, 1987).

Safety Issues

There is a range of suggestions in the practice literature about how to keep abused children safe while they are being looked after, most of which emphasise clear family rules and boundaries. These include having locks on doors, monitoring the child day and night, avoiding family nudity, exercising care in the choice of babysitters and avoiding foster fathers bathing children or being the sole minder (Burch, 1991; Macaskill, 1991). Macaskill found that foster mothers tried to protect foster fathers from children's sexual advances and that safe caring placed additional burdens on foster mothers. However, Devine and Tate (1991) believe that it should not be the foster mother's task to police children when with their husbands or to protect foster fathers from the children in their joint care. In addition, sensitivity is needed at bedtime when some children were abused and foster carers are encouraged to keep a written log of daily events to which they can refer if their care is brought into question (Nobbs and Jones, 1989).

Stress on Caregivers

Macaskill (1991) found that caring for a sexually abused child created enormous stress and this was heightened if there were disclosures or court appearances (Davis et al, 1991). The sexual abuse of a child could arouse intense feelings about the trustworthiness of men, the child's sexual touching could lead to feelings of powerlessness for caregivers, and the foster carers' sexual relationship could be affected (McFadden, 1987; Burch, 1991). A similar impact could be experienced by social workers. Carers' willingness to discuss difficulties in their sexual relationship, which had arisen as a result of looking after a sexually abused child, was influenced by the gender of the worker (Macaskill, 1991). Feelings of revulsion towards the child or the abuser could also arise for caregivers (Macaskill, 1991; Fitzgerald, 1991). Some male carers detached themselves from the child and the fear of sexualised behaviour could sometimes lead to embarrassment and withdrawal by carers (Macaskill, 1991). Guidelines on safe caring suggest that some young people can become attached to a worker in residential care and fantasise about them sexually, leading to distress for the worker. In addition, some staff may find that they develop a voyeuristic interest in young people's sexual experiences (Scottish Office, 1995).

Foster carers quite often found that their friends retreated, unable to handle issues connected with the abused child (Macaskill, 1991), although conversely visitors sometimes took an unnatural interest in children who had been abused (Roberts, 1989). Decisions about whether the school should be told about a child's abuse were contentious (Macaskill, 1991). Volume 4 of the Children Act Guidance and Regulations (Department of Health 1991) states that "it is essential that staff caring for children who have been abused receive specific training and supportive professional supervision" and that consideration should be given to the provision of external consultancy in such cases. Certainly Macaskill (1991) considered that the absence of training impaired the ability of carers to respond to children, opportunities for the children to talk about their abuse were missed and carers were unable to protect themselves. In the same study a third of foster carers said that they had needed more specialised knowledge than had been available.

Mix of Children in Substitute Care

Concerns about the impact of sexually abusing young people on other children with whom they live in substitute care have brought questions of "mix" back into focus. Earlier discussions about the combinations of children who could or could not satisfactorily be placed together in institutions had centred around the advisability of mixing offenders and non-offenders, and concerns about prisons as "universities of crime" had been voiced for some time in relation to adult offenders. However, there is little research on which to draw in exploring this issue in respect of children in substitute care.

The one robust research finding about mix relates to foster care. The early studies of foster care all found that placements were more successful when the foster carers did not have children of a similar age or younger than the placed child in the same household (Trasler, 1960; Parker, 1966) and this finding was confirmed in Berridge and Cleaver's study (1987). In George's research (1970) one of the variables which was related to breakdown was the presence of foster parents' own children regardless of age. Triseliotis (1989) in a review of foster care research concluded that breakdown was more likely when a foster child's behaviour threatened the well-being of the foster carers' own children, even older ones. A study of permanent placements in middle childhood by Quinton and colleagues (forthcoming) has also shown that problems in placements were often associated with the presence of resident children. Research that has looked at the views of the children of foster carers shows that they can feel pushed aside because of the demands of the fostered child (Martin, 1993; Part, 1993).

Research on residential care has examined child cultures and their relationship to institutional goals (Lambert, Bullock and Millham, 1975; Millham, Bullock and Cherrett, 1975) but this approach does not provide information about the advisability or impact of combining particular kinds of children with others. Yet clearly children's experience of residence will be considerably affected by the other children in the setting. Whitaker and her colleagues (1984) found that 30 out of 34 children in four children's homes reported having experienced physical abuse, verbal torments, intense aggravation with other children and/or alarm at witnessing aggressive exchanges between other children. Half the children were observed by the researchers to bully others and the same children were often the target of bullying, whilst quiet children felt insufficiently protected by staff. A few children were isolated because there was no one of the same sex or of a similar age.

There is little information about the extent to which children are at risk of sexual abuse from other children while in substitute care. On the other hand sex between pupils of different ages in single-sex and co-educational boarding schools has been examined (Lambert with Millham, 1968) and, in a study of children in residential schools for pupils with emotional and behavioural difficulties, Grimshaw with Berridge (1994) found that 19% of the 67 children in their sample were reported to have experienced sexual abuse in the previous year. In an internal survey of the NSPCC teams' experience of children who had been abused (mostly sexually abused) whilst living in a residential or educational setting, it was found that half of the main perpetrators were other children (Westcott and Clement, 1992). It was noted that 42% of the children abused in these settings had been placed because of previous abuse, whilst the particular vulnerability of children with disabilities was highlighted by the finding that 35% of abused children had a learning difficulty. In

Macaskill's study (1991), in 51% of the placements the abused child initiated sexual activity with another child in the foster or adoptive family.
The findings of the last two studies should be treated with caution because neither of the samples was representative. Nonetheless, they do
point up some of the potential difficulties of these placements and the
need for more reliable figures about the levels of abuse by children in
substitute care.

In response to growing concern about the risks posed by abusing
young people in care the report *Children in the Public Care* (Utting, 1991)
advocated the principle that "victims of abuse should be separated from
children who are perpetrators of abuse". However, this is a difficult
area. At the time of placement a child's past abuse may not be known to
professionals, and when a history of abuse is known it is generally not
possible to predict which of these children may themselves abuse
others.

These issues were examined in the *The Report of the Committee of Enquiry
into Children and Young People Who Sexually Abuse Other Children* (National
Children's Home, 1992) which explored some of the dilemmas raised by
the placement of abusing children. The report suggested that it could be
argued that other children in a residential setting have a right to know if a
child has abused others in order to keep themselves safe. It was noted
that the use of "cover stories" by young abusers could become part of
their system of denial and cognitive distortions. It was also stated that
decisions about placement in residential care need to take account of
abusive behaviour and the vulnerability of other children and that children needed to be encouraged to speak openly about sexual harassment
by other young people. The report states that "Children or young people
known to have abused should never be placed in a residential setting
where their abusive behaviour will not be addressed, managed or
worked with in any way". Yet this is frequently the case. It was also
suggested that there was a need for secure therapeutic specialist residential provision for young abusers who need high levels of security. The
report notes that foster placements should only be made as part of a plan
which includes specialist resources for the abusing child and intensive
support and specialist advice for the carers and that the foster carers
should always be informed about the child's abusing behaviour. How far
such provision is made will be explored in the research which follows.

Research by Martin (1993) showed that children in foster families
wanted as much information as possible about a sexually abused child
who was placed with them, particularly as abused children often first
disclose their abuse to other children. Such information would prevent
the situation where child confidants are uncertain whether they should
pass on their knowledge to the carers. It would also help resident young

people to protect themselves from allegations by abused children. Nonetheless, Martin found that for two 14-year-old boys in her study fears about the possibility of allegations by a sexually abused girl had been unhelpful to them at a stage when they were preoccupied with their own sexual development.

The Placement of Sexually Abused Children with their Siblings

Macaskill (1991) found that sexual activity between siblings occurred in eight out of the 14 sibling groups in her study. In spite of this somewhat worrying finding, there has been little research or practice advice on the advisability of placing sexually abused siblings together in care. Smith (1989) has also commented that the feelings of siblings after a child in the family has disclosed are generally not addressed.

A guardian *ad litem* drew attention to this issue in a letter to the editor of *Adoption and Fostering* (Head, 1993). She pointed out her concerns that abused siblings may keep the abuse alive for each other, that carers can find themselves blaming one sibling and exonerating the other and that the combined difficulties of two or more abused children can present a considerable challenge to carers. A subsequent study of the placements of 51 sexually abused children on care orders showed that in 70% of the cases siblings were separated and in the remainder there was often sexual activity between the siblings (Elgar and Head, 1997).

On the basis of clinical experience, Smith (1996) believes that when sexually abused siblings are placed together as a whole sibling group there is a high likelihood of sexual activity, sometimes involving the foster carers' own children. If the sibling group has been manipulated to establish abusive hierarchies in which they abuse each other, this behaviour is likely to continue. It should also be noted that some children have derived comfort from sexual contact with their siblings and this may continue to be a motivating force.

In a review of the literature on the sibling relationships of children in the care system Kosonen (1994) noted that "much more needs to be known about the complexity of sibling relationships for children separated from their families". Developing this theme, and on the basis of clinical experience, Hindle (1995) suggests that not all children who are looked after should be placed with their siblings, nor should they necessarily remain together. Decisions need to be made on the basis of an assessment of the child and of the sibling group and the specific circumstances of each. In relation to sexually abused children McFadden, Ziefert and Stovall (1984) suggest that when there is sibling sexual activity, the power differential and the degree of risk to the younger or weaker sibling should be considered when decisions are made.

Contact with Families for Sexually Abused Children

Until recently the literature on contact for children separated from their parents has not drawn out those groups of children for whom contact may be problematic. Indeed, Smith (1995b) comments that in a recent summary of research into contact and permanent placement by Ryburn (1994) abuse was only mentioned once.

On the basis of their clinical experience Jones and Parkinson (1995) and Smith (1995b) argue that contact with the abusing parent after placement can impede the child's recovery by keeping the traumatic material alive. A court decision to order contact with an abuser may place the parent's desire for contact above the best interests of the child. A period without contact with the abuser ensures that the child is not pressured to retract. It also ensures that the child's developing capacity to have a say in their own life and to feel anger about the abuse are not challenged before they are fully established. Continued contact can mean that the child does not feel protected and even non-verbal messages can be used by an abuser to reinforce his power. Supervised contact may be used as a compromise when it is difficult to prove the abuse (Jones and Parkinson, 1995), but if supervision is by relatives who do not accept that the original abuse occurred, then it is unlikely to be effective. It is clear that some children are re-abused during supervised contact with their abusers. Jones and Parkinson (1995) suggest that pressure may be put on a child to retract through the siblings who see the perpetrator, and for this reason they suggest that access to all siblings may need to be denied. If the child is clearly afraid of contact visits then access may need to be supervised or suspended.

Jones and Parkinson (1995) question the assumption which is often made in court that if sexually abused children can have a relationship with their perpetrator, which is free from further abuse, it will be desirable. They point out that the fact of abuse means that the relationship has been distorted through the parent's misuse of power and that sexually abused children need to work through the trauma of the abuse before they are in a position to decide about contact with the abuser. In the meantime contact by means of letters, photographs or telephone calls is possible if the child needs help to make sense of the past.

Another aspect of contact for sexually abused children which has received even less attention is that parents of abused adolescents may forbid contact with their siblings in order to maintain the fiction that the abuse did not take place (Elgar and Head, 1997). Smith (1995b) suggests that the law should be used to secure continued contact with siblings as otherwise the only way in which some abused children can continue their relationships with them is if they retract the allegation. The literature has little to say about contact for sexually abused children with the non-abusing parent or about the extent of rejection by some parents after a disclosure, which effectively closes off the possibility of contact.

SUMMARY

This brief review shows that there has been very little systematic research on the management and needs of sexually abused and abusing children who are taken into substitute care. The fact that there is a growing practice literature in this area suggests that it is one which practitioners and caregivers see as problematic, but the ideas that have been generated in this way have no basis in research. The study that follows is an attempt to bridge that gap.

2

AIMS AND METHODS OF THE STUDY

While there has been little systematic research on the management of sexually abused and abusing young people in substitute care, the large body of practice literature on this topic discussed in Chapter 1 suggests that it is an important issue for practitioners and caregivers. The study was accordingly planned as an exploratory and descriptive exercise in an under-researched area.

Its general purpose was to provide systematically gathered information about the placements of sexually abused and abusing children in residential and foster care. There were a number of more specific aims:

- To describe the characteristics of a consecutive sample of sexually abused and abusing children in substitute care and to set these characteristics in the context of the wider population of children looked after.
- To carry out more intensive study of a sub-sample of sexually abused and abusing children, their caregivers and social workers in order to:
  - examine the characteristics and placement patterns of the children
  - explore the issue of the mix of children within settings, and how vulnerable children were protected
  - consider the ways in which children were managed during the placements and in particular to explore how sexual issues were manifested and dealt with; and to consider the supports available to caregivers in looking after these children
  - examine the range of care and treatment offered to children and to evaluate placement outcome.

METHODS

The Setting

The study was carried out in two local authorities which both had large multi-racial urban populations as well as suburban and rural areas. The fact that both had substantial residential care sectors made them particularly suitable for the study. The main features of the organisational framework of the participating local authorities that have a particular bearing on the study are described below.

Children's services in local authority 1 were organised in two divisions: Juvenile Justice and Children and Families. Of particular interest for the study was their specialist scheme for older children and adolescents with difficult behaviour. This scheme was located within the Juvenile Justice division and was established in response to a review by the Welsh Office to target those children, generally in the 10 to 16 year age group, who displayed seriously challenging behaviour leading to the risk of family breakdown. It had two complementary areas of provision: community (that is foster care and work with children at home) and residential care. A comprehensive assessment of physical, developmental and emotional needs leading to a clear child care plan and the targeting of appropriate resources was seen as a precondition of admission to the scheme. The primary aim of the scheme was to work in a supportive rather than interventionist way with children and their families to prevent them, where appropriate, being looked after or to work towards an early restoration home.

Placements within the scheme were provided by six specially contracted and supported foster carers and four residential units. Foster care was provided on either a planned or emergency basis in respite or longer term placements. The primary aim of residential care was to modify existing patterns of behaviour with the aim of reunification of children with their families, or where this was not possible, placement in foster care or independent living.

Those children who qualified for inclusion in the scheme were offered a comprehensive and well-funded service. However, admission to the scheme was based on strict criteria and children who did not qualify were offered a residential and fostering service with much lower levels of funding and support. The fostering service outside the scheme, for example, had no link workers. Children for our sample were drawn from both specialist and non-specialist schemes.

In its policy guidelines local authority 2 placed a strong emphasis on assessment and planning for children at the time of admission to care, particularly with regard to whether the child's interests would be better served by living at home or with a relative or friend. Foster care was seen as the first option to be considered, and residential care as the final choice for a minority of young people whose particular needs would be best met by the specialist skills of residential workers or where it was the young person's specific preference. Residential care was seen as inappropriate for children under the age of 12 years.

This authority aimed to provide a variety of residential accommodation suitable for the different needs of a range of children and to this end undertook a review and restructuring of its foster and residential care services during the study. The primary aim of this restructuring was to expand and diversify specialist fostering schemes, particularly for teen-agers, children with disabilities and young people needing some degree of residential educational provision as well as to improve its smaller residential care sector. It was anticipated that the new structure would need no additional funding.

The new arrangements included the establishment of a 12-week emergency/reception foster care scheme with intensive support for care-givers and enhanced payments based on carers' skills. It was expected that foster carers would be involved in assessment and reunification work or preparation for longer term placement. It was anticipated that the majority of new admissions to care would go through this route, thus reducing the number of potentially disruptive admissions to residential units. In principle young people would be provided with the choice of a foster home or residential placement.

In addition, an improved second tier specialist fostering project was developed out of the pre-existing adolescent care scheme to meet the needs for long-term placement of "difficult to place" children, primarily but not solely aged 12 or over. Caregivers in this project were expected to have the specialist skills to work with the young people in their care towards reunification or independence and were paid at an enhanced rate on the basis of their skills. Out-of-hours support was provided by foster-ing support workers based in residential units rather than by the Emer-gency Duty Team.

In the residential sector a number of homes were closed during the course of the study, others were refurbished with an emphasis on provid-ing single rooms where possible, and three were designated as special units. Of these three, two were developed as short stay admission units in order to address the problem of emergency placements disrupting settled resident groups in the other community homes. The other was designated as a Special Care Task-Centred Unit with enhanced levels of staffing. The reorganisation led to a sense of instability and uncertainty, particularly among staff in the residential sector, which in some cases had an unset-tling impact on the children in the study.

Operational Definition of Child Sexual Abuse and Abusing Behaviour

The subject of child sexual abuse is a highly complex and sensitive area to study. Accurate descriptions of sexual behaviour and events are often elusive and difficult to define and throughout this study we have had to grapple with our own and other peoples' sometimes equivocal notions of what is normal and acceptable. For this study an inclusive definition was needed which would capture all those young people whose involvement in sexual abuse or abusing behaviour had given rise to concern, whether or not such behaviour was the reason for their admission to substitute care. For the purposes of this study, sexual abuse or abusing behaviour was operationally defined as *professional concern having been noted on file about one or more sexual incidents in a child's life*. The "professional concern" could have been expressed by a medical professional or teacher and noted by the social worker. Alternatively, the social workers might have been sufficiently worried themselves to report the disquiet of a parent or other adult about such an incident, or they might have made a record of their own observations. This approach had the advantage of allowing the researchers more accurately to identify children whose abuse had taken place at some time in the past and to make their own assessment of the probability of abuse or abusing behaviour having occurred where there was no disclosure, no admission of guilt or any forensic evidence.

Selecting Young People for Inclusion in the Study

Two samples of children and young people were selected: *the case file sample* and *the interview sample*. For the study to have value it was important that the young people in the intensive interview sample should be representative of the total population of sexually abused or abusing youngsters in substitute care in the local authorities concerned. Attempts to use the child protection register or to ask caseworkers to identify suitable children proved unsatisfactory. It became clear that the only reliable way to draw an inclusive sample was for the researchers to examine the files of a whole population of children being looked after and to make operational judgements about whether or not they met the research criteria.

The Case File Sample

To draw the case file sample 250 files of newly looked after children were scrutinised, 121 in local authority 1 and 129 in local authority 2.

In local authority 1 the file search included all children who had been newly looked after over a six month period between March and August 1993. This exercise showed that there was a considerable proportion (40%) of looked after children for whom some sort of sexual abuse or abusing behaviour had been an issue at some time in their lives. It also became clear that there was a great deal of variation within this group in terms of their histories of sexual abuse or abusing behaviour, levels of intervention by social services and histories of other adversity. Since local authority 2 was larger, two social services areas were selected as the primary focus and a cohort of children newly admitted over a shorter period was scrutinised (September–December, 1994). A more recent period in this local authority was chosen with the intention of identifying some children for follow-up who had only very recently begun to be looked after, as it seemed likely that the issues for children soon after their initial placement might differ from those for children who had been looked after for a longer period before the time of interview. The proportion of children classified as abused or abusing in local authority 2 was 37%, only slightly lower than in local authority 1. These children were a similarly diverse group. Altogether, the case file sample yielded 96 young people who met the operational definition of sexual abuse or abusing behaviour, that is 38% of all the newly looked after children.

Permission to use these social service department files required lengthy negotiations. Apart from concerns about safeguarding the confidential information contained in the files, senior managers were alert to the way in which social workers might feel exposed by such a scrutiny of their practice, particularly in the sensitive area of sexual abuse. In local authority 2 the researchers were allowed to use the computerised database containing key demographic and placement information. However, senior managers felt they did not have the right to allow access to the children's case files without the consent of the parent (or the child if aged 14 or over) even when the authority had parental responsibility. We therefore wrote to all the children over 14 or to the parents of younger children to seek permission. We had surprisingly few refusals (5%) and several parents or young people agreed to their files being seen after we were able to reassure them about the purpose and confidential nature of the study.

The Interview Sample

The criteria for inclusion in the sub-sample of young people selected for more intensive study were as follows:

- A history of sexual abuse or abusing behaviour, that is that professional concern had been noted on file about one or more sexual incidents in a child's life.
- Looked after in residential or foster care.
- Still in the placement or having moved only within the previous three months, so that placement issues were easier to explore.
- Aged 10 years or over.

Of the 96 children who had been identified in the file search as meeting the criterion for sexual abuse or abusing behaviour, 61 were aged 10 or over, of whom 31 were still in the placement.

It was agreed that, where possible, we would contact the parents of children aged 10 to under 14 years in order to ask their permission for the child to participate in the study. Older children were considered to be able to give their own informed consent about participation. In order to contact the parents and children we initially approached the child's social worker who either took a letter about the study when they next visited or agreed that we would write direct. It was important to maintain a degree of flexibility and in some cases we delayed our approach at the social worker's suggestion because of current difficulties or crises in the child's life. Only six of the cases originally selected for inclusion were not available for a variety of reasons: two parents and one foster carer refused permission and three young people, all older girls, absconded from the placement and were impossible to trace. There seemed to be no consistent pattern to these refusals which might have led to bias in the sample.

However, this left only 25 cases still in the placement and available for interview. As 40 was felt to be the minimum number necessary for the subsample we subsequently selected 15 additional cases from children newly looked after in local authority 2 in a second period in our first two areas, as well as in a third area chosen because of its ethnic diversity. The interview sample then contained 40 children, 16 from local authority 1 and 24 from local authority 2. Figure 1 illustrates the derivation of this sub-sample.

Methods of Data Collection

For the case file, review information was collected in all 250 cases on the child's demographic and family background, abuse and placement career, history of other adversities as well as detailed information on the reasons for the current placement. These data were noted on pre-coded schedules on which we recorded 239 items of information.

In the second phase of the study, our main source of data was from intensive semi-structured interviews with caregivers, social workers and

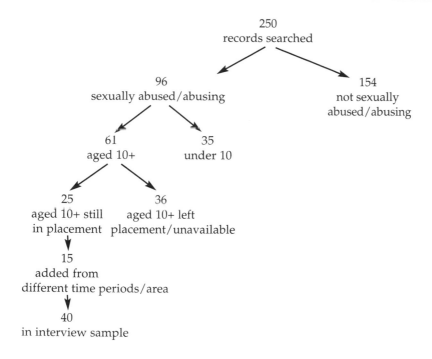

Figure 1 Composition of the interview sample

the young people themselves. In addition we used a range of stand-ardised measures relating to the children's behaviour and emotional well-being.

We also conducted a second interview with the children using the revised Looking After Children Assessment and Action Records (Parker *et al*, 1991; Ward, 1995). These are designed specifically for use with children looked after by the local authority and aim to measure children's progress and assess the quality of care they receive across seven dimensions. In addition, social workers were asked to complete a brief schedule documenting the aims and methods of their work with the child.

The main interviews were lengthy and took on average two hours. They were tape recorded and subsequently transcribed verbatim. During the interview, care was taken to avoid asking leading questions. When responses were unclear, the respondent's account was probed more deeply.

The young people received a small payment to thank them for their participation in the study. This also appeared to be helpful in differentiating us from social workers. Caregivers and social workers were not paid, although a few foster carers expressed the view that payment for their time would have been welcome.

Development of the Interview Schedules

The interview questionnaires were designed specifically for the study and covered a range of key areas relevant to the research objectives. Four separate schedules were produced, one for each category of respondent. A separate questionnaire was produced for foster carers and residential workers. The schedules were designed broadly to cover the same key areas, but each also focused on issues specific to that respondent. Thus, for example, in the foster carer interview we asked about fostering allowances and the impact of the child on their family and in the residential carer interview we asked about staff turnover and other organisational issues. This design meant that for the analysis we were able to compare the different views of the respondents on the same issues, (for instance the preparation for placement or therapeutic intervention) as well as having a rounded picture of the placement process from each different perspective.

During the development phase the interview schedules were piloted and subsequently amended and refined. Issues of reliability were addressed by cross-checking the interview recordings made by the researchers. These checks suggested that the quality of data did not vary significantly according to who conducted the interview.

Other Measures

We used a number of measures employed in other studies in order to facilitate comparison. We planned, in particular, to undertake some comparisons with data from the Institute of Child Health evaluation study of specialist treatment facilities for sexually abused children and young perpetrators (Monck and New, 1996) and research by Skuse and colleagues (1996) on the links between early experience of sexual abuse and later sexually abusive behaviours.

Children

The measures chosen for the children were:

- The Achenbach Youth Self-Report Schedule (Achenbach, 1991b), measuring child behaviour and adjustment.
- The Kovaks and Beck Child Depression Inventory (Kovaks and Beck, 1977), measuring levels of depression.
- A self-esteem checklist based on domains identified for use with children and adolescents (Harter, 1985; Harter, 1987), which also included the 10 items of the Rosenberg Self-Esteem Inventory (1965), measuring self-esteem.

- A brief life events checklist based on the Holmes and Rahe Social Readjustment Rating scale (1967) and used in a feasibility study of the prevalence of child sexual abuse in the UK (Ghate and Spencer, 1995), to assess other potential stresses in the children's past lives.
- The Locus of Control Questionnaire for Children (Nowicki and Strickland, 1973), which measures how far children see events in their lives as within their control.

Caregivers

The caregivers were asked for their views on the children's behaviour using:

- The Achenbach Child Behaviour Checklist (Achenbach, 1991a) as the adult corollary of the Youth Self-Report Schedule.
- The Child Sexual Behaviour Inventory (Friedrich *et al*, 1991; Friedrich *et al*, 1992; Friedrich, 1993), a 35 item checklist which elicits the frequency of sexual behaviours shown in the previous six months.

Social workers

Social workers were asked to complete an Aims and Methods schedule which documented the main objectives of the work with this child and the methods used to achieve these aims. This schedule was developed for use in a previous study by one of the researchers (Farmer and Owen, 1995).

Analysis

The Case File Data

The case file material was coded and entered on to a computer data base and analysed using SPSS for windows. When correlations were examined to look for significant associations, differences were regarded as statistically significant when $p < 0.05$ using a chi square test. The information from this part of the study served two purposes. First, it provided a quantitative framework for the interview sample which enabled us to determine whether the children whom we followed up differed in any significant ways from the total population of sexually abused and abusing children looked after in the two local authorities during our study period. This was important as it allowed us to make an assessment about how far we could make general statements on the basis of the findings from our interview sample. Second, we were able to establish the prevalence of past sexual abuse or abusing behaviour in a total looked after population and compare this "hidden population" with looked after children who had not been abused or shown abusing behaviour, in order to determine whether or not they were significantly different on any dimension. We were also able to establish whether there were differences between children who were sexually abused and those who had demonstrated abusing behaviour.

The Interview Sample

The interviews with respondents in the intensive study were transcribed from tape and then summarised using criteria developed for the study. The wealth of material contained in the transcripts and summaries was then scrutinised in order to draw out and describe key themes relating to the objectives of the study. The advantage of using transcripts for the analysis was that the material could be read several times in its original form, allowing nuances and meaning to emerge. It could also be read and analysed by more than one person.

During the course of the study the two principal researchers met regularly to discuss the data collection and to share their views of the material and themes as they emerged. Discussions were also held at regular intervals with members of the advisory committee and others with helpful knowledge and experience. Cross-referencing several sources of data was useful both in arriving at clear working definitions of sexual abuse and abusing behaviours and in establishing some certainty about the occurrence of events and behaviour. The case files proved to be an invaluable reservoir of information, particularly about events in the children's lives that had been forgotten or denied. Without these data we would have missed a great deal of important information.

Approaches to Respondents

Children

We were able to complete interviews with 38 of the 40 children. One young woman had left care and could not be traced. In addition one of the children was profoundly deaf and as he could not yet use sign language had great difficulty in communicating even with the help of his specialist teacher. He was also uncomfortable about talking to us and so the interview was discontinued. The children were interviewed between two and twenty months from the start of the index placement, that is the one which was current at the time of the interview. The average time between the start of the index placement and the interview was 12 months. Having consulted the social worker about the child's current circumstances we approached the children and their caregivers at the same time by separate letters to arrange a time for interview. We paid particular attention at all times to ensuring that the children did not feel pressurised to talk to us and at the start of the interview rehearsed with them how they might decline to respond to questions which they did not wish to answer.

While all the interviews with participants were confidential we were bound by ethical concerns about child protection. We therefore stressed to the young people at the outset of the interview, that if they told us anything which suggested that they might currently be at risk of harm that was not already known to the appropriate agencies, then we would discuss with the children what steps were needed to ensure their safety. This situation did not arise, although following one caregiver interview we contacted the social services team manager about our disquiet that a child's risky behaviour did not seem to be generating appropriate concern on the part of his caregiver.

Caregivers

Altogether we interviewed 34 caregivers. Two sets of foster carers refused to be interviewed, one because of illness in the family and the other because they were new carers and did not feel confident enough to discuss their work. We were unable to approach four residential workers because they had moved from their units by the time we tried to contact them.

For the caregiver interview we chose to talk to the main carer in the index placement. This was either the foster carer with the main responsibility for the young person or the key worker in the residential units. More than a quarter of the foster carers (5/19) were single parents. Four fostering couples chose to be interviewed together, and this provided a rich source of information. Three of the main carers in foster placement were men, one of whom was single. Where the residential unit or other specialist placement did not have a keyworker system, we interviewed the adult in the placement who knew the child best, usually the head of home or head teacher. Chapter 5 gives further information on the sample of caregivers.

Social Workers

Thirty four social workers were interviewed. Five of them had responsibility for more than one child in the sample. One social worker was unavailable because of long-term sickness. We talked to social workers after interviewing the young people and their caregivers, although by the time of the interview we had usually had several informal contacts with them. The level of co-operation was high and no social worker refused to talk to us despite the pressures on their time and the length of the interview. The social workers are described in detail in Chapter 5.

In what follows the names and some of the details of the individuals who are described have been changed in order to preserve confidentiality.

SUMMARY

1. The study was a descriptive one whose general purpose was to provide systematically gathered information about the placements of sexually abused and abusing children in residential and foster care. The characteristics of a consecutive sample of looked after sexually abused and/or abusing children were compared with those of the wider population of looked after children. An intensive study of a subsample of sexually abused and/or abusing young people explored such issues as the mix of children within substitute care settings, management problems, the range of help and treatment offered and children's views about what they valued.
2. "Sexual abuse or abusing behaviour" was operationally defined as that "professional concern had been recorded on file about one or more sexual incidents in a child's life".
3. The study was set in two large local authorities. It was in two parts. First a case file sample was drawn of 250 young people newly admitted to substitute care during defined periods. Records were scrutinised in order to obtain details of the young people's backgrounds and to identify those who met the operational definition of sexual abuse or abusing behaviour. Ninety-six children (38% of the total newly looked after sample) met this definition.
4. Second, an interview sample was drawn of sexually abused or abusing young people who were over 10 and were still in the placement at the time of the research. Only 31 met these criteria, of whom six refused or were unavailable. To obtain a sample of 40 children, 15 additional children from one of the local authorities were added. Thirty eight children, 34 caregivers and 34 social workers were interviewed, using a mixture of specially designed schedules and standardised measures.

II

CHARACTERISTICS OF THE CHILDREN, THEIR CAREGIVERS AND SOCIAL WORKERS

3

THE CASE FILE SAMPLE: THE CHARACTERISTICS OF SEXUALLY ABUSED AND ABUSING CHILDREN IN SUBSTITUTE CARE

The previous chapter described how a case file sample of 250 newly looked after children was drawn from two local authorities. They came from 203 families. Just over half (51%) were aged under 10 at the time of admission. Boys accounted for 57% and girls for 43% of the sample.

This chapter first describes the characteristics of the sexually abused and/or abusing children ("the abuse group") in comparison with the remaining population of newly looked after children ("the non-abuse group") about whom no information had been revealed about sexual abuse or abusing behaviour. Of course, it is possible that in this group there were abused children whose past was not known. The chapter goes on to explore differences within the abuse group.

Ninety six children met the research criterion for the abuse group: that professional concern had been expressed about one or more sexual incidents in the child's life. Of these 96 children, the information from the files suggested that 72 (75%) had been sexually abused only, seven (7%) were only known to have sexually abused another child, whilst 17 (18%) had both sexually abused another child and had themselves been abused.

THE SEXUALLY ABUSED GROUP
Evidence of Abuse

We divided the 89 children who had been or were suspected of having been sexually abused into three groups according to the level of certainty that abuse had taken place.

Professional Consensus about the Abuse

The first group comprised children where there was professional consensus that sexual abuse had occurred, usually because the child had made a disclosure which had been believed or because there was additional evidence or other corroboration of the abuse. Fifty three of the abused children (60%) fell into this group. For example, Valerie was interviewed after her half-sister's disclosure of sexual abuse. Valerie told the investigating team that she had been sexually abused by her half-brother Stewart between the ages of 9 and 13, involving regular sexual intercourse with him. Her other brother had also abused her once, as had three other boys. Her brothers were prosecuted.

Professional Concern about Abuse or the Risk of Abuse

The second group contained children where there was professional concern about either a high risk of abuse or that a child had been sexually abused, often because there was an accumulation of concerns about the sexual risks in the child's environment or about the child's sexualised behaviour. Fifteen (17%) of the abused children fell into this group. For example, Kevin aged 11 was seen by professionals as likely to have been abused. His younger sister had disclosed that she had been sexually abused by her father who was a Schedule One offender and Kevin masturbated constantly and developed bulimia.

Suspicion Only

The third group included children where there were professional suspicions that the child had been sexually abused, but the issue remained uncertain in the absence of a disclosure from the child or confirmatory evidence. Twenty one (23%) of the abused children fell into this group. For example, Tracey was 4 years old when she went to a foster home because of physical and emotional abuse. Her foster mother saw her as very sexually aware and noticed a mark around her vaginal area. When she started school, it was reported that she was stroking the legs of staff.

The Number of Perpetrators

Of the 89 sexually abused children, the records suggested that 57% were thought to have been abused by one perpetrator, 28% by more than one and the remaining 15% had, in addition to abuse by more than one perpetrator, been exposed to a variety of other harmful sexual activities, such as involvement in prostitution or pornography or inclusion in adult sexual activity.

Whilst it may be that for some children re-victimisation (that is abuse by more than one perpetrator) will have especially severe consequences, it should be noted that many children in each of these groups had suffered adversities other than the sexual abuse. For example, Jack was aged 9 when he disclosed sexual abuse by a family friend who was subsequently convicted of the offence. Although he was only abused by one perpetrator the file shows that he had been subject to other difficulties in his life. He was made a ward of court after his twin brother died at the age of 3 months and he lived in a chaotic and emotionally distressed household with his mother who had many different partners.

The children who had been abused by more than one perpetrator and had been involved in other harmful sexual activities had often lived in very sexualised environments. An example was Jane, who was aged 7 when it was alleged that her father had sexually abused her. By the age of 12 she was involved in prostitution and at the age of 13 she complained that she had been indecently assaulted. Sharon had almost certainly been sexually abused at the age of 5 by a 13-year-old boy who baby-sat for the family and many other families in the area. She had contracted gonorrhoea. At the age of 12 she had oral sex and suffered an attempted rape by a man in his twenties, who was a stranger to her. Her mother was a prostitute and it was noted on the file that her brother had taken videos of the children in the bath when she was aged 8.

THE SEXUALLY ABUSING CHILDREN

Certainty

We grouped the 24 children who had shown sexually abusing behaviour using similar criteria of certainty.

Professional Consensus about the Abusing Behaviour

A much larger proportion of the sexually abusing children fell into this group where there was professional consensus that the behaviour had occurred (20 or 83% of children), largely because the abuse of other children often came to light when it was observed or discovered by an adult or because of a disclosure by the victim. For example, Donna's long-term sexual abuse of her younger brother was discovered when he disclosed it to their mother. She was 14 by then and he was 9.

Likelihood that Abusing Behaviour had Occurred

The second and only other group for the abusing children included those where abusing behaviour seemed likely to have occurred. We employed this category when the information available from the file was too sparse to allow us to be completely confident about the behaviour reported. There were just four children (17%) in this group. For example, Will, who had been sexually abused at the age of 5 by a female cousin, was reported at the age of 6 to have shown inappropriate sexual behaviour at school with a little girl. Whilst the existence of reports on file makes it fairly likely that these events occurred, the lack of detail serves to place them in this less than certain category.

What we have referred to as sexually abusing behaviour covers a wide variety of activities. Fourteen of these children would fit the categories of *"sexually reactive children"* or *"children who engage in extensive mutual sexual behaviours"* (Cavanagh Johnson, 1993). According to Cavanagh Johnson, children in these groups have been over-stimulated sexually and cannot integrate these experiences in a meaningful way. This can lead them to act out the confusion in the form of sexual behaviours and a heightened interest in sex. When they engage in sexual behaviours with other children the difference in age is usually not great and they do not force other children into these behaviours. The children described as engaging in extensive mutual sexual behaviours have a more pervasive and focused sexual behaviour pattern than the sexually reactive children. Of these 14 children seven were only known to have abused one child and another seven had abused more than one child. The other 10 children could be described as *"children who molest"*. According to Cavanagh Johnson children in this group show a compulsive quality to their abusing behaviour, coercion is used and there may be a considerable age difference between the abuser and victim, with many of the molesting children nearing or having reached adolescence. Of these 10 children half were only known to have abused one child and half had more than one victim.

HOW DID THE SEXUALLY ABUSED/ABUSING CHILDREN DIFFER FROM THE REMAINDER OF THOSE LOOKED AFTER?

We were interested to explore whether the 96 children who had raised concerns amongst professionals about sexual abuse would emerge as significantly different in any way from the other 154 children in the case file sample who were looked after. Did they constitute a "hidden population" with particular needs or difficulties in common that might not be apparent to their caregivers?

The children in the abuse group tended to be older than those in the non-abuse group, with 59% aged 10 or over, compared to 42% of the non abused children in this age group. They had also entered care at older ages (mean 10.8 years compared to 8 years).

Nearly half of all the girls (48%) who were looked after in the case file sample had raised professional concerns about a sexual incident in their lives, as opposed to fewer than a third (31%) of the boys. Girls therefore tended to be over-represented in the abuse group (54% compared with 36% in the non-abuse group) and boys under-represented.

Of the abuse group 87% were white and 13% black or of mixed race. Twenty of them (21%) had a disability. Three children were physically disabled, 14 had learning difficulties and another three had severe learning difficulties. The proportions of non-abused children who were black and disabled were very similar.

Previous History of Care

Children in the abuse group were significantly more likely to have had a previous admission to care than those in the non-abuse group (40% as compared with 28%, p<0.01). Children in the abuse and non-abuse groups were equally likely to have experienced respite care, but the abuse group had more previous admissions for other reasons – 16% had four or more previous care episodes compared with only 5% in the non-abuse group (p<0.001). They had also spent significantly longer in care previously – 14% had spent more than one year (compared with 5%), and a quarter had spent more than four months (compared with 11% of the others). The older age of the abuse group accounted for some but not all of these differences.

At the time of these previous periods in care, 19% of the abuse group had been subject to care orders, interim care orders or wardship (as compared with only 6% of the non-abuse group). Of the abuse group 10% had previously been looked after because of the discovery that they had been sexually abused, whilst none had previously been looked after because of their abusing behaviour.

Previous Interventions and Registration

Prior to this admission to care, interventions from agencies other than social services departments had been provided as often for the children in the abuse group (for 41% of them) as for the remainder (for 42%). Professionals from the child guidance service had been involved with 13% of the families in the abuse group and 7% of the other families, whilst workers from the health service had engaged 9% of the former and 13% of the latter group. The other services involved with the children included the NSPCC, probation and psychologists from the education service.

Children in the abuse group had significantly more often been subject to child protection registration at some time (54% as compared with 34% of the non-abuse group). However, as Table 1 shows, registration was under several categories besides sexual abuse. In spite of the greater use of the register in relation to the abuse group, 40% of them had never been on the register. Clearly, in spite of the level of professional concern about many of these children, registration was often not seen as an appropriate intervention.

Background to the Current (Index) Admission

Legal Status

The great majority of the children in both groups (82% and 88%) were accommodated under section 20 of the Children Act, 1989. Of those subject

Table 1 The children on the child protection register at the time the data were collected

	"Abuse" children %	"Non-abuse" children %
Child never registered	40	64
Previously registered but no longer on the register	16	11
Still registered: Category:		
Sexual abuse	13	1
Physical abuse	6	5
Neglect	7	11
Emotional abuse	3	3
Category not clear	9	3
Not Clear	6	2
	N = 96 100%	N = 154 100%

to statutory proceedings, children in the abuse group were somewhat more likely to be subject to a care order (13% as against 5%), and somewhat less likely to have been admitted under an emergency or police protection order.

Household

The children entered the index placement from a wide variety of households. Few were with both birth parents (7% of the abuse group compared with 16% of the remainder). More were with lone parents, usually mothers (37% compared with 43%) and about 28% of both groups had moved from one parent and a step-parent, usually a mother and step-father. Another 9% of the abuse group had been living with other relatives (compared with 6% of the others) and the remainder moved from friends, another placement or from hospital.

The households of the abuse group were slightly larger than those of the other children, with almost half (46%) having five or more members (as compared to 39%). Fifteen per cent of the households of the abuse group had adults other than the parents or adult siblings in them (as opposed to 10% of the others). These other adults not infrequently posed risks to the children, since we noted that in 11% of the cases of the abuse group and 6% of the non-abuse group there were concerns on file about the child's contact with a Schedule One offender who was living in the household. About half of these offenders was the father or the mother's partner. In addition, concerns were expressed about 8% of the abuse group and 4% of the remainder who had contact with a Schedule One offender who lived outside the household.

The possibility that other children in the household had been sexually abused was often raised. Concerns were expressed on file about sexual abuse to other children in 39% of the households of the abuse group and in 15% of the remainder. There were similar levels of concern in the two groups about physical abuse and neglect to other children in the family (31% in the abuse group and 26% in the non-abuse group). It was also noted that 21% of the mothers of the abuse group children had themselves suffered sexual abuse in their childhood compared with only 5% of the mothers and 2% of the fathers or stepfathers of children in the non-abuse group. Although this difference seems large it might be accounted for by selective reporting in relation to the parents of children in the abuse group, where this issue might more often have been raised.

Reasons for Admission to Care

Children whose sexual abuse or abusing behaviour was the immediate reason for their entry to care accounted for fewer than one in five (17 children) of the admissions in the abuse group. For 13 of them the reason for admission was sexual abuse to the child and for four others the child's sexually abusing behaviour. Since the Cleveland Inquiry (Secretary of State 1988) there has been a clear expectation that when sexual abuse is suspected the preferred course of action is for the alleged abuser to leave the household and in this way allow the child to remain with the other parent. The low proportion of admissions for reasons of sexual abuse suggests that local authorities have heeded the recommendations of the Inquiry.

In 56% of cases there had been professional concerns or suspicions of sexual abuse in the past, but the current admission was for other reasons. Another 13% entered care because of concerns about their sexual behaviour which was seen as beyond control (highly undesirable and/or that they were being exploited) and involving risks to them, that is, they were admitted because of what used to be called "moral danger". Four per cent of the children only disclosed their abuse after being placed, and 9% of children were either sexually abused or showed sexually abusing behaviour for the first time after they were placed in care.

Thus the majority of the abuse group entered care for reasons other than sexual abuse, as Table 2 shows. Respite care for various parental needs was the most common reason, but over one in 10 was placed because of physical abuse or neglect or other concerns about the child's welfare. In about one in five cases the child's behaviour was the reason for admission, because of offending or being beyond control. The reasons for the admissions to care of the abuse and non-abuse groups were not very different except, of course, that none of the latter group was admitted for reasons of sexual abuse.

Current Adversities and Behaviour Problems

These data about reasons for entry to care can only go so far in describing the children and their circumstances. We therefore collected information on a range of 33 other concerns relating to the child's behaviour and current family circumstances which were noted at the time of their placement, if not directly connected with the admission. These included, first "Adversities", or data describing deficiencies in the young person's "care-taking environment", (for instance, violence in the home, offending or drug and alcohol misuse by the parent, multiple changes of house or parental partner, psychiatric and physical illness in a parent, sexual and physical abuse and neglect of the children). Second were "Behaviour Problems" or data about behavioural difficulties shown by the young people themselves (for instance, non-attendance at school, bullying, self-harm, criminal activity and drug and solvent abuse).

Table 2 Primary reason for the children being looked after

	"Abuse" children %	"Non-abuse" children %
Sexual abuse or abusing behaviour	18	–
Moral danger	13	–
Sexual abuse to another child of the household	–	2
Break for parents	20	24
Parent hospitalised or unable to care	13	27
Beyond control, including non-attendance at school and drug misuse by the child	15	17
Physical abuse or neglect	6	14
Offending	3	3
Child's request	4	1
Poor home conditions	2	2
Drug or alcohol problems of parent	2	2
Other concerns about child's welfare	3	5
Not clear	1	3
	N = 96 100%	N = 154 100%

For the majority of all the children (72%) there were one to five (and for a fifth, six to 16) adversities and behaviour problems at the time of their placement, whatever the reasons for entry to care. These children clearly came from situations of considerable and sometimes overwhelming adversity, which was not always apparent simply by looking at the reasons for admission to care. There was no evidence of adversities or behaviour problems in respect of only 7% of the children.

There were more concerns about children in the abuse group than in the non-abuse group. For the abuse group the mean number of adversities and behaviour problems was 4.8 at the time of entry to care, as compared with 3.0 for the non-abuse group. When concerns which were directly connected with sexual abuse or abusing behaviour were excluded from the analysis, the difference between the means of the two groups decreased but was still apparent. The adjusted mean was 3.7 concerns in the abuse group and 3.0 in the non-abuse group.

Previous Adversities

We also gathered information on how often the same range of adversities and behaviour problems had been of concern *prior* to the admission to care – that is at any time in the child's life – and combined these with those that had been evident at the time of admission. In both groups, as might be expected in this population, the levels of previous adversity were high. However, there were significantly more prior concerns about the children in the abuse group than about the others, with a mean of 7.8 for them and 4.1 for the non-abuse group. This still held true after excluding those concerns which dealt with sexual abuse or abusing behaviour, with a mean number of concerns of 5.7 for the abuse group and 4.1 for the non-abuse group. Overall, half the former had five or more such prior concerns as compared with only 30% of the latter ($p<0.001$).

Some adversities and problems were common in both abuse and non-abuse groups. As Table 3 shows, a substantial proportion of both groups of children had lived in families where there was violence between their parents, mainly violence by the man to the mother, but also occasionally violence by the mother to the father figure or violence on both sides. Physical abuse of the child was high in both groups, and psychiatric illness and parental misuse of drugs and alcohol occurred in substantial proportions.

However, some previous adversities and behaviour problems were significantly more common in the abuse group (Table 4). The sexually abused or abusing children were significantly more likely than the others to have had severe educational problems (that is non-attendance and school exclusion, serious behaviour problems at school, being bullied) and to have experienced rejection and disrupted parenting (that is multiple separations from their main parent, a parent who had many partners, care which adversely affected their emotional development, a

Table 3 Previous adversities and behaviour problems that were common in both the abuse and the non-abuse groups. (Differences not statistically significant)

Adversity	Abuse group %	Non-abuse group %
Violence between parent figures	38	39
Physical abuse to child	45	42
Child offending	22	14
Alcohol or drug misuse by the child	16	9
Alcohol or drug misuse by parent or parent's partner	19	25
Psychiatric illness of parent	19	25
Physical illness of parent	7	12
Child bullying others	10	7

Table 4 Previous concerns and adversities which occurred significantly more frequently in the abuse group than in the non-abuse group. (All differences significant at p< 0.05)

Events before and at the time of entry to care	Abuse group %	Non-abuse group %	Level of significance
School exclusion	17	8	p<0.04
Non-attendance at school	29	13	p<0.001
Severe behaviour problems at school	35	20	p<0.007
Child bullied	9	3	p<0.04
Multiple separations from main parent	34	14	p<0.0001
Parent has had multiple partners	13	7	p<0.01
Management of child damaging to child's emotional development	40	24	p<0.009
Parent/parent's partner offending	31	19	p<0.02
Psychological/emotional distress of child	40	20	p<0.0008
Beyond control at home	59	40	p<0.003
Pregnancy of child (as % of girls)	15	4	p<0.03

parent figure who offended) and to have been seen as troublesome (that is serious behaviour problems and being beyond control at home). In addition, the girls were more likely than others to have become pregnant.

It is also worth noting that a considerably greater proportion of abused or abusing children harmed themselves (9% as compared with 4%) and experienced neglect (42% as compared with 31%), although these differences, unlike the others, did not reach statistical significance. The only adversity that was significantly more likely to occur in the non-abuse group was violence between non-parental figures such as lodgers and children (29% v. 16%).

The greater prevalence of adversities and behaviour problems in the abuse group is in accord with our earlier evidence about their higher number of previous admissions to care, the longer periods of time children had been previously looked after and the larger proportion who had been on care orders. Certainly the difference was not simply due to the extent to which the two groups of children were known to professionals, since similar proportions had had previous involvement with social services departments (81% of the abuse and 78% of the non-abuse group). What the data appear to suggest is that *sexual abuse or sexually abusing behaviour when combined with placement in care may often be a marker for parenting environments which, in a variety of ways fall far short of those which are optimal for children's development.*

The children in the abuse group were particularly characterised by their high level of behaviour problems. They had only a slightly higher average number of previous adversities in their environments (3.5 as compared with 3.0), but a significantly higher number of previous behaviour problems (2.4 compared with 1.4 p<0.001). There were no differences between boys and girls on either of these measures.

The children in the abuse group were therefore more likely to have shown emotional and behavioural difficulties which were of concern to professionals as they grew up, and moreover these difficulties cannot simply be accounted for by the fact of having a more severely adverse environment. The higher rates of previous disturbance in the abuse group could either be connected with the incidents of sexual abuse which the children had experienced, as previous research would suggest (Beitchman *et al*, 1991, 1992; Kendall-Tackett, Meyer Williams and Finkelhor, 1993, Smith and Bentovim, 1994), or to other features of the children's environment which we could not discern from these data. Whatever their cause, these emotional and behavioural difficulties were potentially likely to have long-term effects on the children's lives, particularly in terms of their educational attainment and social functioning. They were also likely to have implications for their care and management.

Seen as a whole, these findings suggest that sexually abused and abusing children are likely to be especially disadvantaged when they enter the care system. When we come to look at the children whom we followed up in depth in the intensive sample, it will clearly be important to consider how far the range of adversities to which they had often been subject are fully taken into account, not only at the time of their placement but also in terms of what is done for them by way of intervention in their care settings.

Placement

Just under a third (31%) of the abuse group were first placed in a children's home and a little under two thirds (63%) in foster care. The remainder went first to secure units or prison. Slightly fewer of the non-abuse group went into residential care (21%) and more into foster care (69%), as would be expected since they were a younger group. When the effect of age was taken into consideration there was no difference between the two groups. Rather more of the non-abuse group were placed with one or more siblings (36% compared with 21%), but this difference did not reach statistical significance.

All the looked after children moved frequently between placements within the care system. Of the whole sample 38% had more than one placement in the first four months after admission and 13% had more than three placements in the same period. When respite placements were excluded, the abuse children experienced more moves in care in the first four and six months after admission, but this was partially due to their older age.

A substantial proportion of all the children (17%) moved between different *types* of placement, for example, between foster and residential care. This type of movement was higher in the abuse group (25%) than in the non-abuse group (12%). The abuse group had higher rates of placement breakdown than the other children, 9% compared with 4%, but this difference was not statistically significant. Had we been able to follow up the children beyond six months the difference in breakdown rates between the two groups might have been greater.

The main difference to emerge during the index placement was that the children in the abuse group were significantly more likely to demonstrate *new* behaviour problems: 51% did so, as compared with 21% of the others, which was highly statistically significant ($p < 0.0003$). These new types of problems included absconding, alcohol or solvent abuse and inappropriate sexual activity. It seems likely that this difference was linked to the high rate of previously existing behavioural difficulties. This has implications for careful management in both residential and foster care, particularly since this is a more than usually mobile and disrupted group of children.

Plans Made on Entry to Care

We noted the plans that had been made for the children within six months of their entry to care. For a considerable number, plans were either not clear or were to depend on the progress made in placement. Reunification with their parents was less often planned for sexually abused and abusing children (3%) than was the case with the non-abuse group (13%), whilst a long-term placement or adoption was more often sought for the abuse children (21%) than for the others (14%). This may have been because these children were more behaviourally difficult than their non-abused counterparts or in some cases that the presence of an abuser in the family made return for some of the sexually abused children impossible. Regular respite care was the plan for 14% of the abuse group and this figured in 8% of the plans for the non-abuse children. In keeping with the larger number of plans to restore non-abuse children to their families, 46% of them had returned to live with a parent by the time we gathered the data on the children, as compared to 34% of abuse children.

Clearly, although plans were not often made to reunite the abuse children with their families, many of them did return, possibly as a result of positive changes in household composition.

Risks in Care

The files yielded information on some of the risks to the abuse group once in care, as well as the risks that they posed to others. Nonetheless, the more detailed examination through interviews with the follow-up sample suggests that a considerable amount of information was not recorded on file; so the following figures should be regarded as underestimates. The files showed that 10% of the children in the abuse group sexually abused other children or involved them in sexual activity whilst in care. Seven of these instances occurred in foster care, one in a children's home, one in both residential and foster care and in one case the location was not clear. Another 5% of children made sexual approaches or sexually abused a child at school. Thirty nine per cent of the children in the abuse group had, either when at home or in care, displayed sexualised behaviour such as compulsive masturbation or made sexual approaches to adults.

Eleven per cent of the young people had at some time been involved in prostitution and 10% had participated in other kinds of sexual activity which exploited them, including involvement in making pornography and in adult sexual activities. Three per cent of the adolescents were recorded as having procured other young people from their care settings for the purposes of prostitution. Indeed, one young person who regularly worked as a prostitute and whose mother was a "Madam" was recorded as having associated with at least seven of the young people in our file sample and contact with her generally meant that she had introduced another child to the world of prostitution. This represented 8% of all the children admitted during a six month period in her local authority. Since such information is not generally recorded on the case files her influence is likely to have been much more extensive. It was also recorded that at some stage almost a third of the young people in the abuse group had had intercourse under the age of consent.

In addition, two children were sexually abused while in care. One 5-year-old girl was abused by another foster child while in respite care and a boy of 12 alleged abuse by another boy in residential care. A third girl who was 12 alleged that a male resident tried to have sex with her. (Again, we know from our detailed follow-up study that other children were abused while living in care and that this was not recorded on file.) Two other children were sexually abused by a youth worker during their time at home, one of whom had learning difficulties. A further two children aged 5 and 7 were sexually abused by foster children at the time when their parents were acting as foster carers. This made seven children who were noted as having been sexually abused in connection with care placements. It was also clear from the case notes that at least three other children, after allegations of sexual abuse by a family member, remained at home without adequate protection.

Whilst they were in care seven children made an allegation of sexual abuse by an adult, two in respect of foster carers, two in relation to residential workers, and three in relation to other people. There was also one allegation of physical abuse made against a residential worker and two allegations about other aspects of care made in relation to caregivers, one of whom was a foster carer and one a residential worker.

DIFFERENCES BETWEEN CHILDREN WHO HAD EXPERIENCED SEXUAL ABUSE AND CHILDREN WHO HAD ABUSED OTHERS

Of the 96 children in the abuse group, 72 were only known or suspected of having been sexually abused, while 24 had abused others. (Of the latter 17 had also experienced abuse, but the numbers are too small for separate analysis.)

The gender distribution of the "abused" and "abusers" was significantly different. Three quarters of the abusers were boys, while nearly two thirds of the abused children were girls. The abusers also experienced more learning difficulties (29% v. 14%, $p<0.08$).

Previous adversities and behaviour problems tended to be more common among the abusers than among the abused children (mean 9.2 v. 7.2). In particular, the abusers had significantly more often displayed inappropriate sexualised behaviour and emotional distress. They had more often witnessed the sexual activity of parent figures and their parents had more often had psychiatric problems. There was a tendency for them to have been more often exposed to multiple sexual activity, to have experienced poor parenting and to display severe behaviour problems at school.

There is also a suggestion in our data that the sexual abuse suffered by the 17 child abusers who had also been sexually abused included a higher proportion of multiple abuse than did that of the other abused children. Eighteen per cent of these child abusers had suffered abuse by two or more perpetrators and been involved in other exploitative sexual activities, as compared with 5% of the abused children, but the numbers are too small to permit firm conclusions.

Professionals appeared to have felt more concern about the child abusers in the past, as evidenced by higher rates of previous child protection registration (50% of abusers as compared with 26% of victims) and of statutory orders (29% of abusers as compared with 13% for the abused children). The high rates of prior registration of the abusers before the abusing behaviour was noted suggest that the abusing behaviour may have come to light partly as a result of the scrutiny exercised in relation to children on the register. Certainly, few of the abusing children were registered after their abusing behaviour became known (4%) in contrast to registrations for the abused children (21%).

These low rates of registration after sexually abusing behaviour occurred were no doubt linked to the low rates of investigation for child abusers. There had been an investigation in only 21% of all cases of sexually abusing behaviour by a child, as compared with the investigation of 44% of the cases of children who had been sexually abused by an adult. Similarly, a child protection case conference was held in respect of only 29% of all the children who had shown abusing behaviour, (even though half of them were already on the child protection register), as compared with 45% of conferences held on the cases of abuse by an adult. This evidence serves to show that in relation to child protection procedures low priority is given to children who abuse other children, in spite of the guidance in *Working Together* (Home Office *et al*, 1991) which recommends that abusing children should be subject to child protection procedures. In addition, prosecutions were rarely undertaken when abusing behaviour occurred, even though children had more often admitted to their actions than had the adult abusers. Only one child was prosecuted, and this was for a serious offence of rape.

Abusers and abused children had very similar chances of being placed in residential care, with about a third in each group initially being so placed. However, in the first four months after placement the abusers were moved rather more often. Forty six per cent of the abusers had two or more placements in the first four months after entry to care as compared with 29% of the abused children. They may have been seen as more difficult to place or may have become so as a result of their abusing behaviour. Certainly the prospects for returning children to their families were seen as less favourable for the abusers. A third of them were bound for long-term care or adoption compared with fewer than one in five of the abused children.

Thus, while both groups had troubled histories with many adversities, the abusers seemed to be further along a continuum of difficulties than the abused children.

We were surprised to find that there was no information on file about the nature of the abuse inflicted in relation to 46% of all the sexually abused children, about the frequency of the abuse in relation to 50% of them or about its duration in relation to 69%. As a result, the information which could be passed on to caregivers when the children entered care would be deficient. Yet full information is crucial for the safety and welfare of both children and their caregivers.

Counselling after the incident came to light was recorded as being offered to only a quarter of the abusers and one in five of the abused children. These are low levels when the long-term consequences of sexual abuse are considered. Clearly, the risks which the abusers posed to other children were not being addressed in the majority of cases.

SUMMARY

1. Of the 250 children in the case file sample of newly looked after children, 96 were identified as sexually abused and/or abusing ("the abuse group"). The remaining 154 children were treated as a comparison group ("the non-abuse group").
2. Information from records suggested that 72 of the abuse group (75%) had been sexually abused only, 7 (7%) were only known to have sexually abused another child, while 17 (18%) had both sexually abused another child and had themselves been abused.
3. Comparison of the sexually abused and abusing group with the remainder revealed some striking differences. The sexually abused or abusing children were significantly more likely to have demonstrated a range of behavioural problems in the past. They were also significantly more likely to have had severe educational problems and to have suffered poor parenting and multiple separations from their parents. Both groups had experienced high levels of physical abuse, violence between their parent figures and neglect. In addition, children in the sexual abuse group were significantly more likely than the others to have been placed on the child protection register, to have had one or more previous placements in care and to have spent longer there than the other children.

   In the index placement they showed significantly more *new* behaviour problems than children in the non-abuse group. Once in care a considerable proportion showed sexualised behaviour, were involved in prostitution or other exploitative sexual activity, sexually abused another child or were themselves abused. This evidence suggests that sexually abused or abusing children are a particularly disadvantaged group, who require extensive care and attention if these difficulties and deficits are to be addressed while they are separated from their parents.
4. Within the abuse group, there were some differences between the 72 who were only known to have suffered abuse ("abused") and the 24 who had abused other children ("abusers"). Boys were over-represented among the abusers and under-represented among the abused. While both groups had troubled histories, the abusers seemed further along a continuum of difficulties.

4

THE YOUNG PEOPLE IN THE INTERVIEW SAMPLE

So far we have used information recorded on case files to describe the characteristics of a population of young people admitted to substitute care who aroused professional concern because of sexual abuse or abusing behaviour. In this chapter we describe the sample of young people who were interviewed for the study and their placements.

Chapter 2 explained the composition of this "interview sample". In drawing it, we tried to ensure that the children selected for interview would be representative of the total population of sexually abused or abusing children in substitute care who were aged 10 years or over in the local authorities that took part. This involved checking for any significant differences between the 40 children included in the interview sample and the remaining 36 sexually abused or abusing children in the case file sample aged 10 or over who were not included.

There were no significant differences between the interview sample and the remainder in terms of gender, age, race, physical disability and learning difficulties. Nineteen were in foster care and 21 in various forms of non-family substitute care. The children in the interview sample were somewhat more likely to have been placed initially in foster care (53% v. 44%) but the differences in placement patterns were not marked. However, the interview sample had generated more professional and legal intervention than their counterparts. Five times as many were looked after on care orders and more had been placed on the child protection register (57% v. 36%). Children in the interview sample had somewhat more severe experiences of abuse: half had been abused by more than one perpetrator (compared with 36%), and the level of certainty about the abuse was higher. The interview sample, therefore appeared to fall at the more serious end of the continuum of difficulty and disturbance experienced by the total group of sexually abused and abusing young people in care.

THE CHILDREN AT THE TIME OF THE INDEX PLACEMENT

The "index placement", the focus of the interviews with the young people and their caregivers, was not always the first placement in the current care episode if this was short-lived. In fact, 21 of the 40 children in the interview sample had changed placements at least twice within four months of the initial placement.

The age and gender distribution of the interview sample is illustrated in Table 1. There were slightly more girls than boys, and the girls were slightly older than the boys at the beginning of the index placement (mean age of girls 14 years 1 month, boys 13 years 6 months).

Eleven of the children (28%) had a mild to moderate learning difficulty and there was one child with a physical disability. All the children were British. Thirty-four were white, five were mixed race and one child was black African-Caribbean.

Seventeen of the 40 were placed in local authority foster care placements. A further two were placed in Regulation 11 foster placements with the parents of friends who had been registered specifically for the purpose of looking after them. Thirteen of the young people were placed in local authority children's homes. The other eight were placed in a variety of specialist placements as shown in Table 2. For the purposes of many of our analyses, we aggregated all foster care placements in the category of "foster care" (n = 19, 47%) and all institutional or non-family placements in the category of "residential care" (n = 21, 53%). Girls were somewhat more likely than boys to be in residential care (57% v. 43%) but the difference was not significant.

At the time of interview 13 young people had been in the index placement for six months or less, 15 had stayed between seven and 12 months, 10 for between one and two years and only one child had been in her placement for more than two years.

During the index placement 27 of the children were accommodated, but 13 were subject to full or interim care orders. The names of 16 (40%) were on the child protection register and another seven children had

Table 1   Age at time of index placement

Child age in years	Girls	%	Boys	%	All	%
10–12	5	23	4	22	9	22
13–15	15	68	12	67	27	68
16 and over	2	9	2	11	4	10
Total	22	100	18	100	40	40

Table 2   Type of index placement

Type of placement	No. children	%
Foster care	17	42
Foster care (Regulation 11)	2	5
Residential unit	13	33
Independent living unit	2	5
Secure unit	2	5
Residential special school	3	8
Flat with residential worker	1	2
Total	40	100

previously been registered. When these proportions are compared with the legal status of adolescents in children's homes in Berridge and Brodie's study (1998), slightly fewer of the young people in our study were accommodated and, as would be expected, more were on the register.

Eight of the children (20%) were looked after in this care episode because of concerns about sexual abuse to them and a further three children (8%) were looked after because of concerns about their sexually abusing behaviour. Concerns about the child putting *themselves* at sexual risk was the reason for admission in a further seven (18%) cases. The other main reasons for admission were the child's difficult behaviour (18%) or concerns about physical harm to the child (15%). The remaining children were looked after for a variety of reasons such as their parent being unable or unwilling to care for them or the child offending. In only five cases (13%) was reunification intended at the time the child began to be looked after, and long-term placement or adoption was planned for 30% of the children. Only one child was placed with a sibling.

Sexual Abuse and Abusing Behaviour

Thirty six (90%)of the young people had been sexually abused at some time in their lives (15 boys and 21 girls). Of these, 18 had also demonstrated some form of sexually abusing behaviour (11 boys and seven girls). Four of the young people were not known to have been abused in the past but were included in the sample because they had exhibited sexually abusing behaviour (three boys and one girl).

Of the 11 children who had learning difficulties, *nine* had previously shown sexually abusing behaviour. Nine of the 22 sexually abusing children had learning difficulties (41%) compared with only two of the 18 abused only children (11%).

Just over two thirds of the children in the abused only category were placed in residential care, compared with only one third of the children in the abusing category. In contrast, almost two thirds of the abusing young people were in foster placements but only one third of the abused children.

Sexually Abused Children

Information about the history of abuse of the 36 sexually abused children was collected from the case files and where possible from the interviews with the social workers, caregivers and the young people themselves. Detailed information was not always available, particularly in cases where the abuse had happened some time previously. In some cases, although it was clear that there was professional consensus that an abusive episode had occurred, key information such as the identity of the perpetrator or the age of the child at the time of the abuse was missing. We attempted to construct as full a picture as possible of abusive events in the past in order accurately to classify the young people in the sample.

In nine cases (three girls and six boys) the type of sexual abuse was not clear. For the remaining 27 abused children (18 girls and nine boys) the most commonly reported type of abuse was full vaginal intercourse (nine girls) starting in one case before the age of 3 years. The most common type of sexual abuse known to have been experienced by boys was anal intercourse (3/9) or masturbation of the child by the offender (3/9), see Table 3.

Information was available about the frequency of the abuse to only 25 children. For 10 of these young people the abuse had been perpetrated on a regular or frequent basis.

Table 3   Type of abuse (most serious episode)

Type of abuse	No. sexually abused children	%
Vaginal intercourse	9	25
Anal intercourse	4	11
Simulated/attempted intercourse	3	8
Digital penetration	1	3
Sexualised touching/kissing	4	11
Masturbation of child	4	11
Sexual touching of alleged offender	2	6
Type of abuse not clear	9	25
Total	36	100

Table 4 shows that 15 (of the 35 for whom there was information) had been sexually abused by more than one perpetrator including seven children who had been multiply abused by three or more perpetrators. One 13-year-old girl had been abused by at least six different men. Girls were nearly twice as likely as boys to have been abused by three or more perpetrators.

Table 5 gives the identity of the "main" perpetrator. This was usually the perpetrator of the most serious abuse, but occasionally where the abuse had been prolonged this abuser was taken to be the "main" perpetrator. Fathers and stepfathers/male cohabitees formed the largest group of perpetrators (30%), followed by other non-relative adults (27%). Seven children (20%) had been abused by siblings or other young people at school or in previous placements. Three children (8%) had been abused by their mothers or grandmothers. Adult males formed the largest group of perpetrators (24 out of 36), followed by males under 18 (7) and a small number of adult females (4).

Table 4   Number of known perpetrators

No. of perpetrators	No. sexually abused children	%
1	20	55
2	8	22
3	4	11
4	1	3
5	1	3
6	1	3
Not clear	1	3
Total	36	100

Table 5   Identity of main perpetrator

Perpetrator identity	No. sexually abused children	%
Father	6	16
Stepfather/male cohabitee	5	14
Mother	2	6
Male sibling/step-sibling	2	6
Grandfather	3	8
Grandmother	1	3
Other non-relative adult (known)	7	19
Other non-relative adult (stranger)	3	8
Other child	5	14
Not clear	2	6
Total	36	100

Eighteen (of the 34 cases where information was available) were abused by perpetrators living outside the household. The remaining 16 young people were abused by household members. Following discovery of the abuse there was a child protection investigation in 22 cases and 16 (44%) of the 36 abused children were registered as a result. The names of a further seven children (20%) were already on the child protection register. Over a third of the children (36%) were not registered as being at risk following the disclosure of abuse.

Prosecution of the perpetrator was relatively infrequent. In only nine of the 36 cases for which information was available was the alleged perpetrator prosecuted. All these prosecutions were of adult men. None of the sexual abuse by women had been investigated by the police.

In addition to collecting information about the known details of the abuse we made a separate rating of the level of substantiation of the abuse. Using the rating described in Chapter 3 the children were divided into three categories according to the level of certainty that abuse had taken place. As can be seen in Table 6 nearly two thirds of the 36 sexually abused children fell into the category of "professional consensus" that abuse had taken place.

Thirty three of the young people in the interview sample filled out Life Events questionnaires. Nineteen (58%) of these revealed that they had been sexually abused and 14 made no mention of it. Of these 14, 11 (five girls and six boys) had almost certainly suffered sexual abuse. The majority who divulged sexual abuse (16/19) felt that it had affected them "a lot". Just two children felt that it had only affected them "a little" and one that the sexual abuse had had no effect on him. Even where there might not have been professional consensus about the occurrence of the abuse, the majority of the young people themselves remembered and were affected by what had happened.

The Sexually Abusing Children

Of the 22 young people who had shown sexually abusing behaviour, 17 (12 boys and five girls) had shown such behaviour *prior* to the current

Table 6 Level of certainty about the occurrence of sexual abuse

Level of certainty	No. children	%
Professional consensus	23	64
Professional concern	6	17
Suspicion only	7	19
Total	36	100

placement and seven (three boys and four girls) exhibited this behaviour *during* the placement. Three of these young people had shown abusive behaviour both in the past *and* in the index placement. The other four (one boy and three girls) exhibited abusing behaviour for the first time in the index placement. One boy abused another child in a *subsequent* placement. Eighteen of the 22 young people had also been sexually abused at some time in the past. Four of the abusing children (three boys and one girl) had no known history of sexual abuse. In this section the children's abusing behaviour both before, during and subsequent to the index placement will be described.

The nature of the abusing behaviour shown varied from full vaginal intercourse with a 10-year-old girl, to sexualised touching of another child, as can be seen in Table 7. The most common type of abusive behaviour was sexualised touching and kissing. For example a 14-year-old girl in a residential unit got younger boys to sit on her lap and sexually caress her breasts and body.

Description of Known Victims

The victims of these young abusers were all other young people, with an age range of 3–14 years. There was one older victim who was a 16-year-old boy with severe learning difficulties in a residential school. Just over half the known victims were girls. As Table 8 shows, three fifths of the young abusers had abused more than one child and in half the cases the abuse was known to have constituted more than one isolated incident. Although we rarely had detailed information about the ways in which these victims were targeted, these sexually active young people evidently posed a considerable threat to other children of both sexes with whom they came into contact.

Table 7   Nature of abusing behaviour (most serious episode)

Type of abusing behaviour	No. young abusers
Vaginal intercourse	1
Anal intercourse	1
Digital penetration	3
Simulated/attempted intercourse	3
Masturbation of other child	2
Sexualised touching/kissing	8
Indecent exposure	2
Exposure of other child to adult sexual activity	1
Not clear	1
Total	22

Table 8   Number of known victims of young abusers

Number of known victims	No. young abusers
1	9
2	8
3	2
4	2
9	1
Total	22

Half of the known victims were children in children's homes, residential school or foster care and just over a quarter were siblings, step-siblings or other relatives as Table 9 shows. It therefore appears that children in both the family *and* substitute care were at risk of abuse from these young people.

Investigation of these abusive incidents was rare and occurred in only four of the 13 cases for which we had sufficient information. None of the young abusers was registered as a result of social services investigations, although 12 of these young people were already on the register for other reasons. Prosecution of the young perpetrators was rarer still. Only one young abuser was prosecuted (for indecent assault of his cousin), resulting in a supervision order. This lack of official intervention meant that there was little documentary evidence of the abusing behaviour. Poor documentation meant that the behaviour could be easily forgotten or overlooked at a later stage when placement decisions were being made or therapeutic interventions considered.

Despite the low levels of documentation, investigation and prosecution there was little contemporary professional *doubt* about the occurrence of the abusing behaviour. In four fifths of the cases there was substantial

Table 9   Identity of known victims (most serious abuse)

Victim identity (all under 18 years)	No. young abusers
Sibling/step-sibling	3
Other relative	3
Neighbour's child	2
Child at school	2
Foster carer's child	4
Child in residential unit	6
Child in residential school	1
Other	1
Total	22

consensus at the time that it had occurred, either because it had been observed by an adult or convincingly disclosed or corroborated by the victim.
In the remaining four cases the information available on the file was too
sparse to allow us to be completely confident about the behaviour reported,
although it seemed fairly likely that the events described had occurred.

History of Other Adversities

When the young people's wider social history was considered from information on the case files and from interview material, it became clear that
sexual abuse was only one of a whole range of adversities with which
they had had to contend. Twenty seven out of 40 (68%) had suffered
previous physical abuse, 14 (35%) had been subject to neglect and four
children were considered to have been emotionally abused. Children in
the abusing group were significantly more likely than those in the abused
only group to have been previously neglected (p <0.035).

Twenty two of the children (55%) came from backgrounds where violence between caretaking adults had been noted. This is likely to be an
underestimate as violent domestic relationships often go unrecorded
(Farmer and Owen, 1995). Previous social services involvement with the
families of these children was the norm. Only seven of the children (18%)
came from families previously unknown to social services. Eleven (28%)
of the young people had previously been the subject of a care order and
almost all of these were children who had abused others.

Breaks in continuity of care were also common. Nineteen had previously spent time in care, and 12 of these had experienced three or more
care episodes. Children in the abused/abusing category were twice as
likely to have previously spent time in care compared with children in the
abused only category. Twelve of the young people (30%) had experienced
multiple separations from their main caregiver.

Ten of the young people (25%) had suffered significant bereavements
in the past. Five children had lost their father or mother and a further five
children had lost a significant grandparent, sibling or foster sibling. It was
rare for bereavement counselling to have been offered, and the significance of these losses for the children often went unremarked by social
workers, although the children frequently referred to them in our interviews. Apart from losses by death, separations from significant parent
figures through divorce or loss of contact were also widespread. Seventeen of the children had lost contact with a parent, usually a father, in this
way and many of these separations seemed also to have been unresolved.

Given these figures it is not surprising that few of the young people
came from intact families at the point of their current entry to the care

system. Disrupted families of origin are not unusual in care populations (Bebbington and Miles, 1989) and the children in this sample were no exception. Only five of the 40 children had been living with both birth parents. This figure is substantially lower than the 25% reported by Bebbington and Miles. Fourteen of the children had been living in reconstituted families with a step-parent (usually mother and stepfather) and a further 19 children had been living with lone mothers. Two children had been living with single fathers. Almost all the children (93%) had experienced several changes of carer, house or placement.

Within the family and peer group, tensions or difficulties were often recorded. A substantial majority of the children (32) were described as having been so behaviourally disturbed that they had been beyond control at home at some time in the past. Severe rejection or scapegoating of the child was recorded in half the cases. Five of these cases of rejection were specifically linked to the disclosure of sexual abuse in the family of origin. These children were often blamed for having been responsible for the breakdown of relationships in the wider family or for causing tension in parental partnerships. In over half, parental management of the child was thought to have been damaging to the child's emotional development.

Eleven young people (seven boys and four girls), or over a quarter of the sample, reported being bullied in placements at some stage, of whom 10 were in the residential sector and one in foster care. The majority of the children who were bullied were aged under 14. Some of the bullying was severe and had not been known to staff. In at least two instances the bullying was a repeat experience of prior victimisation. For example, in one case a girl, who had entered care because of physical abuse by her mother, ended up as the only girl in her children's home and was bullied and assaulted by two boys who used a lighter to singe her hair. In addition, nine young people (five boys and four girls) bullied other children. The bullying took place in seven residential placements and two foster homes. Most of the incidents involved threats of violence or actual physical assaults on other children. It is noteworthy that most of the reported bullying took place in residential care. From the point of view of bullying, foster care provided a great deal more safety for children.

In addition, 10 of the young people had been bullied at school or had bullied others there. Some had been suspended or excluded because of their violent behaviour to other children at school and quite a few refused to attend because of their fear of being picked on. When these incidents were put together 16 of the young people had bullied others or been bullied in placements and this rose to 21, or over half of the young people, when bullying in school was included. Another four young people identified themselves in the Assessment and Action Records as getting picked on by other children where that information had not emerged from interviews. That made 24 (60%) children in all who had been bullied or had bullied others either at school or in their placements.

Enmeshed relationships between mothers and sons occurred in the case of nine out of the 18 boys in the study. Of these, four were thought likely to have had an incestuous sexual element. These enmeshed relationships were characterised by mutual difficulties in both living together *and* separating and the boys frequently had difficulties in settling in their placements. In one extreme case a 14-year-old boy repeatedly absconded from his rural residential school and walked 30 miles to rejoin his mother who, while caring for him, had difficulties in managing his frequently menacing and violent behaviour. Such relationships appeared to cluster among the sons of single mothers who had been or were currently in relationships with violent men.

Seven of the young people had a parent who was recorded as having had a personality disorder or psychiatric problem, including schizophrenia and depression. While only one of the young people was described as possibly having suffered from a psychiatric illness in the past, over half the children were reported to have experienced significant psychological or emotional distress. Nine of the young people (23%) self-harmed or attempted suicide during the index placement. Another 14 had cut themselves or attempted suicide in previous placements. Thus 23, or almost three fifths of the young people, had self-harmed or made one or more suicide attempts. In many cases these incidents were not known to the social workers or to the child's caregivers. A quarter of the young people were reported to have been abusing solvents, drugs or alcohol and 12 out of 40 had offended.

High levels of educational disruption were common. More than half the children were recorded as having exhibited severe behaviour problems at school and just under half the young people had a history of non-attendance at school. Nine had been suspended from school at some time and 13 had a history of school exclusion. During the index placement two fifths of the young people (14 of the 34 of school age) did not attend school, a slightly higher proportion than the third of children not attending schools in a study of residential care by Sinclair and Gibbs (1998).

Psycho-Social Problems of the Young People

Standardised measures were used to assess the emotional and behavioural problems of the young people at the time of interview, and a short summary of the main findings will be included in this chapter. It is intended to publish more detailed analysis of the material separately.

Primary caregivers or keyworkers were asked to complete the Child Behavior Checklist (CBCL, Achenbach, 1991a), and the young people completed the Youth Self-Report (YSR, Achenbach, 1991b) as described in Chapter 2. These include measures of *internalising* problems, such as anxiety and depression, and *externalising* problems, such as delinquent and sexually inappropriate behaviour. The young people filled in a self-report of depressive symptoms – the Children's Depression Inventory (CDI, Kovacs and Beck, 1977; Kovacs, 1982), and a measure of self-esteem based on domains identified for adolescents (SEQ, Harter, 1987), which also in cluded the 10 items of the Rosenberg Self-Esteem Inventory (1965). The measures chosen were, where possible, the same as those used in other recent studies of sexually abused and abusing children (for example Monck and New, 1996) in order to facilitate comparison. The young people also filled in a Locus of Control questionnaire (Nowicki and Strickland, 1973) to see how far they saw events in their lives as within their control.

Emotional and Behaviour Problems

Twenty-six out of 40 caregivers returned completed CBCL questionnaires (65%), and 33 (83%) of the young people themselves returned the YSR. Table 10 summarises the findings. It can be seen that based on the caregivers' ratings, a much higher proportion of children were seen to have serious emotional and behaviour problems (typical of levels that occur in clinically treated populations) than was the case when the children rated themselves. The most likely explanation was the children's denial of problems, found also in other studies (Hymel, Bowker and Woody, 1993; Monck & New, 1996). For this reason a "best estimate" was derived by taking the highest CBCL or YSR score as the "true" estimation. Overall, CBCL and/or YSR data were available on a total of 38 out of the 40 young people in the interview sample.

Table 10 Summary score on measures of emotional and behaviour problems by informant

Informant/scores	No.	Mean	Range	SD	Clinical		Borderline	
					No.	%	No.	%
Carer (CBCL)								
Internalising T	26	64.73	31–81	11.74	18	69.2	2	7.7
Externalising T	26	69.54	53–90	9.50	18	69.2	5	19.2
Total T	26	70.30	52–87	8.84	21	80.8	2	7.7
Child (YSR)								
Internalising T	33	57.78	38–81	9.45	10	30.3	6	18.2
Externalising T	33	61.03	23–87	12.93	15	45.5	6	18.2
Total T	33	60.03	34–81	10.18	12	36.4	7	21.2

Compared with other studies, high proportions of the children were displaying emotional and behaviour problems in the clinically significant or borderline range. As Table 11 shows, 11 (65%) of the 17 children who had only been sexually abused were in this range as compared with 47% in the Monck and New study (1996) of children referred for services in specialist day treatment facilities at the start of treatment. However, the children in our sample were somewhat older than those in the Monck and New research. Sixteen (94%) of the 17 victim-perpetrators and all four of the perpetrators only in our sample were in the clinically significant or borderline range, as compared with 54% of the victim-perpetrators at the start of treatment in the Monck and New study (1996). It was interesting to find that our sample of sexually abused and abusing young people had higher rates of clinical disturbance than the sample in Monck and New's study, all of whom were receiving treatment. However, apart from being somewhat older, all the children in our sample had experienced the disruptions associated with being looked after and often also of previous periods in care.

When the 17 children who had only experienced sexual abuse were compared with the 21 who had exhibited sexually abusing behaviour (whether or not they had suffered abuse), the "abusers" had significantly higher scores on measures of social problems, attention problems and total problems. They also tended to show more aggressive behaviour.

Table 11   Clinical significance of best estimate scores by sexual abuse category

Clinical/ borderline significance	Sexual abuse category							
	Victim		Perpetrator		Victim and perpetrator		Total	
	No.	%	No.	%	No.	%	No.	%
Withdrawn	1	6	2	50	6	35	9	24*
Somatic complaints	4	24	1	25	5	29	10	26
Anxious/depressed	6	35	2	20	10	59	18	47
Social problems	2	12	1	25	10	59	13	34**
Thought problems	4	24	1	25	7	41	12	32
Attention problems	6	35	3	75	10	59	19	50
Delinquent behaviour	12	71	4	100	13	77	29	76
Aggressive behaviour	5	29	2	50	9	53	16	42
Internalising T	11	65	4	100	13	77	28	74
Externalising T	13	77	4	100	15	88	32	84
Total T	11	65	4	100	16	94	31	82*
	N = 17		N = 4		N = 17		N = 38	

Chi square * $p < 0.06$ ** $p < 0.02$

Self-Reported Depression

Thirty four of the 40 children completed the Children's Depression Inventory. Eight of them scored in the clinical range for depressive symptoms, and a further 18 had mild depression, so that three quarters reported experiencing depression. At the time of interview 10 young people admitted to having thoughts of suicide and 10 more had actually considered means of ending their lives in the previous two weeks. These rates are higher than the already high rate of four in 10 young people in children's homes in the Sinclair and Gibbs' study (1998) who said that they had considered killing themselves in the previous month.

The young people in residential care had significantly higher mean scores on the Children's Depression Inventory, with almost half falling into the clinical range, compared with none of those in foster care. They also tended to have thought more seriously about ending their lives.

Self-Esteem

Thirty two children out of 40 completed the Self-Esteem Questionnaire (SEQ). On average, the children's scores indicated they had positive views of themselves. However, the 17 children placed in residential care had significantly lower self-esteem scores than the 15 children in foster care. In general, the children with high self-esteem had fewer depressive symptoms.

Locus of Control

With the exception of the children aged 12 and younger, average Locus of Control scores were over a single standard deviation higher for the young people in the sample compared with average scores for children of the same age. This means that they saw many events in their lives as outside their control.

In summary, these were young people who came from backgrounds of multiple deprivation, instability and uncertainty characterised by frequent separations from familiar people and places together with high levels of educational disruption. Family and peer group relationships were often characterised by conflict and the young people's disruptive and self-destructive behaviour mirrored their emotional disturbance. Sexual abuse was often only part of the complex and deep-rooted pattern of disadvantage which the young people brought with them to their placements. In the placement, they had high levels of emotional and behaviour problems. Depressive feelings were common and on one measure well over half (59%) had contemplated suicide.

In the next chapter we turn to look at the foster carers, residential and field social workers who had responsibility for looking after these challenging young people.

SUMMARY

1. Forty young people, their caregivers and social workers were selected for the interview sample. The young people were broadly representative of the population of sexually abused or abusing children in substitute care in the local authorities taking part in the study, but they appeared to fall at the more serious end of the continuum of difficulty and disturbance.

4. Nineteen of the index placements were in foster care and 21 in a variety of residential placements. At the time of the interview almost three quarters of the children had been in the index placement for less than a year. A third of the young people were subject to a care order and 40% were on the child protection register.

3. There was certainty that the sexual abuse had taken place in almost two thirds of the 40 cases. Almost half were abused by a household member. Most, but by no means all, abusers were adult males. Many of the children had been sexually abused by more than one perpetrator. Over a third of the children were not registered following the discovery of their abuse and there were prosecutions in only a quarter of the cases.

4. Twenty-two of the young people had shown sexually abusing behaviour either before, during or after the index placement. Three fifths of the young abusers were known to have abused more than one child and in half the cases the abuse constituted more than one isolated incident. Formal investigations of these incidents were rare and only one young person was prosecuted. The majority of the young abusers (18) had themselves been sexually abused at some time in the past.

5. Sexual abuse was part of a pattern of disadvantage in these young people's lives. More than two thirds of the children had suffered previous physical abuse and over a third neglect. More than half had experienced violence between their parents or parent figures and multiple separations from parental figures were common. The majority of children had previously been known to social services departments and almost half had spent an earlier period of time in care, with this experience most common among the abusers.

6. Four fifths of the young people had been beyond control at home and half of them had experienced severe rejection or scapegoating. Half of

the boys had enmeshed relationships with their mothers, some of which appeared to include a sexual element. Almost three out of five of the children had harmed themselves or attempted suicide. In addition, a third had been excluded from school and almost half had a history of non-attendance at school. The majority of the children who completed standard assessments were found to be scoring in the clinical range on measures of emotional and behaviour problems, with "abusers" showing more disturbance than "abused" young people. Approaching a quarter had clinically significant depression and 20 of the 34 who answered admitted to considering ending their lives. Children in residential care were more depressed and had lower self-esteem than those in other settings.

5

THE CAREGIVERS AND SOCIAL WORKERS IN THE INTERVIEW SAMPLE

In the last chapter the extent of disruption and behavioural disturbance of the young people in the interview sample was described. These findings would suggest that they required highly trained caregivers with particular skills. How far that was the case will emerge in this chapter in which the characteristics, qualifications and training of the foster carers, residential workers and social workers who took care of them will be described.

THE FOSTER CARERS

We were able to interview 17 (out of 19) foster carers. Just over half of them (nine) were in special schemes for children with challenging behaviour which attracted enhanced levels of payment. Eight of the nine children in the special schemes were fostered by couples, and one by a lone mother who later conceded that the teenage boy in her care "would be better in a family with a husband and wife, with two of them there to take the strain". The ages of these carers ranged from 32 to 53.

Of the eight carers not in special schemes, two were designated carers of specific children (Regulation 11), and one dealt with emergency placements. Carers in this group were in a similar age range to those in special schemes, from 37 to 54, and four of the eight were single parents. One of these was a single man.

The majority of foster carers were white Europeans, the exceptions being an African-Caribbean/white couple and a mixed race woman married to an Italian. A mixed race teenage boy was being fostered by a white single woman, but the young person had a black male social worker who was a valued role model. There was one African-Caribbean foster mother caring for an African-Caribbean girl, but she declined to be interviewed.

Generally, in the case of fostering couples, the woman was considered to be the main carer, sometimes combining this with a part-time job outside the home whilst the man pursued his own employment. However, in two cases the women worked full-time outside the home whilst the men were the main carers. One of these couples said that they were given the most difficult cases to foster (adolescent boys who had been involved in criminal activity) because the husband was recognised as the main carer. In two cases the fostering job was the principal source of income for the couple.

Qualifications and Experience

The foster carers' educational qualifications were varied, ranging from none at all to a university degree. No one had a formal qualification which was relevant to the caring professions, although one foster father had a City and Guilds Certificate in medical skills, and a foster mother had started to train as a State Registered nurse but was unable to continue. One foster father had both a business degree and a teaching qualification.

Six of the 17 foster families had been carers for over 10 years. Three foster carers had less than a year's experience, and a further four families had been fostering for one to five years. The remaining four had been carers for periods of between five and 10 years.

Fifteen of the 17 foster families had raised, or were still raising children of their own. In nearly all cases they cited this as a source of expertise that fitted them for the task of fostering. A couple who had no children of their own had originally intended adopting the child they now fostered, but had found her behaviour too difficult to complete this step. The other caregiver with no children of his own was a middle-aged single man who had worked in middle management and who now fostered three teenage boys.

Those who had been fostering for many years spoke of learning how to cope with difficult behaviour as they went along. One couple had cared for 29 children over 14 years, and another still had their original foster child living with them after 16 years, during which time they had also cared for many other children. In a few instances the early or current careers of carers complemented their caring skills. One foster father had been a residential carer and a foster mother worked full-time in a residential home for adults with learning difficulties. In the latter case the husband was regarded as the main carer, and he had been influenced to take up fostering by his own parents who were themselves foster carers. One foster mother brought to the job the knowledge gained from three years as a full-time social work assistant at a family centre, a job which she still performed.

Training

The majority of foster carers felt that the training they had received was good and that they could not get enough of it:

"You never know too much and things change all the time."

"I don't think foster carers could ever have enough knowledge."

However, two sets of carers felt that more training was offered than they required whilst another couple, who attended as many courses as they could, found a considerable number to be "irrelevant". Foster carers generally agreed that the opportunities for attending courses were plentiful, and if one was missed through, for example, illness or no vacancies, it was usually repeated six months later. Only one carer stated that there were not enough courses on offer.

A foster mother who worked in a residential home found that she could use the in-service training there to assist her in the foster care role, and she also chose courses under the fostering scheme which were useful in her work. Some foster carers had attended courses on the Children Act. One foster carer had also been on training sessions with social workers and carers from a children's home, but had found this experience of little use to her as conditions for them were so different.

In the unique case in our sample of the would-be adopters who were fostering the child, the carers said that they had learnt "through the back door". This was because they had attended a three-day adoption course and had obtained a lot of reading and video material. They had also attended workshops run by voluntary agencies which they would not have been able to attend if they had not been considering adoption.

Training Needs

Several gaps in training were highlighted by carers. The two Regulation 11 foster families who were approved to care for a specific child both said that they had received no formal training to assist them. They felt that the social services departments relied on their goodwill. The single mother concerned expressed a wish to attend general courses and, in particular, something that would help her to deal with her foster son's self-harm, but nothing had been arranged and she felt she had been left to cope alone. She told us that the social worker's response when she requested such a course was:

"Oh we see it as attention-seeking behaviour and ignore it." She added:

"I can't believe that someone can say that to me . . . I do wonder sometimes if they're just relying on the fact that I can cope, you know . . . I feel there are occasions when someone else would have fallen to pieces."

The other couple wanted more information on general fostering matters and they were worried about their lack of knowledge about where they stood in terms of responsibility for the child. Their social worker told them:

"If later on in time you do decide that you want to foster – not a specific child – then we'll put you on an introductory course."

Two fifths of the foster carers interviewed (seven) wanted more advice on dealing with sexually abused children, although six had already attended some courses on the subject. Particular aspects of this issue which needed further attention included how to deal with a child's disclosure and how to counsel abused children. Four carers wanted more courses on dealing with difficult behaviour. Another thought a course on communicating with children would be useful. The lone foster father wanted training and information about children with learning difficulties. Other courses that carers felt would be helpful included: working with outside agencies, practical first aid, coping with children with HIV, court work with children and drug awareness. This last-mentioned course had been requested by a foster father but it did not materialise, leaving him to track down leaflets for his own instruction.

A single foster mother had found her "brief" foster care course of one week too short, and other courses too far apart. She wanted foster carers to get together more to share their ideas and methods and suggested that spreadsheets should be available on subjects such as anorexia and bullying. She said that there was a need to access specific advice more easily, without having to make an appointment with a busy social worker.

In general, carers were eager to take up the training that was offered to them, although some had difficulty in attending the courses due to their work commitments or constraints on their time, or found it impossible to get baby-sitters who were willing or vigilant enough to look after difficult or abusing children when training occurred in the evening.

THE RESIDENTIAL WORKERS

As described above, 21 of the 40 young people in our interview sample were living in residential placements. Thirteen were accommodated in ten different children's homes, three were in residential schools one of which cared for deaf children, two were placed in secure units, two girls were in independent living units and one boy lived in a flat with his own residential social worker. In 15 cases we interviewed the child's keyworker and in one case we spoke with the head of a children's home where the keyworker was on extended sick leave. We also interviewed the head teacher of a residential school for children with educational and behaviour difficulties. Ten of the residential workers were women and seven were men. We were unable to conduct interviews with the keyworkers for four children in the sample, which included a young person in secure accommodation, and one who had moved on to a hostel.

The ages of the residential workers ranged from the early 20s to 60, the majority being between 30 and 45. They were mainly white European with one African-Caribbean and one black African keyworker.

Experience

The least experienced care worker had been in paid employment for just 10 months. Seven residential carers had 2–5 years' relevant experience, four had 5–10 years' experience, and five had over 10 years of experience.

Voluntary work had preceded entry into paid residential care employment for nearly half of the residential workers. The settings for this voluntary work included residential units, hospitals, hostels for the homeless, and working with teenagers in youth clubs. In the case of one voluntary worker, the month he spent in a children's unit led him to leave the army to take up this employment permanently.

The head of home who was interviewed had a background in residential care for nursery children and further experience in co-ordination of pre-adoption and fostering services before caring for 6–16-year-olds with challenging behaviour. The worker who looked after a young person in a flat had been a teacher and worked in probation before working in sheltered accommodation for aggressive young people. A senior residential worker at a specialist secure unit had been a secondary school teacher. Two keyworkers had previous experience in the caring professions, one as a psychiatric nurse and the other in working with adults with learning difficulties.

Qualifications

Twelve of the keyworkers (71%) had no formal qualifications which related to their employment, although one was undertaking an NVQ course in supported living, and another was a qualified teacher.

Of the five residential workers whose qualifications were relevant, the head of home had a certificate in social studies and had trained as a nursery nurse. One residential worker had an Open University diploma in working with young people with behaviour problems and another had a City and Guilds certificate in community care and an NVQ in working with people with learning difficulties. The senior residential worker had diplomas in counselling and social learning theory whilst the headmaster of the school for children with educational and behavioural difficulties had a degree in education, specialising in emotional difficulties.

Training

The head of home said that many of her staff were untrained, but she added that the local authority offered many in-service training courses. She encouraged her staff to attend these to the extent of paying them overtime to go on their days off, since it was not possible to cover their shifts during working hours unless they were attending NVQ courses. Another worker said that numerous courses were offered by social services and the National Children's Home, and that it was the fault of the staff if they failed to take advantage of them: "It's there if people apply to do these things."

However, three workers said that they had had to use their own initiative to find the courses that they required. One who said that he and his colleagues needed more specialised knowledge was constantly looking for suitable courses and putting himself forward. Another who realised that the majority of residents in her independent living unit had a history of sexual abuse sought out a session run by the NSPCC on techniques for dealing with sexually abused young women.

Some of those who were eager to attend courses had experienced difficulties because of lack of staff cover or financial constraints. A worker who had applied to attend college was told that there were no staff to cover for her. She was very upset about this because she saw the training as part of her job.

Only five of the 17 residential workers interviewed (29%) said that they had attended courses or seminars which dealt specifically with sexually abused children. Three workers had attended "Challenge in Residential Child Care" courses and one had, as part of her course project, produced booklets on leaving care. A criticism of this course by one worker was that various aspects such as fostering, communicating with young people and looking after sexually abused children had been dealt with too briefly. Courses dealing with drug-taking had been attended by two workers, and three others had learned self-defence and methods of physical restraint which helped to reduce staff injuries. The worker at the residential school for deaf children had benefited from in-service training, and a worker who had had numerous intensive training courses mentioned one on working in partnership with other agencies which she had found very useful.

Other courses which had been attended by one or two workers included working with children and young people, children's development, and managing violence and aggression. One worker was about to attend a course designed to help young people who were involved in police inter-views, entitled "Appropriate Adult in a Police Interview Situation".

The majority of workers said that the courses they had attended were useful. Four others mentioned that reading was an important element of their skills development, two of whom said that their units had extensive library material. One of these residential workers referred to "the shelf" in her office which contained agency procedures and Children Act guidelines. This was required reading for the staff although this worker said:

"I haven't done it, I must confess. But now when I have supervision he'll say read so and so, and I've got to read it."

Only two workers expressed no desire to further their training or knowledge and one other who had attended "many courses" said that they were "too much social work and rubbish".

Six residential workers told us that they had developed their skills through a combination of life experiences, listening to the advice of col-leagues, training courses, and learning on the job. One felt that the necess-ary skills had been developed mainly through her own efforts. She said, "It's kind of instinctive I think". An African-Caribbean worker said that had she not been able to draw on her own life experiences, she doubted whether she would have lasted a week in residential work, due to the lack of awareness of racism in her children's home.

Several gaps in training were identified by the residential workers. Five expressed a need for more knowledge to enable them to work with sex-ually abused young people. One other worker explained that although there was a lot of information on dealing with the disclosure of sexual abuse, he needed guidance on working with sexually abused young people in a more therapeutic manner. The difficulty of dealing with this aspect of their jobs is illustrated in the following quotations:

"I don't think I was particularly skilled at drawing out stuff that she might want to tell me but couldn't."

"There are situations that arise and I feel, I think, I'm not actually qualified to cope with it, and therefore extra knowledge or training would be useful."

"At the moment I don't feel too confident about opening something up that I might not be able to deal with or contain . . . I mean it might cause more damage in saying something to Katy than not saying it."

Courses on counselling young people were requested by four workers. Other subjects in which carers wanted training included working with young people using drugs, communicating with children, methods for teaching young people assertiveness, and in the case of an African-Caribbean residential worker, anti-racism training for staff at her children's home. One residential worker thought that all residential staff in her children's home would agree with her when she said that there was a need for more training in *every* aspect of the job.

THE SOCIAL WORKERS

We interviewed 34 social workers who were working with 39 of the 40 young people in our interview sample. Five workers each had responsibility for two children in the study. We were unable to interview the child's social worker in one case. Almost three quarters (25) of the social workers were female of whom one was black. She was the worker for a white male youth and a black girl. There were nine male social workers of whom two were black. Both were working with white children. The majority of social workers (20) were in the 36–45 year age group, seven were aged 20–35 and seven were over 46. The youngest social worker was 23 and the oldest 61.

Qualifications and Experience

Social work qualifications, either a Certificate of Qualification in Social Work or a Diploma in Social Work, were held by 32 (94%) of the social workers. Six also had university degrees in, for example, psychology or social sciences, one held a certificate in counselling, and another had a diploma in psychiatric social work. One worker had been awarded a Certificate in Social Studies (CSS).

The longest serving social worker had been practising for 25 years since she qualified. Nine workers had had 10–20 years experience and 12 had practised for 5–9 years. A further 12 workers (35%) had been qualified for less than five years. Five workers in this group had had 1–2 years' experience and one had been qualified for just six months. Although the most experienced worker was at the top end of the age range at 61, those with least experience were not necessarily the youngest. Eight who had been qualified for less than five years were in the middle and upper age ranges.

Teams and Caseloads

Two of the social workers interviewed were employed in specialist youth justice teams. One of our interviewees was a child care team manager who was dealing with the case during the prolonged absence on sick leave of the social worker. Her team carried "a very mixed caseload" including children looked after long-term, child protection and preventive work.

Most of the social workers operated within specialist long-term or short-term child care or children and families teams, which included elements of child protection and investigation. A few teams dealt with a mixture of long- and short-term child care cases. A male worker in a long-term team dealt solely with older adolescents with challenging and of-fending behaviour. We were told that, because of pressure of work in the long-term teams, cases were often held by the short-term teams for longer than they should have been.

Caseloads were often described as "very busy" or "heavy" but one social worker said that hers was unusually low to enable her to fulfil her obligations to undertake court work. A worker whose caseload consisted of 18 families pointed out that this involved a very large number of children, since some of the families contained six or eight youngsters. Twenty two of the children on his caseload were on the child protection register.

Training

Of the 34 social workers interviewed, 14 felt that their training had been complemented by a combination of other factors which included their own life experience, learning on the job, and advice from colleagues. The following quotation represents these views:

"Part of it is through your own life experience isn't it, bringing up your own children. And part of it is from stuff you get – learning from colleagues and training courses you go on. It is a mish mash of lots of different experiences really."

Ten workers said that they had accumulated the knowledge necessary to work with the children in our sample from having previously dealt with similar cases, and a Family Centre placement for one worker whilst at college had proved an asset. It was widely held that certain skills could only be acquired from working directly with young people.

Most social workers felt that there was sufficient post-qualifying train-ing, particularly in the child protection field, although their views varied as to its effectiveness. Court work had prevented one worker from attend-ing a child protection course and he had found that the in-service training he had received was "not relevant" to the type of case he was handling because it had been confined to basic Working Together courses covering the implementation of the Children Act. In-service training offered valuable opportunities for one worker to up-date on practice and issues of legislation, and she attended several courses each year. Three social workers found their post-qualifying training unsatisfactory because it had been limited to general child care issues.

Two social workers highlighted the training anomalies for members of a child and family team who were working with adolescents. They had had no training courses in working with adolescents because in the department there was a clear division between people who worked with adolescents (for example, the youth justice teams and the scheme for difficult behaviour) and those who worked in the section responsible for children and families. Because of this, training about adolescent issues had been difficult for them to access. For this reason they felt that adolescents got a poor service from their teams.

The worker who was attached to a youth court team had discovered that his original training for a career in probation work was inappropriate for his present role because he had vital gaps in his knowledge of child development and care, essential for work in the children's division. However, he saw himself as "learning fast".

Training Courses Attended

Eight workers (24%) mentioned that they had attended courses dealing with sexual abuse, and whilst three thought that they had been useful, the other five had reservations. The main complaint was that the courses lasting two or three days were too brief. In one case the worker said that sexual abuse was not an area in which she felt comfortable, and although she had done courses through social services and with the NSPCC, which included direct work with sexually abused children, the opportunity to use this training had never presented itself. One of the workers who was happy with the courses added that there could never be enough training about abuse and that she would go on any course that she had not done before because "there's so many different aspects of abuse to look at".

Courses specifically aimed at training staff for direct work with sexually abused children had been attended by two social workers, one of whom stressed that her course concerned children who were still being abused. Training in preparing and using video evidence for child sexual abuse cases had been useful to two social workers. One had altered her method of working as a result of the course because she had learnt so much about how she looked and sounded to other people:

"One watershed thing for me was the video evidence training . . . that was quite a momentous training for me because it hurt when I saw myself as others might see me."

Three workers had attended counselling courses but one had done so "off her own bat" when she sought out a social services course which contained a module on counselling skills with young people. Another worker had discovered that the counselling training which she had received when working with a community alcohol team had proved useful in her work with young people who drank excessively, as did the girl in our sample.

A social worker in a specialist team for disabled children had undergone disability awareness training which dealt with communicating with children with learning difficulties. His post-qualifying training had hitherto been confined to child protection work. Three other workers had taken courses specifically dealing with communication skills in work with adolescents. A course entitled "Working in Partnership" had been very useful to a social worker who said that it had changed the way in which she worked with our subject child. She believed that the course had "shifted people's attitudes" and that there was no longer a demand that children be adopted in order to provide permanence "and never mind the contact". Training aimed to facilitate life-story work with children had helped one social worker to undertake such work with a particular child.

The NSPCC were praised for their training. One worker described their course on planned work with adolescents as the most interesting of her in-service training. It was very practical, with lots of ideas and practical ways of explaining things:

"That was very helpful because the idea of things is fine – it's the actual doing of them that's often the most difficult."

A worker, who had a current case involving a Schedule One offender in the family, described attendance at NSPCC sessions with the family as "brilliant training" for her. She also found that she gained valuable knowledge by seeking out information to give to the mother concerning the effects of abuse on her daughter.

Training Needs

One worker highlighted the fact that apart from training in practice teaching, there was:

"No other type of training for people who are three, four or five years qualified, or for experienced people. There is a big gap."

This worker said that his child protection training had been very basic when he started, and that more in this field, to include assessment of risks and investigations "would be way at the top" of his agenda. He said:

"It is something we are doing all the time but we have never given it any formal thought, or application of theory or relating it to any research. There is just not the opportunity to do that."

Seven workers (21%) wanted more training for working with sexually abused children. Training in interpreting the behaviours they showed and a greater knowledge of how best to then respond to them was called for by one worker.

One worker said that she needed more specialised courses because so far the training had been "run of the mill stuff". Post-qualifying training had thrown up nothing new on the subject of sexually abused children for one social worker who had thoroughly researched the area for her university course, and she found that her learning about the subject – signs, symptoms, cause and effect – came from working with the cases. The following quotation illustrates another worker's wish for more training in this area:

"I have got a lot of experience in working with young people. I would like to have some more experience in the area of sexual abuse . . . there is not that much around on sexual abuse."

Three workers wanted training on working with sexually *abusing* young people. One whose caseload included a number of young abusers was trying to get onto the next available course because he felt that he needed to know how much of their behaviour was appropriate, how much was experimentation and how much was actual abuse. Another social worker wanted to know how to assess future risk and whether a girl's past would "always make her an abuser". She had written to various experts for advice.

Two workers wanted courses which covered children with special needs. Three called for a greater knowledge of substance misuse and one wanted a self-defence course, in this case to protect her from a mother. An older female social worker wanted training in assertiveness with "stroppy teenagers". An area of training which eluded two workers centred on helping families. For example, a social worker who felt comfortable with the individual work that she did with the young person was not so confident when it came to working with the family:

"When you have to take on board everybody else in a family, then it's a different area and I'm not that experienced in that."

The other worker wanted training for social workers who work with families on a long-term basis which involved exploring attachment and moving on. She wanted to learn how to effect change in families. Two social workers wanted training in one-to-one counselling and group work, one in family therapy, and another wanted a course on domestic violence and mediation work. Two other workers wanted training for working generally with adolescents and ideas on building up young people's self-esteem were sought by one worker who said:

"That would be a useful area . . . some direct work ideas around how you work on self-esteem of young people and how you raise difficult subjects that are very painful, that they use different strategies to avoid . . . I'd really benefit from more training around how to tackle those things with young people."

A need for more knowledge in *every* area was identified by six social workers who thought that training should be ongoing. The following quotations illustrate their views:

"You constantly feel unskilled or de-skilled because every situation is new."

"You can never have enough training, it is always helpful, it can always give you an extra insight."

One worker thought that refresher courses should be available "so that work continues to be meaningful".

Only one social worker told us that she could think of nothing that she lacked by way of training. She had undertaken all the courses that she wished to do and had found them all very useful. By contrast, three social workers said that their post-qualifying training had not helped them to work with our sample cases, and three others had found that their in-service training in general was insufficient.

However, not all workers were able to attend the in-service courses which were provided in their authorities. One worker who had qualified 15 years earlier described her training since then as very sparse, apart from "a couple of workshops". The lack of training opportunities for one social worker who had been qualified for two years had been the subject of "heated debates". She had been prevented from attending a three-day course on communicating with children, because she was on a temporary contract.

Shortage of time was a major constraint on attending training courses. Four social workers cited this as the key issue for them. A worker who told us that management was willing to pay, the Principal Social Services Officer was willing to release her, and there were lots of courses to choose from, still was not able to get the training she desired. This, she told us, was due to the immense amount of time that she had to devote to writing up cases and to contact work. Likewise, another worker said:

"Having the time to go on the training courses is my problem, because I have got so many . . . complex cases that I am working with at the moment."

Another social worker said that the sheer volume of basic courses on offer made it difficult to single out those that would really benefit her work, given the constraints on her time:

"I do hear about most of them . . . Often time is a factor. I actually felt swamped in the last couple of years . . . having difficulty keeping up with recordings or deadlines, and management overview of that. And just feeling that I can't take on any more."

In general our impression was that while social workers, residential workers and foster carers were available and willing to improve their knowledge and skills in their work with the sexually abused and abusing young people in their care the existing training opportunities were provided on a piecemeal basis rather than being provided as part of a well-resourced and co-ordinated strategy. There was a considerable need for specialist and advanced courses that would help experienced caregivers and social workers build on their existing skills to develop their practice and feelings of competence.

SUMMARY

1. Of the 19 foster carers 17 were interviewed. The foster carers were appreciative of the training offered by their authorities, with the exception of the Regulation 11 carers who received none. Two fifths of the foster carers wanted more advice on dealing with sexually abused children.
2. Of the 21 residential caregivers 17 were interviewed. Twelve of the 17 residential workers had no formal qualifications which related to their employment and access to in-service training varied according to the availability of staff cover. Over a third of the residential workers wanted more training on working with sexually abused young people.
3. Thirty four social workers were interviewed who dealt with 39 of the children in the study. The majority of social workers were white (31)

and almost three quarters were female. Most of the social workers had a social work qualification. One in five wanted more training in working with sexually abused children and three in working with children who were abusers. Shortage of time was a major constraint on attending training courses.

4. Training opportunities appeared to be provided on a piecemeal basis rather than as part of a well-resourced and co-ordinated strategy. There was a considerable need for more advanced courses that would help more experienced caregivers and social workers to develop their practice in working with sexually abused and abusing young people.

6

SEXUAL BEHAVIOUR INSIDE AND OUTSIDE PLACEMENT

Now that the characteristics of the children, their caregivers and social workers have been described, we will examine the sexual behaviours displayed by the 40 young people in the interview sample once they had arrived in the index placement. There were 18 boys and 22 girls.

DEFINITIONAL ISSUES: WHICH BEHAVIOURS ARE DEFINED AS UNACCEPTABLE?

Sexual behaviours are generally not very visible, they are intended not to be observed by outsiders, and even when they do come to the notice of others the nature of what has occurred may never be clarified. It was not uncommon, for example, for caregivers and social workers to hold different views on whether particular young people were having sexual intercourse with their partner or partners. Moreover, even when such behaviours are visible they are filtered through the perceptions of caregivers, social workers, school staff and others. Similar behaviour may be defined as normal adolescent sexual exploration, problematic sexual behaviour or pathological activity depending on the viewpoint of the adult who discovers the activity. Sexual norms, and in particular, ideas about normal sexual behaviour in adolescence change over time. There is also a lack of reliable normative research data about the sexual behaviour of children (Grocke, 1991).

Over and above this there are complex definitional issues about what is or is not interpreted as sexual abuse or sexually abusive behaviour. Researchers and specialised professionals rehearse and alter their definitions at various stages of their work. The pragmatic definitions or interpretations employed by caregivers, social workers and other professionals in their day-to-day contact with young people will vary depending on a number of factors, such as their own attitudes to sexuality, the extent of their training and experience in this area and, more pragmatically, the power which they can invoke to alter the behaviours of the young people for whom they have a measure of responsibility. Moreover, some caregivers and professionals who work extensively with sexualised young people may come to develop high thresholds for what is acceptable behaviour and may be slow to define as abnormal behaviour that which would be seen as very concerning in a less disturbed population of adolescents (see also Farmer and Owen, 1995).

Another powerful determinant of the constructions made about sexual behaviour is the gender both of the young people involved and of their caregivers and other professionals. At its simplest, sexual advances made by males to females are more likely to be constructed as abusive than are sexual advances made by females to males, unless the age gap between the girl who initiates sexual activity with a boy is very large.

Whilst some sexual behaviours are self-evidently harmful to young people, others are more borderline and can be subject to different interpretations. For example, Frank was aged 17 when he developed a relationship with a girl of 11. His foster carers saw this as potentially sexually abusive behaviour and requested his removal because they considered that he could pose a risk to their 5-year-old daughter. Whilst this decision may have been reasonable, since Frank had learning difficulties, this relationship was in line with his mental age and not as inappropriate as it appeared at first sight.

However, on the whole, the interpretations put on the sexual behaviours of the young people in the sample by their caregivers and social workers were not generally in the direction of pathologising behaviours which many would have considered normal in adolescence. It was much more usual to find that sexual behaviours which appeared to put young people at risk were normalised. One example was a girl of 12 who on a number of occasions was seen outside her children's home getting into cars with known Schedule One offenders with whom she stayed out overnight. This behaviour led to no action from the residential workers. In contrast, her mother was alarmed and tried to take out a private prosecution against the men concerned.

In addition to these issues of the interpretation of behaviour, information about any one child's sexual behaviours may be known by individuals or held on case records but not systematically shared when children move to a new placement. Important information may therefore not be known by residential workers or foster carers at the time of the young person's arrival in placement.

The description of behaviours in this chapter has been derived from the full range of sources of information available in the study, that is the child's case file and interviews with the young person, their placement caregiver and field social worker. Inevitably, it covers only those behaviours which were known to the respondents and about which they were prepared to talk. We have attempted to be rigorous in our classification of sexual behaviours, but the choice of grouping for some behaviours is difficult to make. There can be a fine line between, for example, overtly sexual behaviour and sexually abusing behaviour. These definitional difficulties bring home the complexity and sensitivity of the task facing caregivers and social workers who deal with sexual behaviours in substitute care.

THE DIMENSIONS OF SEXUAL BEHAVIOURS SHOWN BY THE YOUNG PEOPLE

The sexual behaviours which were in evidence during care placements varied on a number of key dimensions. The first was the type of sexual activity itself, which could be non-contact (such as exhibitionism), contact without penetration (such as sexual touching of another's body) or penetrative contact (vaginal or anal intercourse). The second dimension was the age and/or power difference between the participants and the third was how far the activity was consensual or had been subject to coercion. A fourth factor was whether the sexual activity was exploitative in the sense that adults systematically used a young person for their sexual gratification (for example, involvement in prostitution). The fifth factor which differentiated among sexual behaviours was whether the young person acted alone (such as in masturbation), with other young people or with adults. The sixth and final dimension was the location of the sexual activity. The critical distinction was between behaviours which took place in the placement and those which occurred off the premises, whether in the community, at school or back in the child's family during contact visits. The intersection of these dimensions of sexual activity are shown in Table 1.

THE RANGE OF SEXUAL BEHAVIOURS SHOWN OR EXPERIENCED BY THE YOUNG PEOPLE

After they were placed in residential or foster care what sexual behaviours did the young people in our interview sample show or experience from others in the index placement?

Young Person Only

Masturbation

Starting with sexual activities which did not involve approaches to others (non-contact) five of the young people masturbated compulsively. Three

Table 1   Classification of sexual behaviours

	Types of sexual behaviours	
	In placement	Outside placement (in community/school/family)
Young person only	Sexual self-harm	Masturbation in public
Young person and other young people	*1. Non-contact* Sexualised behaviour to children in placement	*1. Non-contact* Self-exposure
Dimensions: • Type of contact: Touching to penetrative sex	*2. Contact* 13-year-old girl offers sexual contact to male residents in children's home	*2. Contact* 10-year-old boy aggressively touches boy's genitals at school
• Age and/or power difference	14-year-old boy rubs genitals of 3-year-old child of foster carers	10-year-old boy has sexual contact with younger brother on a contact visit
• Consensual to coercive/aggressive	Consensual sexual relationship between boy and girl in children's home	Boyfriend–girlfriend relationships
	Long-term sexual abuse of boy (up to age 16) in residential school by another male resident with intimidation	16-year-old girl raped by known male peer in park
Young person and adults	*1. Non-contact* Sexualised behaviour with caregivers or visitors to placement	*1. Non-contact* Sexualised behaviour to staff at school
Dimensions: • Type of contact: Touching to penetrative sex	*2. Contact* Child stimulates self on caregiver's lap Child seeks sexualised physical contact with caregiver	*2. Contact* Sexual activity with adults outside placement
• Consensual to coercive	Sexual abuse by residential worker	Sexual activity with Schedule One offender Rape by acquaintance
• Exploitation		Prostitution Procurement of young people from placement Involvement in pornographic activities

of the boys in this group frequently masturbated when with others either in the living room or in one case during bus journeys with his social worker. A fourth child was a girl who would masturbate whilst sitting on the lap of one of her foster carers or riding piggyback with them.

Whilst self-stimulation which took place in private would not generally come to adult attention, it had done so in two cases where children were known to insert objects into themselves. One boy inserted objects into his anus and the sexual self-harm of the girl already mentioned was known to her caregivers because of the bleeding which resulted from insertion of objects into her vagina.

Young Person and Other Young People

Sexualised Behaviour by the Young People

Five of the young people, all girls, showed sexualised behaviour to other children in their placements.

Four girls showed non-contact behaviours such as offering themselves to boys in their residential homes or dressing provocatively to attract attention. Examples were a girl who would dress scantily and drape herself across her bed when a new male resident was admitted to the children's home and a girl in foster care who dressed only in her bra to do the ironing when there were boys in the house. A fifth girl frequently tried to kiss her foster carers' 17-year-old son.

Sexually Abusing Behaviour by the Young People

However, seven young people in the sample (three boys and four girls) showed sexually abusing behaviour towards over 13 children, in that they targeted, sexually touched, or in one case, penetrated a younger child apparently without consent and sometimes involving coercion. The victims were younger siblings either in a shared foster care placement or on a contact visit, the younger sons of the foster carers and other children in either residential or foster care. An example was Zoe aged 10 who was found with her foster carers' 6-year-old son naked from the waist down in bed with Zoe masturbating him and rolling to get on top of him. Another example was Fiona aged 13 who got the boys in her children's home to fondle her, encouraged younger boys to sit on her lap and offered herself to them sexually in exchange for cigarettes. There was also one case of a boy of 14 in the study who was arrested on suspicion of rape whilst at home after being suspended from his residential placement.

Sexual Abuse to the Young People

In addition, two adolescent girls alleged that they suffered sexual abuse by another young person. One alleged sexual abuse by a boy in her children's home but subsequent investigation did not substantiate the allegation. The other girl alleged rape by her friend's boyfriend when she was out one evening. There was insufficient evidence for an investigation but it seems likely that unwanted sexual intercourse did take place. The lack of official action after her allegation may have been connected to the fact that she had made previous allegations of sexual abuse which were considered to be fabricated.

Sexual Activity with Peers Outside Placement

Not all sexual contact, of course, was unwanted. It is likely that a considerable number of the adolescents in our interview sample were involved in consensual sexual activity during their stay in care, but this was mentioned as an issue of concern only in relation to girls. Concern was expressed about the sexual activity of eight of the girls in the sample, generally because they had many different sexual partners and were seen as "an easy lay" or "boy mad". Some were the subject of gossip and even graffiti at school because of their sexual availability. Sometimes they drew other young people from the placement into their sexual activities and thereby put them at risk. Others were already the target of sexually predatory young people before they started to be looked after and this continued in placement.

There are considerable gender differences in what is considered appropriate sexual activity for adolescents, with high levels of sexual activity or numbers of partners seen as a matter of concern in relation to girls but not boys. Part of this difference is no doubt connected to the risk of pregnancy for girls and pregnancy arising whilst a young person is in the care of the state is likely to be seen as particularly undesirable. Moreover, since most of the girls were under 16 at the time of placement, penetrative sex constituted unlawful sexual intercourse, a charge which could be brought against their male partners. Girls who have been sexually abused may have low self-esteem and an expectation that their social contacts with members of the opposite sex will involve sexual activity. They are also vulnerable to being used as sexual objects by others because of their past experiences.

Sexual Relationships Within Placements

In addition to sexual activity outside the placements it was reported that at least five young people (three boys and two girls) had a consensual sexual relationship with a fellow resident in their children's home during their stay. Of course, there may have been other such relationships which were never made public. A sixth child, a girl, rebuffed sexual advances made to her by two boys in her children's home. The five sexual relationships were heterosexual in four cases and lesbian in a fifth. When these relationships came to light it was usual for the young people to be told to desist from sexual activity in the residential home itself because of the impact on other residents and often one of the young people was moved out.

Any institution will need policies on how to handle sexual relationships between residents, whether of the same or opposite sex. However, these questions achieve a particular salience when one or both young people have previously been exposed to sexually abusive experiences.

Pregnancy

Four of the 22 young women (18%) in the study became pregnant whilst placed in care, three of whom were aged under 16.

Young Person and Adults

Sexualised Behaviour by the Young People

There were 13 young people (nine girls and four boys) who displayed sexualised behaviour towards adults. Five were in foster care and the remainder in residential settings. Six girls showed non-contact sexualised behaviour, such as exposing themselves or flirting with male residential staff or men whom they met outside the placement or acting in what was described as a "sexually provocative" manner with male visitors. One boy was verbally sexually aggressive to girls and women he passed on the street, calling out to them, "How you doing, bitch?". For another six young people the sexualised behaviour involved contact (three girls and three boys). The girls sexually touched or hugged residential workers and foster carers, usually but not always focusing on the male caregiver. The boys kissed, hugged and touched female residential workers in their placements or staff at school. For example, one boy tried to suck the necks and touch the breasts of female residential workers in his children's home. Some of the boys' approaches were seen as comfort-seeking behaviours whilst others were construed as sexually expressed aggression.

Sexual Abuse to the Young People

In contrast to these behaviours which were initiated by the young people, three others had (or were alleged to have had) an experience of sexual victimisation by an adult. One girl alleged that she had been sexually abused by a male residential worker who had rubbed against her, another was raped by a man who she met in a pub garden and a third became the object of sexual gratification for her grandfather who bought used items of underwear from her.

Prostitution and Other Exploitative Sexual Activity

During their stay in the index placement five young people appeared to be involved in prostitution. Another young woman had been actively involved in prostitution during the current care episode but had been placed in a secure unit and so was not currently sexually active. Two of the five young people were actively engaged in prostitution during the index placement, one a boy and one a girl. The other three (all boys) were frequenting the meeting point where rent boys made contact with their clients and were at the very least on the fringes of such activity. The young people who were known to be actively involved in prostitution not infrequently procured young people from their placements to service their clients, an issue to which we will turn in Chapter 10. Some had been involved in the making of pornographic videos for money and involved other children whom they met in placement in these activities. In addition, as we have seen, a sixth girl regularly associated with Schedule One offenders while she was in residential care.

Having described the range of sexual behaviours shown by the adolescents in our sample, Table 2 summarises the combined sexual behaviours

Table 2 The sexual activity and sexual experiences of the young people in the interview sample during the index placement

Sexual activity	No. of boys	No. of girls	Total	%
Masturbation	4	1	5	13
Overt sexual behaviour	4	11	15	38
Sexually abusing behaviour	3	4	7	18
Sexual activity with peers noted as of concern, excluding exploitative sexual activity	3	10	13	33
Prostitution and other exploitative sexual activity	4	2	6	15
Sexual abuse to the young person	0	4	4	10
Pregnancy (% of girls)	0	4	4	18

and experiences of the young people alone, with other young people and with adults. Some young people showed sexual behaviours or had sexual experiences with both peers and adults, for example three young people were involved in overt sexual behaviour with both their peers and adults and one was sexually abused by both a peer and an adult. In this table such multiple activities are not shown within individual categories of behaviour because the child is the unit being counted.

As can be seen 13% of the young people masturbated a great deal in public or inserted objects into themselves, and nearly two fifths (38%) showed overt sexual behaviour to adults and/or children. The sexual activity of a third of the young people was a source of concern to their substitute carers either because of the number of sexual partners involved or because sexual relationships took place in the placements. Almost one in five of the girls became pregnant and one in seven of the young people worked as prostitutes or were involved in another form of exploitative sexual activity during the placement. One in 10 of the adolescents disclosed sexual abuse to them during the time of the placement and almost one in five sexually abused another child within the placement or in one case outside it. In all, over two thirds of the young people (27) were involved in one or more of these sexual activities. It is interesting to note that in spite of their backgrounds a third of the adolescents were not reported in interviews as showing any of these sexual behaviours.

While some sexual behaviours occurred predominantly within the residential or foster placements, others generally took place away from the care setting. The masturbation reported was mostly within placements, but occasionally a child also masturbated elsewhere. Overtly sexual behaviour to peers and adults was especially noticeable when directed at other residents and caregivers, but it too was apparent with other children and with staff at school. Whilst most of the sexually abusing behaviour which came to attention was observed within placements, some occurred outside, such as one boy who sexually abused his younger brother during a contact visit.

Consensual sexual activity with peers and with adults mostly took place during evenings out or during periods of absconding. However, some children had sexual relationships with other residents inside their placements. Prostitution took place away from the placements, although contacts were sometimes made from children's homes and children were picked up by their clients from the doors of their residence. The allegations of sexual abuse related to two incidents within placements and three outside them.

THE REVISED CHILD SEXUAL BEHAVIOUR INVENTORY

In addition to scanning the case records and asking caregivers and social workers about any sexual behaviours exhibited by the young people a

36-item measure of sexual behaviours was used with caregivers. This questionnaire was used to gain the fullest information possible from caregivers, because when they were asked about sexual behaviours some actions would not have been recalled without a prompt and other behaviours might not be defined by them as sexual. The measure chosen was the revised Child Sexual Behaviour Inventory devised by Friedrich (Friedrich *et al*, 1991, 1992; Friedrich, 1993). The inventory was designed for children aged 2–12 and it is intended to discriminate between sexually abused and non-abused children in this age group. Its usefulness for our study was that it specifies 36 separate sexual behaviours which can be used for descriptive purposes. It has also been shown not to demonstrate systematic differences when used with substitute carers and birth parents.

Some of the difficulties in gathering good quality information about a sensitive subject such as sexual abuse were demonstrated by the fact that only 22 inventories were completed on the 40 children in the sample. Some caregivers refused to fill it in because of its sexual content, commenting that such issues were "private" or more vocally complaining that the questionnaire was "disgusting". Occasionally a substitute carer said that they did not know a child well enough to fill in the form, a large number of forms were not returned and in a few cases it had not been possible to interview a caregiver who knew the child. The young people whose forms we did receive were, however, fairly representative of the whole sample in relation to their gender and the type of placement they were in. There was clearly some bias in that amongst the young people whose forms were not returned were some whose substitute carers were particularly uncomfortable in talking about sexual issues.

As expected, the sexual behaviour inventory revealed more incidents of particular behaviours on some items than had been described in interviews. This suggests that the sexual behaviours previously described should be taken as an underestimate of those which would have been shown in the index placements. The inventory also revealed a wide range of specific behaviours, which substitute carers had had to manage. In Tables 3–6 the behaviours have been grouped according to the type of activity described.

Table 3 Masturbation recorded on the CSBI-R

Activity	(No)	%
Touches sex (private) parts when at home	(6)	27
Touches sex (private) parts when in public places	(5)	23
Rubs body against people or furniture	(5)	23
Inserts/tries to insert objects in vagina or anus	(2)	9
Makes sexual sounds (sighing, moaning, heavy breathing, etc.)	(3)	14

Seven of the 22 young people (32%) for whom forms were returned showed one or more of the masturbatory behaviours described in Table 3.

Table 4 Weak interpersonal boundaries recorded on the CSBI-R

Activity	(No)	%
Stands too close to people	(11)	50
Overly friendly with men they don't know well	(10)	45
Hugs adults they don't know well	(10)	45
Kisses adults they don't know well	(8)	36
Talks in a flirtatious manner	(7)	32
Touches/tries to touch women's breasts	(5)	23
Tries to look at people when they are nude or undressing	(5)	23
Kisses other children they don't know well	(4)	18
Touches other people's sex (private) parts	(3)	14
Tries to undress other children or adults against their will (opening pants, shirts, etc.)	(2)	9
Tries to put mouth on women's breasts	(1)	5

As many as 18 of the 22 young people for whom we had forms (82%) showed evidence of having weak interpersonal boundaries (Table 4).

Table 5 Self-exposure recorded on the CSBI-R

Activity	(No)	%
Shows sex (private) parts to adults	(2)	9
Shows sex (private) parts to children	(5)	23

Six of the 22 young people (27%) for whom inventories were completed had exposed themselves during placement (Table 5). Ten of the young people, or just under half of those for whom there were forms, showed one or more of the other sexual behaviours shown in Table 6.

Table 6 Other behaviours recorded on the CSBI-R

Activity	(No)	%
Talks about sexual acts	(8)	36
Asks to look at nude or sexually explicit TV shows or videos	(3)	14
Imitates the act of sexual intercourse	(2)	9
Touches animals' sexual parts	(1)	5

An invitation on the form for respondents to describe other sexual behaviours revealed that one boy talked about wanting to be the opposite sex, one girl dressed like a boy and one boy defecated into his pillowcase and stored the faeces.

HOW PREDICTABLE WERE THE SEXUAL BEHAVIOURS WHICH WERE SHOWN IN PLACEMENT?

As we have seen, the information from interviews and case files showed that, in all, during the index placement over two thirds (27) of the 40 young people in the follow-up sample either sexually abused others, were themselves sexually abused or became involved in sexual activities which were of concern to their caregivers. Were there any connections between the children's sexual abuse histories or previous manifestations of sexually abusing behaviour and the behaviours shown in placement?

Four of the young people in the sample had no known history of sexual abuse to them. The remaining 36 of the 40 children had such a history. Twenty of them had been sexually abused by one perpetrator and of these, 65% (13) were involved in sexual activities of concern during the index placement, including sexual abuse to and by them. This included 15% (three) who sexually abused another child. Sixteen of the young people had been sexually abused by more than one perpetrator and a slightly higher proportion (75% or 12 young people) were involved in sexual activities in placement, were abused or abused others. This included 19% (three) who sexually abused another child and four (25%) who were themselves sexually abused while placed. There was therefore a slightly heightened risk of sexually abusing behaviour and of revictimisation among the children who had been sexually abused by more than one perpetrator.

It is perhaps of even greater concern to investigate whether the likelihood of a young person sexually abusing another child can be predicted on the basis of their history. *Of the 36 young people in our sample who had been sexually abused in the past, half (18) sexually abused another child at some stage,* either when they were living at home or in one or more of their substitute care placements. Of these 36 young people, seven (19%) sexually abused a child in the index placement.

When we related the past sexually abusing behaviour of the young people to their abusing behaviour in the index placement the findings had a similar predictive value. *Seventeen of the adolescents had sexually abused other children prior to arriving in the index placement and of these, three (18 %) repeated this behaviour in the residential or foster placement* which was the main focus of our study. The very close supervision exercised in a number of the index placements probably had the effect of containing the abusing behaviour of some of the other children for that period.

This evidence suggests that when young people with a history of sexual abuse are looked after in substitute care consideration should always be given to the possibility that they may sexually abuse other children. A history of sexually abusing behaviour should also lead to caution and careful supervision. As we will see in Chapter 7, sexually abusing children who are placed with siblings who have been abused by the same perpetrator are at high risk of continuing sexual activity and require either very high levels of monitoring and work on their behaviour or separate placements.

Looking at the overall histories of the 22 young abusers in our sample, five children sexually abused others only at home or school and another 11 children only showed sexually abusing behaviour when in one substitute care placement. However, three children sexually abused others both when they lived at home and in one or more care placements and three others showed sexually abusing behaviour in a series of placements. This is shown in Table 7.

What this glance at the overall histories of the young people shows is that over time 17 of the 40 children in the sample, or 43%, sexually abused another child in substitute care, whilst five children had only done so at home. However, in only six of the 17 cases (just over a third) had there been previous known incidents of sexually abusing behaviour *before* the child arrived in placement which could have been used as a warning sign.

In all, then, over two thirds of young people were involved in one or more sexual activities during the index placement. The findings from the Child Sexual Behaviour Inventory suggest that this proportion may well be an underestimate.

Half of the sexually abused children went on to abuse another child at some stage and just under one in five did so in the placement which was the focus of our research. In addition, almost one in five of the abusing young people abused a child again during the index placement. This suggests that careful consideration should be given to the mix of children in any new placement when young people with a history of

Table 7 Sexually abusing behaviour at home and in placements

Location	Number
At home	5
At home and in one or more placement	3
In one placement	11
In more than one placement	3
Total	22

sexual abuse or abusing behaviour are looked after, because of the high risk that they will sexually abuse another child during their stay. Moreover, the absence of sexually abusing behaviour in one setting does not mean that it will not occur in another.

SUMMARY

1. Of the 40 young people in the interview sample over two thirds (27) were reported in interviews to be showing sexual behaviours in placement (which were of concern to their caregivers). However, the extent of such behaviour was difficult to assess as it was often kept secret, was difficult to define and depended on the perceptions of the adult who discovered it. Data collected from the Revised Child Sexual Behaviour Inventory, suggested that this figure was an underestimate.
2. Sexual advances by males to females were more likely to be seen as abusive than were sexual advances by females to males, unless the age gap was very large. Likewise, high levels of sexual activity or numbers of partners was considered more inappropriate for girls than boys. Often sexual behaviour which appeared to put young people at risk was normalised by caregivers and social workers.
3. Sexual behaviours in evidence during placement were categorised on a number of dimensions, including the type of sexual activity itself, the age and/or power difference between the participants, whether coercion or exploitation was involved, and whether the young person acted alone or with other young people or adults. There was a critical distinction between behaviours which occurred in the placement and those which occurred off the premises.
4. Compulsive masturbation in public was shown by five of the children, and over a third (38%) showed overt sexualised behaviour to children and/or adults. Seven young people showed sexually abusing behaviour towards at least 13 other children either in foster care or residential placement, or on a contact visit; whilst sexual activity with peers was noted as a concern in relation to a third of the young people.
5. Four young women became pregnant whilst accommodated, three of whom were under 16.
6. Five young people appeared to be involved in prostitution during their stay in our index placements. Not infrequently they procured young people from their placements for their clients and also involved them in the making of pornographic videos. One other girl regularly associated with Schedule One offenders whilst in residential care.
7. Four of the young people alleged that they were sexually abused during the course of the placements.

8. The data were analysed to see whether a child's sexual behaviour whilst in placement could be predicted from past sexual abuse or abusing behaviour. Half of the 36 sexually abused young people abused another child at some stage, but only one in five did so during the index placement. Of the 17 adolescents who had sexually abused other children previously, just under one in five (18%) repeated this behaviour in the index placement. Almost half of the child abusers were under close supervision during this period of their stay in care and this may have prevented further incidents of abusing behaviour.

9. This evidence suggests that careful consideration should be given to the mix of children in any new placement when young people with a history of sexual abuse or abusing behaviour are looked after because of the high risk that they will sexually abuse another child during their stay. The absence of sexually abusing behaviour in one setting does not mean that it will not occur in another. Sexually abusing children who are placed with siblings who have been abused by the same perpetrator are at high risk of continuing sexual activity.

III

MANAGING THE CARE OF SEXUALLY ABUSED AND ABUSING YOUNG PEOPLE

7

PLANNING AND PREPARATION FOR PLACEMENT

Having described the sexual behaviours shown by the young people in the interview sample we now examine the basis on which decisions were made to place them and how well the caregivers were prepared for their arrival. We begin by considering whether the young people were placed with their siblings and go on to describe the kinds of placements they were in and how these related to their backgrounds of sexual abuse or sexually abusing behaviour.

PLACEMENTS WITH SIBLINGS

Only one child was placed with a sibling. The great majority were not. This is usual in an adolescent looked after population (Berridge and Brodie, 1998; Packman and Hall, 1998; Sinclair and Gibbs, 1998). In addition, it was not uncommon for the young people in our sample to have been singled out for rejection, scapegoating or sexual abuse. Not only this but eight of the young people had sexually abused a sibling or younger relative so placement with a sibling had often not been considered as an option.

The one child who was placed with her younger sister sexually abused her in foster care, in addition to abusing the 6-year-old son of the foster carers. In spite of this the placement continued and later the sisters were placed together in an adoptive home. Two other young people had been placed with siblings in the past and in both cases they had sexually abused their siblings in those placements. Each was now placed separately from his siblings, but one of these boys re-abused his younger brother during a contact visit, where the high vigilance practised by his foster carers was not replicated in the younger brother's placement.

This evidence suggests that sexually abused and abusing adolescents are often not placed with their siblings but that, when they are, very high levels of vigilance are needed if further sexual activity between them is to be avoided (see also Smith 1995a, 1996). It seems likely that when more than one child has been sexually abused by the same perpetrator, the children may become sexually active together. In these situations considerable caution is needed if siblings are placed together or have contact with each other. The presence of a sibling may act as a trigger for further sexual activity.

THE PLACEMENTS OF THE SEXUALLY ABUSED YOUNG PEOPLE

At the point at which the index placement was made 22 of the young people were known only to have been sexually abused. These were the 18 sexually abused young people described in Chapter 4 who did not show abusing behaviour together with four other abused children who first showed sexually abusing behaviour only after entering the placement. This was a predominantly female group (17 girls and five boys) of whom two thirds (14) were placed in residential care. All but three of those placed in residential care were girls. Only eight of the sexually abused only group were looked after in foster care. There was therefore no pattern of foster care being used to afford protection for young people who had a history of sexual abuse. All but one of the children's homes were mixed units and some would have housed other young people with histories of abusing behaviour.

In practice, as we saw in Chapter 6, only one young person alleged sexual abuse by another resident, an allegation which was not substantiated, although another five young people had what appeared to be consensual relationships with a resident in their children's home.

THE PLACEMENTS OF THE YOUNG PEOPLE WHO HAD SEXUALLY ABUSED OTHERS

When we looked at the placements of the young people who were known *before* the index placement to have sexually abused others, (whether or not they had themselves been sexually abused) a quite different pattern emerged. This was a predominantly male group (12 out of 17 were boys) and the majority (11) were placed in foster care (seven boys and four girls).

This preference for foster care for the abusing children, seemed to be connected to their sexually abusing backgrounds. Nonetheless, most of the abusing young people shared their foster placements with other children, some of whom were at risk from them as we saw in Chapter 6. In only two foster homes was the placed child the only child or the youngest with considerably older children. Both of these children, nonetheless, found other victims to abuse, in one case the son of a friend of her foster mother and in the other his younger brother on a contact visit.

Only two of these young people went to ordinary children's homes. The other four, all of whom were boys, were offered specialist placements because of their previous abusive behaviour. Two were in residential schools, one in a specialist secure unit and one in a segregated flat where he was the only child. Of the boys in specialist placements, one boy in residential care could not be contained and he returned home. Another boy was accused of rape while excluded from his residential school. The boy in the secure unit was subject to extremely close supervision and the boy in a flat was effectively segregated from other young people. There was one other young person who went on to sexually abuse another child in foster care *after* the index placement in a children's home had ended.

BEDROOM SHARING

Ten of the 22 young people who at the outset were known only to have been sexually abused shared their bedroom with another child, four in foster care and six in children's homes. Three of the four in foster care shared with one of the foster carers' own children.

More than half (10) of the young people who had previously sexually abused another child shared a bedroom in their placement, and most of these did so in foster care (7). Of these seven, four shared with one of the foster carers' children and three with another foster child. In one placement, two fostered boys shared a bedroom, both of whom in addition to sexual abuse in their backgrounds had sexually abused other children. Another boy with a history of sexually abusing behaviour and severe physical abuse shared his bedroom with the foster carers' son who was his age. He did not sexually abuse him, but subjected him to a series of physical assaults, leading to placement breakdown.

In the event, none of the children who was abused in the index placement had been sharing a room with the young person in the study. However, this had occurred in previous placements. One young man who had sexually abused the 3-year-old grandchild of his foster carers returned to his former children's home where he was placed in a shared room. He quickly sexually abused his room mate, a possibility which should have been taken into account when the room arrangements for his return were made.

Sharing a bedroom could also bring a range of other problems. When we examined bedroom sharing in the whole sample we found that two of the young people in the study were bullied or assaulted by the adolescents with whom they shared and one frequently physically attacked the child whose bedroom he shared. Disputes arose between five other looked after children and those with whom they shared, as a result of which one daughter of the foster carers was beaten up by the foster child's friends at her behest, one girl was cautioned for a knife attack and the police became involved in another case of assault. Three other children kept those with whom they shared awake at night because of their nightmares or noisy masturbation.

ASSESSMENTS

Children are not generally automatically assessed before being looked after, but some of those in our interview sample had been subject to an assessment which could have proved useful in making placement decisions and in providing information for the caregivers. As we have seen one of our local authorities ran a separate service for challenging adolescents and no child was admitted to the foster care schemes or children's homes within that service without an assessment. As a result, nine of the young people would have had such an assessment. However, by the time of the index placement those assessments could be quite out of date, and this was the case for at least two young people. The assessment on one of these children had been completed 18 months earlier before the worst of her acting out behaviour.

Six young people had had a psychiatric assessment at some stage, including one who had also been assessed by the specialist scheme. Four children had had educational assessments in preparation for residential school placements, one of whom had also been subject to a psychiatric assessment. In addition to an educational assessment, one of the boys who went to residential school had been the subject of a multi-professional assessment which was not passed on to his school until the case was allocated to a new social worker who had participated in the assessment and noticed this gap. Thus an assessment had been completed at some stage on 17 of the 40 young people.

WERE THE PLACEMENTS PLANNED?

The distinction that is frequently made between emergency and planned placements conceals the fact that, in practice, there is a continuum between placements made at a few hours' notice, placements made with a few days' notice, those planned over a matter of weeks and those planned over a number of months. For all placements, except those made within the space of a few hours, some planning is possible. For this reason we occasionally found that social workers defined as an emergency placement one which residential workers regarded as planned, because there had been sufficient time for them to plan for the new arrival. In what follows we have used the descriptions supplied by the social workers.

Emergency placements accounted for half of those made. A slightly higher proportion of the emergency placements were made to residential care. If we exclude the three residential school placements all of which only allowed planned admissions, the proportion of residential care moves which were emergency placements rose to two thirds, as compared with two fifths of foster placements. In some cases a placement was made at only a few hours' notice, in others within a matter of days. In spite of the need to secure a placement swiftly three of the young people visited the caregivers before the placement started.

The other half of the placements were planned, including at least nine in which the child had visited the placement. These included two children who made a number of visits and overnight stays during the preparation period. Almost three fifths of the foster placements were planned as compared with two fifths of those in residential care. If the three placements in residential schools are excluded only a third of the remainder of residential placements were planned.

Altogether fewer than a third of the young people made a pre-placement visit, so in only a minority of cases had steps been taken to minimise the difficulties faced by the young people when they experienced separation. There was no sign that parents had been involved in these visits to placements or in preparing the young people for the move, partly no doubt because the rift between parents and their children was in some cases already deep.

FACTORS WHICH GUIDED THE SELECTION OF PLACEMENTS

Whether or not an assessment of the young person had been carried out, in many cases a considerable amount of background information was available on the young people. We were interested therefore to explore the factors that were taken into account when placement decisions were made.

The Match of the Young Person with Others in the Setting

The context for this exploration is that when a new admission is being considered, no mechanism exists to ensure that the child will be a good match with the children already in placement. The placing social worker will rarely have completed an assessment of the child and will consider only whether a proposed placement might be suitable for the young person. Social workers will not generally consider the impact of the placed child on others already in the placement or the likely impact of children already in the setting on the newly arrived child. Indeed, they will not generally know much about the child composition of the placement (see also Whitaker, Archer and Hicks, 1998). At the point of placement, it is then up to the head of home in a children's unit or the foster carers to say if they think a proposed child is unsuitable. In practice, local authorities vary as to how far heads of home may refuse admissions, with many given little choice but to accept most comers. Foster carers often feel that their choice is constrained either by a desire to please the social worker or the need for payment. In our study there were exceptions. The residential schools gave careful thought to the suitability of proposed new admissions and the leaving care units were able to refuse unsuitable children. Once a child had been placed, subsequent decisions about the admission of other children could and did affect their progress. There were a number of children in the study who were doing well until one or two disruptive children were placed with them, after which the placement failed.

In nine cases some consideration was given to the issue of mix, that is, how the young person would fit in with others in the placement. In four of these nine cases this issue was considered in the light of the sexually abusing behaviour of the placed child and the placements made either involved no younger children, high levels of surveillance or no other children in the placement. Mix was also considered for both of the girls who were placed in independent living units since both units had a committee that screened all referrals for suitability in the light of the group of children already there. Careful thought was given to the placement of one very sexualised girl, for whom a children's home was found which had a predominantly female peer group without older girls and where the child and staff group were stable. In one foster placement it was thought that the absence of other children would allow the carers to devote themselves to the very needy child in their care and in another foster home the carer said that he had considered that the new boy would fit in because he was not an offender as were the other boys there. However, this inexperienced foster carer gave little thought to the possible adverse effect of the other boys on the child in the study and a particularly unsuitable placement was made where a boy with learning difficulties and functioning at an 11-year-old level was placed with hardened young offenders who bullied him mercilessly.

It is probable that the issue of how the young person would fit in with the existing child group was also considered fairly fully for the three young people who were placed in residential schools, although this consideration was hampered in two cases where the boys' history of sexually abusing behaviour was not known to the school. In all then, it appeared that attention was paid to mix in only 30% (12) of the index placements.

Other Factors

A range of other factors was mentioned as having played a part in the decision to place the young people. Ten children were placed outside the local authority area, four in foster care, one in a children's home, three in residential schools and two in secure units. In four cases the placement was chosen because it was an out-of-county placement, either to shield the child from adverse influences in their home area or in one case because the child himself insisted on living at some distance from his physically abusing mother. In the remainder, the chosen placement happened to be outside the authority's area.

Three residential school placements were chosen specifically because they would cater for the educational difficulties and behavioural problems of the children, and two placements in secure units were made because of offences committed by the young people. One setting was chosen to be near the child's school, and two were Regulation 11 foster placements where the children asked to stay with families they knew.

PREPARATION OF THE CAREGIVERS FOR THE YOUNG PERSON'S ARRIVAL

Now that we have looked at how placements were chosen for the young people in the interview sample, we turn to explore how well the caregivers were prepared for their arrival.

Written Information

Much of the information passed on to caregivers about the young people before placement was given verbally rather than in written form. A basic form giving brief details about the child's background was the most that was generally provided in writing, although in five cases the caregivers said that nothing written had been provided.

Access to the Child's Case File

Foster carers were not generally given access to the children's files, but residential carers could look at them if they so wished. However, some residential workers said that it was not made easy for them to see files, although in practice we found that it was rare for them to seek to do so. The maintenance of confidentiality was the dominant reason behind the refusal to show files to foster parents. Presumably this was not seen as a problem with residential workers who were employed by the same authority. However, the tasks expected of foster and residential workers were similar and foster carers had no less need for good quality information than residential workers. Since the foster carers were paid by the local authority social services departments to care for the young people, it is difficult to see what justification there was for not giving them the same opportunity to see a child's file as residential staff.

In one case the foster carers of an extremely disturbed girl pressed to see the file so that they could understand some of the reasons for the breakdown of previous placements. The team manager who dealt with these requests admitted that their protocols were unclear, but decided under continued pressure that she would photocopy minutes of conferences for the foster carers, on the basis that they were acting as the child's parents. She ended up unsure whether she had acted improperly or not:

"I just didn't know who to get consent from within this bureaucracy so I just thought I'd take responsibility and do it."

However, she had less difficulty in deciding to make the files available to the child's therapist who then passed them on to the foster carers. The logic of being able to share confidential information with a therapist working for a different organisation and not doing so with foster carers working for the same authority was hard to understand. The foster carers found it reassuring to see the files because it demonstrated that the way the child behaved towards them had occurred in other placements too (see also Macaskill, 1991). Another foster carer, who unusually was given almost full access to the case records of the child in her care, also found this very helpful:

"Where if you get a child and you have got no background information whatsoever, and they start being disruptive and naughty and their behaviour problems are way out of line, then you think 'Well, what to do, what is going on with this kid? Why is this kid like this?' And you know you are trying to come to your own conclusions which does not always work."

Caregivers' Views of the Importance of Knowing about the Child's History

On the whole it was foster carers rather than residential workers who expressed concern about the inadequacy of the information which they had been given about the young people placed with them. They found that what they were told had been insufficient to enable them to understand the children or had omitted particular behaviours about which they needed to know.

When residential workers considered that they had too little information they were in a position to search for more. Three of them did so. One residential worker chased up a girl's notes from the social worker in her previous local authority and so found out about her highly sexualised behaviour and the pattern of habitual absconding from her former children's home. A second worker telephoned around for information about a new arrival and another residential worker went to the social services office to look at a girl's file in order to try to make sense of her behaviour.

However, a more common reaction among residential workers was not to look at the information that was available on the young people. The reason most often given for not doing so was to avoid prejudging them. Four workers gave this as an explanation, arguing that young people should be able "to leave their baggage behind" or that as staff members they liked to "go in cold and you get chatting to the (young people) and they talk about things on their own". There was no evidence that any of these workers read the notes on the child later after getting to know them. This seemed surprising and unprofessional. Few patients would be satisfied with a doctor who had failed to read their medical notes before examining them. Two other residential workers explained that they had not looked at the notes on the child in their care and clearly did not see it as important to do so:

"I can get hold of the information if I need it. But because I haven't specifically gone out to delve into that work because it's being done by other people, then it's not needed at the moment. I've got a rough outline of what happened but the exact details, no I haven't."

The message which comes across from these interviews is that many residential workers fail to appreciate the importance of understanding a child's background to the provision of good quality care (see also Berridge and Brodie, 1998). This may shed light on the management offered to some young people which we will look at in later chapters, when their behaviour receives superficial attention but no link is made to their past and the likely aetiology of that behaviour.

Contact with Previous Caregivers

In only one case had the social worker put the present caregivers in touch with the previous ones. This rich source of information about children for the most part went untapped. Some foster carers knew the previous caregivers through their own network of contacts or through a foster carers' group and so were able to obtain useful information about a child, but in most cases this did not occur. In contrast, when a child moved between children's homes within the same local authority there were often meetings at which information was shared.

INFORMATION WHICH WAS NOT PASSED ON TO CAREGIVERS
General Information

What kind of information was *not* shared with residential workers and foster carers before children arrived?

The social worker of one young person decided not to provide information to his foster carers about his fire setting. She may later have regretted this because he did set fire to the bedroom which he shared with the caregiver's son. Another boy was admitted to a children's home because of a serious offence of arson. His keyworker knew about this but not whether it was an isolated episode or part of a history of fire setting. Another social worker did not share the information that a girl's sister was involved in prostitution. In this case the staff at her children's home discovered this for themselves and made good use of it in forestalling the sister's influence when she tried to involve the girl in her activities. One foster carer was not told that a boy had a serious ear condition and was phobic about hospital treatment until the boy's mother mentioned it.

However, the foster carers who complained particularly bitterly about information which had not been passed to them were the two families who took in young people who had not attended school for some time beforehand. Looking after a child who is not attending school requires full-time care and one foster mother said that if she had known that the girl was not attending school she would not have accepted her.

Incomplete Information in Order to Secure Placements

Some foster carers believed that social workers would not share full information about children if they thought that by doing so they might not secure agreement to take the child. As one carer put it: "Some of the things [which we were told] were not correct. I think sometimes they are tailored to suit the placements". Another foster carer thought that they had been given little information about previous placement breakdowns because the social services department "knew what a difficult job it was going to be and they didn't want to spoil the chance of a good placement".

Some foster carers had come to the conclusion that they had to ask about the issues that gave them concern because they could not rely on social workers to tell them. One new foster carer had had a sexually abused boy placed with his family, who made sexual advances to his daughter. He was angry that the information on the boy's background had been withheld:

"I said to them 'Why haven't you told me? I should have been told'. And they said, 'Oh well, we weren't sure that we should tell you.' I made it plain that I needed to know, for safety reasons . . . I learned very quickly with social workers to ask the questions. Because if you don't you won't get told". As he said: "I think you need that honesty because you lose trust."

However, in answer to a direct question about the next boy placed, the carers were told that he had not been sexually abused, but no mention was made of his history of sexually assaultive behaviour.

Indeed, some foster carers and a few residential workers felt that they rarely received adequate information about the young people placed with them (see also Berridge and Cleaver, 1987; Macaskill, 1991), for example that full social histories were never provided and that they had to push social workers to get the information they needed. One residential worker considered that social workers treated them as "second best so it's not important that we get information". Another care worker in a residential school said that apart from the child's age and name the information that had been available to her upon the child's arrival had been very sketchy. She knew little about his background, previous separations and even whether he had been in care before.

Information about Sexual Abuse and Sexually Abusing Behaviour

The information which was passed on to caregivers about the sexual abuse and sexually abusing behaviour in the young people's backgrounds was clearly far from complete. When we examined the reasons for this we found that attrition of information occurred at a number of stages in the system.

First, of course, only the young people knew the full situation about the sexual abuse which they had suffered and any abusing behaviour which they had shown, and only some of this information was in the public arena. Most of them, once in substitute care, did not know how much others knew about these experiences. The children's case files were the central record of what professionals knew about them. However, as we saw in Chapter 3, surprisingly often, incidents of alleged sexual abuse had not been formally investigated or conferenced under child protection procedures and so the details of the allegations were often not known.

A lack of investigation was especially a feature of cases of alleged sexually abusing behaviour by young people, in spite of the guidance in *Working Together* (Home Office *et al*, 1991) which makes it clear that child protection procedures should be followed in relation to child abusers as well as their victims. These deficits were further compounded by the lack of agreed definitions of what constituted "abusing behaviour" in the first place. Indeed, only four of the 22 incidents of sexually abusing behaviour by the young people were investigated, four were subject to a case conference and of these only one led to a prosecution.

The lack of investigations and child protection conferences were not, of course, the only reasons for information not being recorded. Information about a child's behaviour in previous placements was often missing from the case records, even though there might be a full record in the children's homes in which the child had stayed. However, if good minutes had been kept of residential review meetings such information would have been available on the file. We found that occasionally individual staff had information which had not found its way onto the case file. One example was a residential worker who had cared for a sexually abused boy immediately after he was first looked after. She told us that he had been subject to a paedophile ring and that there had been extensive sexual activity between him and his siblings, but neither of these facts had been recorded on the file.

However, although important information was missing from some case files they did provide a great deal of useful data. But case files can be long and neither of our local authorities made systematic use of case summaries which would have enabled busy social workers to retrieve key information easily. As a result, information was often lost when there was a change of social worker. Six social workers told us honestly that they had not read any or all of the child's file and there were probably others who were not so forthcoming. Monck and New (1996), in their study of sexually abused children and young perpetrators in day treatment facilities, also found that social workers did not know about the previous sexual abuse experiences of 40% of the children for whom they held responsibility. In our study, when social workers were not familiar with the files, information about past sexual abuse or abusing behaviour by the child was often not known. As a result, the caregivers who took the child often lacked information about it or had not been given crucial details. Other information too was highly likely to be missed, such as details about the child's background, self-harm and depression.

A further problem was that another seven social workers were misinformed about the young people's abuse with the result that they minimised it. Of these, two workers were unaware of the identity or of the number of perpetrators of the abuse. In the five other cases social workers considered erroneously that the sexual abuse had not been serious or had not been substantiated, when it had been severe and was well substantiated, sometimes to the extent of the perpetrators having been imprisoned. As a result, they passed on this misinformation to the caregivers at the time of placement. When we put together the social workers who had factually wrong information with those who had not read the case files we found that at the time of placement 13, or a third of the workers were very poorly informed about the children's history of sexual abuse or abusing behaviour.

The information which was shared with caregivers was generally the latest concerns about the young person, and sexual abuse tended either to be the dominant theme or to have been split off. It was worrying to find that of the 36 young people about whom there were serious concerns in relation to sexual abuse, this had not been passed on to the caregivers in as many as 15 cases or over two fifths of the group. This compares with Macaskill's finding (1991) that 32% of foster or adoptive parents had not known about the sexual abuse in the child's background prior to placement. In our study this lack of information affected seven foster homes and eight residential establishments.

In three instances the information about abuse had not been passed on to residential schools because the arrangements were made by education departments and social services departments took no part in preparing the schools for the children's arrival. In one other case information about abuse to a child had not been passed on because originally the placement was for respite care. However, it had not been shared later even when the placement was made more long-term. The practice of not informing respite or short-term carers and residential schools needs to be reconsidered because, in both instances, carers are deprived of information which is essential to the safety and well-being of the placed child and others. Education departments are unlikely to have much knowledge about sexual abuse and abusing behaviour because social services are the lead agency in this area. Social services departments therefore have a responsibility which they are not currently fulfilling to prepare caregivers in these situations.

Of the 21 cases where some information about the abuse had been conveyed, crucial details had been omitted in six instances. Such omissions could have an important bearing on children's welfare. For example, one caregiver was given few details about a boy's sexual abuse at residential school. He was not told that it had been prolonged, coerced and accompanied by extensive bullying. Had he known this he might have been more alert to the fact that the boy was subject to repeated bullying and humiliation by other boys in his foster care placement, and more supervision might have been provided. The foster carers for a newly arrived girl might also have exercised closer supervision over her activities if they had realised that she had been sexually abused by multiple perpetrators. The social worker failed to mention four of the perpetrators and this girl, who had no idea how to keep herself safe in social encounters, was raped when out for the evening. The general effect of omitting known details about the abuse which children had endured was that the abuse was minimised.

Seventeen of the young people had displayed sexually abusing behaviour before the index placement was made and it might have been thought that workers would have taken pains to pass on this information. However, surprisingly in nine of the 17 cases or over half they did not do so. Six foster families, one children's home and two residential schools were not informed about past sexually abusing behaviour. Again, two placements were in residential schools and social services departments had left it to education departments to prepare the schools and played no part in imparting information. Another placement was to Regulation 11 foster carers, that is to carers who had agreed to foster a particular child who was known to them. Social services departments appeared to feel little obligation to pass on information to these carers. Such findings highlight a substantial shortcoming in practice. Young people who have sexually abused other children may well do so again. In not passing on information about these behaviours local authorities are failing in their duty of care both to the young abusers and to the other children in the placements.

Of the eight placements where some information about the young people's sexually abusing behaviour was passed to caregivers important details were missing in three cases. Again, this could have a considerable impact on other children's safety. For example, Christina's foster carers were told very little about the sexual abuse which she had inflicted on her younger cousin:

"We were just told . . . that she had abused her cousin . . . But that was made very light of at the time. You know I thought it was a one-off. Just dropped in as an after-thought."

It was only when arrangements had been made by the school for Christina to do work experience in a day nursery that social services

intervened and revealed that she had sexually abused her cousin extensively over a four-year period. There was also evidence that four social
workers minimised the sexually abusing behaviour which children had
shown and, as a result, their caregivers did not appreciate its severity.

*When we put this evidence together, we found that information about the sexual
abuse and/or sexually abusing behaviour of 18 young people, or just under half of
the sample, had not been passed on to their caregivers.*

Management Implications

As we have seen, of the 36 children in the interview sample who had been
sexually abused in the past, half sexually abused another child at some
stage. Clearly, if a young person's history of sexual abuse or sexually
abusing behaviour is not passed on then other children in the placement
are placed at risk and caregivers are not able to plan to maximise these
children's safety.

Even when information was passed on it often lacked specificity. Caregivers did not always know if "sexual abuse" meant inappropriate touching or full vaginal or anal intercourse. It was not uncommon to find that the
caregiver and the social worker held different views about the nature of the
abuse to the young person or the identity of the perpetrator. A number of
residential workers did not know what kind of sexually abusing behaviour
certain youngsters had displayed, even when the placement had been
made precisely for this reason. Moreover, in the absence of adequate information about the abuse, caregivers may find that they have unwittingly
recreated aspects of the context of the original abuse (McFadden, 1987;
Davis *et al*, 1991; Macaskill, 1991). For example, Sharon was terrified when
her foster carers' young son came into the bathroom to use the toilet as she
was getting into the bath. This family practice with their younger children
had to be quickly altered as it seemed to have revived memories of
Sharon's original abuse. The foster carers had not been told that Sharon
had been sexually abused in the first place. Situations of this kind can lead
to allegations of abuse from frightened children who misinterpret situations which are similar to their earlier experience of abuse (McFadden and
Stovall, 1984; McFadden and Ryan, 1986; McFadden, 1987).

Advice on best practice (McFadden, 1986; Macaskill, 1991) would suggest that caregivers need to know exact details of the abuse where possible, including the time of day and circumstances in which it took place,
as well as the age, gender and identity of the abuser, the child's age when
it started and stopped, how the abuser gained compliance and silenced
the child and the child's reaction to disclosure. The lack of specific

information given to caregivers clearly placed them at a disadvantage in terms of understanding how young people's current behaviour might link with their past experiences; of avoiding situations which replicated the context of the original abuse; and enabling them to gauge the children's need for counselling. Some caregivers felt strongly that more specific information would have helped them to manage the children more effectively, but others, especially residential staff, as we have seen, were much less concerned to know about the child's background. The link between this lack of information and the possibility of allegations being made against caregivers appeared not to have been fully made by the social workers who arranged the placements.

SPECIFIC PREPARATION WHEN PLACEMENTS WERE MADE

As we saw in Chapter 5 caregivers had had variable amounts of training for their work. For some it had been thorough, but for others it had been partial, whilst Regulation 11 foster carers had received none. This was important because there was little evidence that caregivers were given any specific preparation or advice on how to deal with the young people in the study prior to their arrival (see also Quinton *et al*, forthcoming). Management ideas were not discussed in advance and nor was the issue of how to keep the young people and others in the placement safe.

This chapter has shown the vital importance of providing comprehensive and detailed information to caregivers about the children placed in their care. However, in practice information was lost or minimised at a number of stages and information about the histories of sexual abuse and abusing behaviour was not passed on to the caregivers of as many as 18 of the 40 young people (45%) in the study. In the absence of specific preparation and advice about how to manage the placed children, opportunities to make plans to reduce risks were diminished. In the chapters which follow we will see the impact that this had on the management of the young people. In the next chapter the ways in which residential and foster carers tried to create a safe environment for the children placed with them will be explored.

SUMMARY

1. With only one exception, none of the children were placed with a sibling. However when siblings who have been sexually abused by

the same perpetrator *are* placed together the children will often become sexually active together and high levels of vigilance are required.

2. There were 22 young people in the study who were known only to have been sexually abused and most of them (14) were placed in residential care. The majority of the abused children were girls (17) and all but one of the children's homes to which they went were mixed units which would also house other children with histories of abusing behaviour.

3. In contrast, the majority of the 17 young people who had sexually abused others (mostly boys) were placed in foster care. Only two of these young people went to ordinary children's homes. Four boys had specialist residential placements. Most of the child abusers shared their foster placements with other children, some of whom were at risk from them.

4. More than half (10) of the young people who had previously sexually abused another child shared a bedroom in their placement, and most of these did so in foster care. Bedroom sharing brought a range of problems.

5. Some kind of assessment was made either before or during their placement for only 17 of the 40 young people.

6. Emergency placements accounted for half of all placements, and these formed two thirds of the placements made to residential homes. Three fifths of the foster care placements were planned, but this was true of only a third of those in residential homes. Fewer than a third of young people made a pre-placement visit.

7. When a new admission was considered there was no mechanism to ensure that the child would be a good match with the other children in the placement. Heads of homes were not always allowed to refuse unsuitable admissions and foster carers did not always feel able to do so. In contrast, the suitability of new admissions to the leaving care units was considered by a panel and by the head teacher at residential schools.

8. Pre-placement information was generally given to caregivers verbally. Foster carers were not usually given access to children's files for reasons of confidentiality while residential carers had the option of looking through files, although they rarely did so. In only one case were caregivers put in touch with previous caregivers, thereby leaving a rich source of information about the child unused.

9. Many residential workers did not appreciate the importance of an understanding of children's backgrounds for the delivery of good quality care. Just three residential workers had searched for additional information about the child in order to help them to understand the child's behaviour.

10. In the group of 36 young people about whom there were serious concerns regarding sexual abuse, information had not been passed on to the caregivers in 15 cases (42%). Of the 21 cases where some information had been conveyed, crucial details were omitted in six cases.

11. Information concerning sexually abusing behaviour was not passed on to the caregivers in 9 of the 17 cases (53%). Of the 8 placements where some information concerning sexually abusing behaviour was passed on to caregivers, important details were omitted in 3 cases.

12. Overall, information about 18 young people's sexual abuse and or sexually abusing behaviour was not passed on to caregivers. This represents 45% of the sample.

13. There was no evidence that caregivers were given any specific preparation or advice on how to deal with the young people prior to their arrival in the placement.

8

CREATING A SAFE ENVIRONMENT FOR CHILDREN

Now that decisions about placement and the preparation given to caregivers have been examined we turn to look at how the nuts and bolts of providing a safe context for children within placements were managed. But first we need to consider which sexual behaviours elicited most concern from residential workers and foster carers.

Not all the sexual behaviours shown by the young people in the study were regarded as equally problematic. Indeed, when we talked to heads of homes about difficult behaviour generally they never mentioned sexual behaviour. It was aggressive and violent behaviour within children's homes which claimed their attention. From observation we noted that the sexual behaviour which was seen as most problematic and as requiring particularly careful placement and management was sexual abuse of other children. Even then it was only either pervasive sexually abusing behaviour within substitute care or a single incident which had included highly aggressive and coercive elements which received concentrated attention from professionals and caregivers. One-off incidents of sexually abusing behaviour, even occasionally when aggression was involved, were sometimes minimised. The sexually abusing behaviour of girls also received less of a response than did that of boys. Other behaviours which caregivers saw as problematic and managed accordingly were those which occurred *within* placements, such as sexual relationships between residents in residential care, sexualised behaviour directed at staff and masturbation in public.

It was notable that sexual behaviours which occurred *outside* care settings evoked very much less concern and received less attention from caregivers. Sexual activity outside placements, even when young people, especially girls, put themselves at risk, was sometimes minimised by caregivers, although the outcome could be exploitation, early pregnancy or sexually transmitted disease. Little was known about the sexual activity of boys, since this was not perceived as problematic. Prostitution by young people in care was also slow to evoke a concerted response, partly because when the young people stayed out all night or for several days the caregivers did not have to manage their day-to-day behaviour. We should therefore be alert to the fact that behaviours typical of boys, such as aggression and abusing behaviour which put *others* at risk were seen as problematic and evoked a professional response, whereas the behaviours shown by girls, such as indiscriminate sexual activity and prostitution, in which they put *themselves* at risk, were given much less professional attention.

In this chapter we look at the ways in which caregivers tried to make the placements safe for children, particularly by means of rules and routines, the maintenance of confidentiality and the provision of information about sexual relationships.

RULES AND ROUTINES FOR KEEPING YOUNG PEOPLE SAFE

Most placements had some basic ground rules which were intended to keep the young people and others who lived there safe. Some of these involved restriction of contact. Male residential workers were often careful not to be alone with new female residents and avoided physical contact with them. Foster fathers were more variable in their awareness that their behaviour could be misinterpreted by girls with backgrounds of sexual abuse, but two of them showed similar caution, including one man who was never alone with the fostered girls in his family after the experience of an official investigation into an allegation by a previous foster child. In four foster placements young people who had sexually abused other children were never left alone with the carers' own younger children or grandchildren and this entailed very active supervision by the foster carers. In one placement the foster carers were so anxious about their foster daughter's sexualised behaviour that they rarely allowed her to play with other children.

Most placements had rules which prohibited sexual relationships or contact between young people in care settings, but the rigour with which these were enforced varied greatly. In foster families young people were told that they should have "brother–sister" relationships with other adolescents in the household and should seek girlfriends or boyfriends from outside the family. Sexual relationships between residents were also strongly discouraged in children's homes and in both sectors there were rules that children were not allowed into each other's bedrooms at night. Sometimes this rule extended to daytime visits too or the bedroom door had to be left open when young people were in each other's rooms. In one foster family none of the girls was allowed to go to the top of the house where the foster carers' sons had their bedrooms. The foster mother explained: "You've got to protect the men in the house, so you've got to have these sort of rules". Caregivers who had reason to worry about children's activities would sometimes go up to check the rooms. However, there was little that could be done to monitor the activities of young people who shared their bedrooms and same sex relationships did occasionally occur in this context. Many caregivers also prohibited young people from walking around in the house in their nightwear.

Not all caregivers considered the imposition of rules to be sufficient. Two sets of foster carers and one children's home used alarm systems or listening devices to ensure that the rules were obeyed. The children's home had an intercom system so that staff could ensure that young people did not enter each other's rooms at night. The foster carers used a variety of devices of their own choosing in order to protect their children from the unwanted attentions of the young people they fostered. These devices were used either because of the obvious vulnerability of the foster carers' own much younger children or after the discovery of harmful sexual activity or physical cruelty by fostered adolescents to their children. These included placing alarms on a younger child's bedroom door and on the living room door at night, locking their own bedroom door during the day, placing an intercom or baby alarm system in the upstairs rooms so that the foster carers could hear if anything untoward was happening and installing a fire detector after one fostered boy was found setting fires. In addition, two residential settings, both of them residential schools, employed night staff who patrolled the sleeping areas. In one of them the introduction of a "night walker" as this staff member was called, had followed the discovery that a boy had sexually abused a number of boys in the school. However, the head teacher was quick to point out that the boys in the school could engage in sexual activities in many other places which could not easily be supervised, such as the grounds and the lounge area.

Whilst house rules were explicit, caregivers varied in the extent to which they were open with young people about their monitoring activities. Listening devices were sometimes in place without children knowing that this was the case or young people were tactfully withdrawn from situations where they would have been alone with younger children. In a minority of settings, alarm systems or rules about restrictions on contact were openly discussed with the young people.

Generally caregivers did not inform other children in the placement or their own children that a looked after young person could pose risks to them. However, in one children's home this was done and two sets of foster carers did so once they realised the risk of sexual abuse to their children from the girls placed with them. One residential school encouraged children to tell a member of staff if any child did anything to them which they did not like and children did follow this up. One set of foster carers asked the two boys they fostered to keep an eye on each other's activities and to tell them if the other was taking part in activities which could get him into trouble. Since these boys both had histories of sexually abusing other children and were sharing a room this strategy was potentially a sensible one.

In addition to house rules and routines designed, as far as possible, to keep children safe some caregivers went to great lengths to supervise the daily activities of the young people in their care. In secure units and well-staffed residential schools supervision could be made tight and some foster carers exercised these responsibilities with skill and determination. Indeed, one set of foster carers did not go out in the evenings because they considered that no one else would be as vigilant with their fostered children as they were. The vigilance exercised by their caregivers probably prevented some of the abusing adolescents from again abusing a child in placement. However, in other placements supervision was less well organised. In general, whilst as we shall see, a considerable amount of thought had gone into protecting staff from the possibility of allegations being made against them, less attention was paid to helping children to keep themselves safe from other young people who might place them at risk.

ADDITIONAL RESOURCES USED TO MANAGE CHILDREN'S BEHAVIOUR

However, in a few cases, special efforts were made to keep children safe and additional resources were made available for this purpose. The most imaginative of these was the employment of an extra residential worker to shadow one young woman, Alice, who was vulnerable to sexual exploitation in the community and who had frequently absconded from a previous placement. For the first six weeks after her arrival in the children's home there was an extra worker on both day and night shift who had a particular responsibility for Alice when she was away from the home.

The placement of another very disturbed and difficult girl who had been sexually abused from babyhood was supported from the start by a therapist from a private agency which specialised in consultancy and therapy for sexually abused children. She worked intensively with both the girl and the foster carers and without this assistance it seemed likely that the placement would not have survived. After the placements had started, support workers were brought in to work with another two young people, both of whom were involved in prostitution. Whilst both of these adolescents liked their support workers their interventions did not succeed in making the placements work nor in halting the young people's prostitution. In one of these cases, the support worker had been assigned to live in with the girl, but in this case her pattern of absconding and indiscriminate sexual activity was not affected. Over and above this, in another three cases the placements themselves were highly resourced to provide a secure and containing setting. These were the two placements in secure settings and one in a dedicated flat staffed by residential workers.

Obviously, when information about a child's past abuse or abusing behaviour was either not known to the social worker or not passed on to the caregivers, which as we saw in Chapter 7 was not uncommon, no specific preparation or additional resources could be planned.

In ways such as these, caregivers tried to provide a safe environment within their care settings. We turn now to consider how issues of safety were managed when the young people had contact with family members.

CONTACT

Using the Assessment and Action records (Parker *et al*, 1991; Ward, 1995) 30 of which were completed for this item we found that while over two fifths (13 of 30) of the young people had contact with their birth mother at least once a week, nearly another two fifths saw their mothers infrequently and one in five had no contact at all. Contact with birth fathers was less frequent with three fifths of the young people (17), never seeing their fathers. Four fifths of the young people (23) had some contact with their siblings, but while all the sexually abused children had contact with siblings two fifths (6) of the sexual abusers never saw their brothers and sisters. Overall, children in residential care were more likely to see members of their families frequently than were those in foster care.

A third of the young people in the study wanted more contact than they had (see also Sinclair and Gibbs, 1996). However, worryingly, over half (56%) found either some or most of their contacts were unhelpful to them and this compares with a quarter of the children in Sinclair and Gibbs' study of residential care (1996) who mentioned someone of whom they would have liked to see less.

For sexually abused children, contact with family members has particular features which deserve to be noted. On the one hand, some children had suffered rejection because they had disclosed sexual abuse by a family member and the rest of the family had only managed to remain intact by means of extruding the abused child. In these cases, the child in care often had limited or no contact with the family, and parent figures severely restricted the child's contact with siblings (see also Elgar and Head, 1997). At the other end of the spectrum, there were a number of boys who were in enmeshed relationships with their mothers where contact appeared to involve an intense preoccupation more usually found among lovers than mothers and sons. Although these relationships were often considered as likely to be incestuous they had never been subject to investigation and they therefore continued unchecked. At the very least, the boys continued in relationships which clearly lacked appropriate boundaries and which challenged the influence of the more appropriate relationships provided in placements.

Another aspect of contact which required attention was that some of the children had been involved in exploitative sexual relationships as a result of people they had met through family members, such as through their siblings and parents. Where a parent or sibling worked as a prostitute, contact with them was likely to lead to such involvement for the child. These links therefore needed careful monitoring and sometimes reducing or curtailing (see also Whitaker, Archer and Hicks, 1998) and the vigilance of caregivers ensured that some children were protected in this way. Finally, if insufficient action had been taken at the time of the discovery of abuse, or lingering suspicions had not been investigated, then contact with family members could lead to further sexual abuse to the child. There were at least two children in the study where this appeared to be the case.

We turn now to consider how caregivers managed the balance between maintaining confidentiality about the young people's backgrounds and informing others outside the placement who could be vulnerable.

CONFIDENTIALITY OF INFORMATION ABOUT CHILDREN

Caregivers and social workers were aware of the sensitivity of information about children's histories of sexual abuse and abusing behaviour. They were generally in agreement that they would expect a child's school to be told that a child was being looked after, although not necessarily be given the reasons why he or she could not live at home. Selective information was passed to the school by social services or the child's caregiver, in many cases intimating no more than that the child had "had a rough ride". One residential worker said that her children's home gave schools only as much information as it was thought they needed. Another worker chose to deal with only one member of the school staff and stressed the confidential nature of the knowledge she was imparting. Occasionally the wish to keep a child's background confidential could not be fulfilled, as in the case of an abusing girl whose school was going to place her among infant pupils for job experience. Of course, sometimes senior staff at the school were aware of a child's history of sexual abuse through attending a child protection case conference or review.

Whilst some social workers believed that schools did not need to know the details of a child's background, others thought that schools needed more information. On discovering that her predecessor had told only the caregivers about a child's sexual abuse background, one social worker took steps to inform the school. A foster mother also believed that "open information" was essential for the school, and both she and the social worker kept staff fully informed about anything in the child's life which could have repercussions at school.

However, for one boy information in an educational psychologist's report about an incident of sexual aggression to a teacher had proved counterproductive. It had resulted in a number of schools refusing to offer him a place. In another case a boy could not get into school because local head teachers were aware of his history of prostitution. His social worker said: "All the schools know his background. They get to hear."

In general, caregivers did not pass on details of a child's history to friends or neighbours, except in exceptional circumstances. There was an obvious dilemma between keeping a child's background confidential and informing others who could be vulnerable. One foster mother felt compelled to warn her neighbours about her foster son's sexually abusing behaviour because he spent a lot of time with their son. She also warned the couple who were fostering the boy's brother. Another foster mother would warn male visitors to her home to be especially careful around her foster daughter as "she can come on a bit strong".

One foster mother was worried about how she should handle the situation if her sexually abusing foster daughter was asked to babysit, and the social worker of one abusing boy thought that youth club leaders should be told of his background:

"I think people need to be alert . . . I mean obviously not to know his history but to be asked to be a bit more vigilant."

However, where the child posed no threat to others, it was generally felt that there was no need to divulge their history. This opinion was summed up by a social worker when speaking of foster carers as follows:

"They have a particular view, that in a way I have sympathy with, that it's her story. It doesn't belong to the world and people need to know only what they need to know . . . They're very careful about her story. They're not loose about it at all."

However, the children themselves were sometimes responsible for other people learning about their backgrounds (see also Burch, 1991; Macaskill, 1991). A residential worker was worried because one girl would tell strangers about her sexual abuse: "It made her so vulnerable"; and a caregiver said that her foster daughter was so open about her sexual activities that she had probably told everyone about her rape. A young male prostitute regretted agreeing to take part in a television programme which revealed his identity and left him open to violence and bullying by his peers at school.

We turn now to consider how far the young people had sufficient information about contraception and sexual health to maximise their own safety in the relationships which they formed outside the placements.

INFORMATION ABOUT SEX EDUCATION AND SEXUAL CHOICE
The Legislative and Policy Context

Establishments of any kind which shelter adolescents require clear ways of dealing with issues of sexuality. Yet this is an area in which guidelines, procedures and training have often been lacking (Parkin, 1989). Volume 3 and 4 of the guidance to the Children Act are exceptions (Department of Health, 1991). They provide clear guidelines about the needs of looked after young people for education on sexuality and personal relationships:

"The experience of being cared for should also include the sexual education of the young person. This may, of course, be provided by the young person's school, but if it is not, the SSD or other caring agency responsible for the young person should provide sexual education for him. This is absolutely vital since sexuality will be one of the most potent forces affecting any young person in the transition from childhood to adulthood.

Sexual education will need to cover practical issues such as contraception, particularly in view of the spread of AIDS. However, it must also cover the emotional aspects of sexuality, such as the part that sexuality plays in the young person's identity; the emotional implications of entering into a sexual relationship with another person; and the need to treat sexual partners with consideration and not as objects to be used. The emotional and practical implications of becoming a parent also need to be explained in some detail.'' (Department of Health 1991, Vol. 3, p. 97, Vol. 4, p. 107).

The need to address the subject of sexuality is even greater in the case of young people whose early experiences of sex have involved coercion, intrusion and the abuse of power by others. This is recognised in the same guidance which states:

''. . . young people who have been abused, or have been in touch with abused young people, may need special counselling if they are not to regard sexual feelings as a matter for shame or to regard sexual relationships as impersonal and exploitative.''

In addition, Department of Health guidance on children and HIV (Department of Health, 1992a) encourages social services departments to develop policies on sex education that will help looked after young people be confident about their sexual identity and be able to make informed choices about their personal relationships, in order to reduce the risks to them of HIV infection. In the white paper ''Health of the Nation'' (Department of Health, 1992b) sexual health was identified as a key area. Targets were set relating to teenage pregnancies, sexually transmitted diseases and HIV infection. Sex education was seen as one of the central means of achieving those targets. This is especially relevant to looked after girls whose vulnerability to early pregnancy is much greater than that in the population as a whole. Almost 25% of young women are mothers by the time they have moved to independence or ceased to be looked after, as compared with a national rate of 3% for the 16–19 year age range (Biehal *et al*, 1992).

However, although the guidance to the Children Act 1989 and on children and HIV is clear and places the onus on workers to acknowledge and deal sensitively with children's sexuality and sexual identity, other legislation appears to complicate these issues. On the one hand Section 22 (3) of the Children Act imposes a straightforward obligation on the local authority to safeguard and promote the welfare of young people who are looked after. On the other hand, a House of Lords judgement made in 1985, usually referred to as the Gillick judgement, allows young people of ''sufficient understanding and intelligence'' who understand the implications of medical treatment to consent to treatment on their own behalf. The Gillick judgement emphasised that girls under 16 seeking contraceptive advice should be encouraged to inform their parents, but it upheld the right of doctors to prescribe contraceptives without parental knowledge or consent. Nonetheless the publicity given to this case and the extent to which the final judgement rested on the ability of a medical practitioner to assess a girl's competence to give consent appears to have led to a cautious approach to the provision of contraceptive and other advice to under-age girls. Moreover, it is an offence for a person to cause or encourage the commission of unlawful sexual intercourse with a girl under the age of 16 for whom they are responsible. By consenting to the provision of contraception, therefore, the local authority could in theory be open to prosecution. However, according to the Children's Legal Centre (1992, p. 34):

"The only situation in which it would be unlawful would be where it could be proved that advice was given to a young person (or an adult) with the intention of facilitating sexual intercourse with a girl under 16. In such a case the adviser concerned could be charged with being an accessory to the crime of unlawful sexual intercourse."

Another piece of legislation which is likely to have led to caution on the part of local authorities is Section 28 of the Local Government Act 1988. This made illegal the intentional promotion of homosexuality by local authorities (Evans, 1989/1990). This legislation is sometimes interpreted as prohibiting the provision of information to young people about lesbianism or homosexuality. However, it does not forbid the provision of information or counselling to young people who are or who think they may be lesbian or homosexual. This is particularly important in relation to giving information about sexually transmitted diseases, including HIV/AIDS.

At the time of our study one of our two local authorities had a specific policy document on personal relationships for looked after young people. The document acknowledged that the social services department, in safeguarding and promoting the welfare of young people in its care, should provide advice and access to contraceptive and HIV prevention services where appropriate. It stated that residential workers and foster carers would often be best placed to provide support and information about personal relationships to young people. It went on to say that residential staff and foster carers would need to identify the most appropriate ways of providing access to contraceptive services and consult with the social worker and also with parents unless not "reasonably practicable". Review meetings were to be the key mechanism for ensuring that advice and information was given to young people by means of identifying who would take prime responsibility for having an active role in this area. Training was to be provided for key staff and caregivers to undertake these tasks.

In spite of the policy document in this one local authority there was some confusion in both authorities about responsibilities for sex education (see also Bremner and Hillin, 1994). Parkin (1989) suggests that the roots of such confusion lie in uncertainties about what are public and what are private concerns. She considers that public care cuts across the public and private domain and that policies and guidelines belong to the public world and do not speak the same language or translate easily into the private world of sexuality.

Bearing in mind the local policy context and legislation we now examine how information about sexuality and in particular sex education was handled in the placements in our study. This is particularly important because if caregivers are not comfortable in discussing matters of ordinary sexual development and health, they are unlikely to be at ease in talking about or dealing with sexual abuse.

The Information Provided

Our analysis of the case file material in Chapter 3 noted that sexually abused children are at high risk of not attending school and indeed two fifths of the school age young people in the interview sample did not attend school during the placement on which we focused. Any sessions on sex education offered by the education system might therefore have been missed. It cannot be assumed that parents will have passed on information about sexuality to their children and it was clear that for some their knowledge of the facts of life was rudimentary. For example, one young man thought kissing led to pregnancy and another that having sex twice could lead to twins. Indeed, sexually abused children have the dual disadvantage of premature experience of sex often with a profound lack of knowledge of sexual development, health and relationships (McFadden, 1987). In addition, they do not know what they should or should not know at their age and stage and as a result may be fearful of asking and revealing the state of their knowledge (Smith, 1995a). Yet their abusive experiences make the task of sex education a delicate one as painful memories may be revived. Two young people reacted to discussions of sexual issues with caregivers with disgust, commenting that the material they were shown was "sick" or "dirty".

The Assessment and Action Records showed that more than two fifths of the young people had not been given information about how their bodies change as they grow up; moreover as many as a quarter had not been given information about the dangers of unprotected sex and almost a third felt that they did not know enough about this issue. In addition, one in seven of the young people had not been given information about sex and contraception and a third felt that they did not know enough about this issue. These findings need to be set against a Gallop poll finding of 1990 for the National AIDS Trust that 54% of 16–24-year-olds felt they were at no risk from HIV/AIDS. In addition, one in five of the children in our study had not had any information about sexual identity and a third did not feel that they knew enough about it. Given that adolescents may not want to expose a lack of knowledge, these figures, whilst high, may be an underestimate of the proportion of adolescents with inadequate knowledge about sexuality. In the light of these gaps in basic information a more proactive approach to sex education appears to be needed.

Issues relevant to sex education can be divided into information on sexual and physical development and facts about contraception and sexual health. It was rare for caregivers to say that they had discussed sexual development with the young people in their care, although more may have done so than was reported. The exception was work done with two girls whose vulnerability was evident because of their immaturity, obvious naiveté and overt sexualised behaviour. The work was undertaken in one case by the keyworker in a children's home and in the other by a specialist worker as part of an ongoing programme of support to the child and her foster carers.

Residential workers in different homes tackled the area of contraception and HIV/AIDs in different ways. These variations appeared to be strongly influenced by the attitudes and training of the heads of homes or of individual workers. However, a passive approach was most commonly adopted. This was summed up by one residential worker as follows:

"We've got leaflets. We've got a whole pile of stuff that they can look at. But we're not actually allowed to say, 'I'm going to talk to you about this now'."

The usual approach taken by caregivers, especially by residential staff, was to leave it to young people to raise such issues and discussion most often occurred after watching a television programme. It was frequently said that young people knew that they could talk to staff on sexual matters. General injunctions were given for both boys and girls to remember to practise "safe sex" because of concerns about the risks of HIV/AIDs. In independence units and in one foster care placement when the young people were 16 and over, contraceptives were made available in the bathroom but they were not given out.

This passive stance, which was particularly a feature of the approach taken in residential care, was no doubt the product of a number of factors. In the first place, there is the unease felt by many adults in discussing sex openly, and particularly in doing so with adolescents, especially as sexual activity among adolescents occurs on average at a younger age than it did in the previous generation. In the early 1990s about 35% of girls and 46%

of boys claimed to have had sexual intercourse before their 16th birthday, compared to 2% of girls and 6% of boys in 1964 (Schofield, 1968; Ford, 1991). Second, caregivers face the dilemma of how to prevent unplanned pregnancy or sexually transmitted diseases without appearing to condone sexual activity between young people who are below the legal age of consent. This is of particular importance because the local authority is *in loco parentis*, but given the high levels of sexual activity of some of the young people at the time of entry to care the balancing act is a difficult one. Third, as has been shown, the legislative context is not without complexity.

There were, however, examples of good practice where caregivers or social workers had been proactive in providing sex education. In one children's home the provision of advice and help on sexual issues was incorporated into care plans and the staff group would agree together when and in what form sex education would be offered to individual young people. The approach taken was tailored to the child's needs and could be one-to-one work or could involve the use of videos or another medium. In practice, the residential workers in this home had talked to a sexualised but very immature girl about sex, relationships, adolescent development and appropriate interpersonal boundaries, as well as about contraception. They had been backed up by the social worker who had also advised her on contraception, when the girl herself became concerned that she might be pregnant.

Another children's home showed an even more proactive approach, focusing in particular on helping children learn how to keep themselves safe but also including information about the practice of safe sex. The staff ran regular groups and showed videos from Kidscape to the young people which demonstrated how they could say "no" to unwelcome advances of any sort. This was the only establishment which was involved in this kind of preventive educational work with children.

Foster carers were much less likely to see themselves as subject to restrictions on discussing sexuality, although one newly approved couple had understood from their training that it was not their job to talk to a fostered adolescent about issues relating to sex education, willing as they were to do so. They understood that they could respond to questions, but that they could not give advice. Foster carers were often able to draw on their experience of looking after their own teenage children and sometimes also on long experience of fostering adolescents. Some foster carers made a point of talking to all the sexually active young people in their care about sexual matters and again, television programmes provided opportunities to have family discussions about sex and relationships. Foster parents, especially foster mothers, would talk to young people about the importance of finding a partner who would provide companionship as well as sex; and contraception and sexually transmitted diseases including HIV/AIDs were openly discussed in some households. Indeed, some foster carers, worried about the high levels of sexual activity of the girls in their care, tried hard to ensure that precautions were being taken but, needless to say, young people were not always receptive to such advice. There were only a few foster carers who were obviously not at ease in talking about sex and who avoided the subject.

Social workers did not generally see the discussion of contraception and sexual health as outside their permitted remit, but even here there were considerable variations in practice. Some practitioners took on this role in response to specific concerns about a young person's sexual activity, particularly the possibility of a girl becoming pregnant. Social workers only occasionally gave advice to boys, and this was when the risks attaching to their sexual activity were inescapable, such as when a sexual relationship was occurring in a children's home. However, it was clear that some social workers, like their counterparts in residential care, were not comfortable in taking up this role and avoided doing so. Such discomfort was sometimes compounded when female workers were dealing with young men whose manner was aggressively sexual. Similar difficulties were encountered by some male workers in relation to the girls on their caseloads who were overtly sexualised. There were also social workers who seemed genuinely uncertain about their role in relation to imparting information on sexual topics. As one put it:

"It's the kind of area where we're not clear if we're allowed."

When a situation occurred in substitute care to which social workers had to respond, such as an incident of under-age sex or sexual assault, practitioners might offer counsel about the dangers of under-age sex or the risks of sexually transmitted disease but such discussion often explicitly skirted round the issues of sexual relationships more generally or of contraception in particular. Occasionally young people became worried about the possibility of pregnancy or had a specific health concern and for them the choice of a confidante was influenced by both gender considerations and by the relationships which they had developed with caregivers and professionals. One boy who regularly worked as a rent boy would discuss recurring worries about contracting HIV/AIDs with a hospital worker from a unit for sexually transmitted diseases, with whom he had been put in touch by his social worker.

The influence of parents was sometimes strongly felt in relation to contraception, either when a child feared parental disapproval or conversely when a parent had insisted on contraception for a child, and caregivers thought this to be premature. Moreover, in order to cover themselves, some residential workers ensured that parents were aware of the fact that their children were sexually active:

"We can't actually condone anything until we actually know parents are aware."

It can be seen, then, that the attention given to the sexual knowledge, health and contraceptive needs of the young people was extremely variable. Whilst some young people arrived in placement using contraception, others did not. Arrangements for contraceptive advice from clinics or GPs were rarely made for the latter group until a young person's level of sexual activity had become a matter of concern, and by then it was sometimes too late to prevent conception. Such advice was generally given to girls but not boys even though the impact of unplanned pregnancies by the boys would have long-term consequences if not for them, at least for their erstwhile girlfriends.

In some cases attitudes to the opposite sex were the main source of concern for caregivers or social workers. At least four of the boys saw sex principally as a means of obtaining gratification and exerting power over others. They had already sexually abused younger girls and their attitude to women was misogynistic in the extreme. The equivalent concern in the case of girls was when they made themselves available indiscriminately to a variety of partners and gained the reputations of being an "easy lay" (Lees, 1986). This behaviour and the fact that they sometimes spoke frequently about their past sexual abuse made them the target of both hurtful gossip and in some cases the predatory intentions of boys.

The overriding message from this evidence is that imparting information about sexual matters is given little priority in residential care and that this is sustained by a lack of confidence in this area among workers about what is allowed and expected and about their own ability to take on this role. Over and above this, there is a lack of clarity about the respective responsibilities of the various workers involved. The picture in foster care is better, but in both sectors there is a need for more attention to be given to sex education in case planning and greater clarity about who would be the most suitable person to undertake it. Given the exploitative context in which many of these young people were introduced to sexual contact, young people may only be able to absorb and use information about sexual choice and control which is provided within the context of a trusting relationship. The position of local authorities is not an easy one, but if young people are to have the benefit of information which will enable them to make choices about their sexuality and about pregnancy the present passive approach will need to be rethought. Whilst this is true of all looked after children, sexually abused young people are an especially vulnerable part of that population. Schools often employ specialist health education workers to undertake sex education and some voluntary organisations now employ a sex and health education worker for the children in their care. It may be that developments in this area would be assisted by specialist workers who would undertake part of the work and act as consultants and trainers.

SEXUAL IDENTITY

One of the aims of any sex education programme should be to assist young people to develop a positive sexual identity. This developmental task can be complicated by the experience of sexual abuse. The compulsive and indiscriminate heterosexual activity of some young people in the study appeared to be connected to their earlier sexual experiences. How often an incident of sexual abuse by someone of the same sex led boys to worry about the implications for their sexual orientation, we do not know. There was little evidence to suggest that this had been taken up in most of the work offered to them. Smith (1995a) has suggested that for some sexually abused young women the choice of a same-sex partner can provide a positive way to explore their sexuality and is less likely to trigger traumatic material connected to their abuse.

Two of the young people in the study were actively exploring their sexual identity. A third young man appeared to have confusion in this area. One was Martin, a 13-year-old boy who was active as a prostitute. He had a sympathetic support worker who discussed his sexual identity as a gay boy with him at length. This worker believed that Martin might be less drawn to prostitution if he could establish a satisfactory relationship with a man which did not involve exploitation. In spite of intensive work by the support worker Martin asked for further counselling about his sexual identity when the worker left. Julie felt clear that she was lesbian. She gained support from a voluntary agency contacted by her keyworker which provided a counsellor for three sessions. At the end of that she felt more confident that the problems lay not in her but in getting her family to accept her sexual orientation. However, she felt that after the keyworker left, her replacement disapproved of her sexuality, although the new keyworker herself intended to express sympathy with the girl's position. Later Julie was placed with an agency which specialised in providing housing for homosexual young people.

Craig, a third young man had suffered teasing and bullying at school because of his effeminate behaviour. He had also been sexually abused by a boy in his former residential school. He had confided to his previous foster carers that he liked dressing in women's clothes. Craig had earlier received a six-month period of counselling after the original sexual abuse which did include attention to issues of his sexual identity and which he had found very helpful. In addition, a support worker had visited every three weeks in his next foster care placement to discuss sexual issues with him.

It appeared that workers were aware of the importance of trying to provide help to young people who expressed a desire to explore their sexual identity and did their best to do so. How the young people themselves dealt with the negative attitudes of family members and others was less clear, but two of the three had endured bullying and teasing at school or in their placements.

The findings from this chapter show that most placements had basic ground rules which were intended to keep the young people and others safe and in some settings listening devices, alarms or night staff were used to monitor night-time activity. Contact with family members posed risks for some of the young people. Considerable emphasis was placed by caregivers on the importance of maintaining confidentiality and they generally did not pass on details of children's histories to schools or to their friends or neighbours unless the children in their care clearly presented sexual risks to other children. However, less attention was given in the placements to providing information and education about sexuality for the young people, which would have enabled them to exercise sexual choice and control in their relationships, although more was done in foster than in residential care. Greater priority was given to issues of sexual identity.

SUMMARY

1. Behaviours more typical of boys, such as aggression and coercive sexually abusing behaviour which occurred *within* placements were seen as problematic by caregivers and evoked a professional response. In contrast, the behaviours shown by girls, such as indiscriminate sexual activity and prostitution, in which they put themselves at risk *outside* placement, were given much less professional attention.

2. Most placements had some basic ground rules and routines designed to keep children safe, however the enforcement of rules varied greatly. Generally, caregivers did not inform other children in the placement or their own children that a looked after young person could pose risks to them.

3. Sometimes, significant additional resources were found to help to protect specific children.

4. Over half of the young people found that contact with family members was unhelpful and some were placed at risk of sexual abuse during contact visits or were reinforced in activities such as prostitution by family members. For others the disclosure of their sexual abuse had led to rejection and cessation of contact with their families.

5. Divergent views were held on whether schools should be informed about children's experience of sexual abuse or abusing behaviour. In general, caregivers did not pass on details of the children's history to their friends or neighbours unless the child clearly presented sexual risks to their children. However, some of the young people told others indiscriminately about their abuse.

6. The attention given by caregivers to the sexual knowledge, health and contraceptive needs of the young people in the study was extremely variable. Many young people lacked basic information and sex education sessions at school were likely to have been missed because of the young people's poor attendance.

7. Imparting information about sexual matters was generally given little priority, especially in residential care. A number of staff believed that they were not allowed to raise issues relevant to sex education with residents and some felt uncomfortable talking about sex.

8. Foster carers tended to be better than residential workers at taking up the issue of sexuality with young people. They were often able to draw on the experience of looking after their own teenage children and their work in fostering other adolescents.

9. The approach of social workers to sex education varied considerably. Some only took on this role reactively for example, when there was a concern that a girl might be pregnant. Contraceptive advice from clinics or GPs was rarely sought until the young persons' sexual activity was a matter of concern and then it was often too late to prevent conception. Discussing issues of sexuality with sexually aggressive boys and overtly sexualised girls was particularly difficult.

10. The issue of sexual identity was given more attention. Three of the young people were exploring their sexual identity and they received sympathetic help from social service practitioners and counsellors from voluntary agencies.

9

MANAGEMENT OF SEXUAL BEHAVIOUR WITHIN PLACEMENTS

Now that the ways in which caregivers tried to provide a safe environment have been examined, in this chapter we look at the management of sexual behaviours which occurred *within* placements and which therefore impinged very directly on residential workers and foster carers. Whilst the focus will be mostly on behaviours in the index placements, where we have information about the young people's behaviours in previous placements, these too will be described.

SEXUALLY ABUSING BEHAVIOUR

As we saw in Chapter 7, 17 of the 40 young people were known to have sexually abused other children before they arrived in the index placement. Three of them abused another child in the index placement. They were joined by four other young people, with no known history of abusing behaviour, who sexually abused one or more children whilst being looked after on this occasion. Of these seven children, four sexually abused others in foster settings and three in residential care. (One other young person went on to sexually abuse another child in a subsequent foster care placement.) As described in Chapter 6 the three boys and four girls showed sexually abusing behaviour towards over 13 children, in that they targeted, sexually touched, or in one case, penetrated a younger child apparently without consent and sometimes involving coercion. The victims were younger siblings either in a shared foster care placement or on a contact visit, the younger sons of the foster carers and other children in either residential or foster care.

As noted earlier, four of the boys with an abusing history were placed in secure accommodation or residential school because of their abusing behaviour and two of the children were in foster homes where there was no other child or the other children were considerably older. The remainder shared their foster homes, or in two cases children's homes, with a number of other children.

Use of the Child Protection Procedures and the Criminal Justice System

As we have seen, as many as 12 of the 22 young people who sexually abused another child either before, in or after the index placement, were or had been on the child protection register at some stage, often because of earlier concerns about them, sometimes but by no means always, centring on the sexual abuse which they had suffered. However, as discussed in Chapter 7, the acts of sexually abusing behaviour, whether prior to or during the index placement, were rarely referred for a child protection investigation or conference, so child protection procedures played little part in attempts to keep other children safe from young abusers (Morrison, 1992) despite the fact that the *Working Together* guidance (Home Office *et al*, 1991) makes it clear that an allegation of sexual abuse by a child should lead to child protection procedures being invoked in respect of the abusing child, and a case conference called.

Indeed, formal investigations were rarely undertaken and even when a police investigation had taken place the outcomes were unlikely to deter the young people. One boy who at the age of 13 had sexually abused his 5-year-old stepsister over an 18 month period, including full sexual intercourse, had not even been prosecuted. This was an unfortunate decision as it allowed him to continued to deny responsibility for his actions. This boy was described by his social worker as "one of the most dangerous kids I've worked with". Two boys had received cautions, one who at age 14 had sexually touched the 3-year-old granddaughter of his foster carers and the other who at the age of 12 had digitally penetrated and threatened a 10-year-old girl in a park who was forcibly held down by two other boys. One of these boys subsequently sexually abused two other children in the residential home to which he went. In the latter case although buggery and assault occurred the police regarded this as a minor incident and no charges were brought. The only young person whose case went to court was given a two-year supervision order as a result of tying down a 10-year-old girl and indecently assaulting her when he was 14.

Experienced practitioners who work with young abusers believe that all incidents should be investigated and that decisions about the use of the criminal justice system should be made in the light of the best way to secure assessment and treatment for the young person (National Children's Home, 1992; Brown, 1993; Morrison, 1994). *Working Together* (Home Office *et al*, 1991) echoes this view suggesting that focused forms of therapeutic intervention are likely to be needed under the orders of the civil or criminal courts. The low level of investigations and prosecutions even for serious offences in this sample does suggest that sexually abusing behaviour is still generally minimised. This meant that the young people had not had to face up to the consequences of their actions and that there was no record of their offences. It also made attempts to offer them counselling or other assistance with their behaviour more difficult, as denial had proved so effective. It is interesting to contrast this low level of involvement by the criminal justice system in sexually abusing behaviour with the common practice in residential care of calling the police if an assault or damage to property occurs. This practice has the effect of rapidly criminalising young people for physical assault or damage to property, whilst leaving those who have committed serious sexual assault with no criminal record.

Assessment

In spite of the guidance in *Working Together* (Home Office *et al*, 1991) that a comprehensive assessment should be made in respect of any child who is alleged to have sexually abused another, as we saw in Chapter 7 very few assessments appeared on the files and only two on the young abusers directly involved child psychiatrists. In one of these cases the young person had been formally assessed by the Tavistock Unit in London. As a result of their report he was placed in a specialist secure unit. Social workers were anxious to get three others assessed. The Gardener Unit in Manchester had been seen as unsuitable for one boy because of his learning difficulties and speech impediment and the Tavistock Unit had not been contacted about another boy because it was thought, probably erroneously, that there was too little concrete evidence of his abuse to others. Yet the latter boy had seriously sexually assaulted his young stepsister. A referral had been considered to a psychiatric unit for a third boy but had not been pursued.

The lack of specialist assessments on these young people put pressure on their social workers who were obliged to plan for them without good quality information about the likelihood of whether they would commit further acts of abuse in the future. One saw it as like "being up against a brick wall". In one further case, lack of information about the likelihood of re-abuse had led to an overcautious approach to contact. Sarah had sexually abused her younger half-sister in parallel with her own abuse by her older brothers. A decision was taken that she would not be allowed to stay overnight with her mother even when her younger sister was away. The social worker was unhappy about this decision, but her team manager was insistent. However, without a second opinion, she had no grounds on which to challenge it.

Therapeutic Intervention

As Chapter 11 will show the provision of therapeutic services for abusing young people was extremely patchy. Of the 22 children who had sexually abused others only five, or under a quarter, received a referral for therapeutic intervention in relation to the abusing behaviour at any time, but in only one case was any ongoing work provided. Although eight girls had shown abusing behaviour only one of the five so referred was a girl. Eighteen of the 22 abusers were known also to have been sexually abused. Eight of them or over two fifths had some intervention which concerned their experience of abuse and proportionately more girls (63%) than boys (37%) were given such direct work.

Management of the Sexually Abusing Behaviour

The sexually abusive behaviour which emerged in placement was managed in a variety of ways. An example of good practice was the work done with Kate. This 14-year-old girl targeted the boys in her children's home as soon as she arrived and got them to fondle her, sit on her lap and come with her to the bedroom. In exchange for a cigarette she allowed the boys to kiss, fondle and touch her. The residential staff worked as a team, supervising her activities closely and teaching Kate about the importance of more appropriate personal boundaries. She received therapeutic help from a counsellor outside the placement and this was supplemented by intensive and committed work by the head of home and Kate's keyworker. The workers were also careful to provide protection for Kate from outside influences. They discouraged an unsuitable relationship she made outside the placement and successfully diluted the influence of her sister who was a prostitute. In addition, once the residential workers had realised that the cause of Kate's depression was her profound feeling of having been let down when no prosecution was pursued against her long-term abuser, they involved her with an advocacy unit whose staff revived the case and referred it back to the Crown Prosecution Service. As a result of these efforts, Kate became happier and less sexually active and she learned clearer and safer personal boundaries. It is also interesting to note that in this children's home the practice was for every incident of serious sexual abuse to be reported to the child protection team.

The work with two boys who were in residential schools was less effective. One boy was observed to target two older boys with whom he would go to great lengths to share a shower. The careworker would try discreetly to arrange the shower rota so that these boys did not share a shower. This approach did not change the boy's behaviour and no other interventions were offered. He would also touch the female careworker's breasts and showed indiscriminate over-affectionate behaviour, which made him vulnerable. This boy was at a residential school which had a visiting therapist, so a referral would not have been difficult. The workers in this school showed little knowledge of how to manage a sexually abused or abusing child and so did not relate his behaviour to his background. An additional problem which had received no attention was that this boy went back every weekend to his family where a relative who was a Schedule One offender lived. The relative had probably sexually abused him in the past. Ongoing sexual abuse to him could not therefore be ruled out.

The other boy Gavin, who was also at residential school, had a very negative view of women and linked sex with violence, gratification and the exercise of power. Although he was seen as dangerous, his sexually abusing past was not known to the residential workers and received no direct attention. An attempt was made to challenge his negative stereotyping of women by the provision of strong female residential staff who could model healthy male–female relationships. However, his behaviour and attitudes received strong reinforcement from his immediate and extended family and did not change. This boy had so little self-awareness that he would make offensive remarks to passing girls. Whilst excluded from the school he was arrested on suspicion of rape, but in the absence of proof, the police were unable to prosecute.

As we have seen, four other young people sexually abused others whilst in foster care. Two girls sexually abused the younger sons of their foster carers, aged respectively 6 years and 12 years, and one, Karen, also abused her 4-year-old sister. One of these foster mothers had particular reason to feel aggrieved about the abuse of her son, since she had been given no information about Karen's background of sexual abuse and of having witnessed sexual activity between her mother and her boyfriends, apparently on the grounds that the placement had started out as a respite placement. She said after the abuse came to light:

"I was just shell-shocked . . . I was in shock for about a day. I just couldn't get over it . . . I would have tackled the sexual behaviour side completely different if I was aware of it, but at the time I wasn't."

The foster mother, after an unsuccessful attempt to get help for Karen and herself at the local child guidance clinic, went on a course on the subject of sexual abuse and used this to guide her management. She asked her own children and Karen's sister, to tell her if she made any sexual advances to them. She also told them Karen's history so that they could protect themselves. Karen therefore knew that her behaviour was being carefully watched. The foster mother tried to teach Karen more appropriate sexual behaviour. Karen's initial reaction was to say "But I can do it", which suggests that she was surprised to find a habitual behaviour pattern subject to censure.

The other foster mother stressed the house rules about the prohibition on bedroom visiting. The son who was abused was somewhat older, so the impact on her was probably less than on the other foster mother. Nonetheless, we need to ask what impact such sexual activity would have had on these boys, especially as it emerged that one had previously been the focus of a former foster girl's sexual attentions. The social worker in this second case did not report the girl's sexual abuse of the foster carer's son because she was concerned that the social services department might overreact. A third girl sexually abused the son of one her foster mother's friends. The foster carers reacted by placing heavy restrictions on the girl's contact with other children, leaving her with few normal peer activities.

The fourth foster child, Robin, was a boy. His foster carers were extremely vigilant because they had a thorough knowledge of his history of abusing behaviour. This was a particularly suitable placement as all the other children were older. At first, in addition to compulsive masturbation in public, Robin targeted one of the fostered girls, trying on three occasions to enter her bedroom. He also pinched the bottom of another of the girls. He was told firmly that bedroom visiting was against the rules of the family and he was never left alone with younger children. With such a highly sexualised child it was no doubt due to the care taken by the foster parents that no incidents of sexually abusing behaviour occurred at first. However, Robin had regular contact with his younger brother whom he had sexually abused in the past. On one of these contact visits, when the brother's foster carers left the two boys alone in the bedroom, Robin re-abused his brother. When this came to light the foster mother talked to Robin about it.

Amongst the other young people who had sexually abused other children in the past, precautions were not always taken to maximise the safety of other children. Room sharing was not uncommon, as we have seen. However, the placements which were of most concern were those in which, as we saw in Chapter 7, the carers were not given background information about the children. One has just been described. Another notable case, already mentioned, was that of a boy of 14 who had committed a violent sexual assault on a girl, including the use of threats and force. He was placed in foster care with a family who had two younger girls, until a residential school place became available. No mention was made of this serious incident of sexual assault. This was extremely negligent of the social services department which might have been held responsible had the boy abused either of the girls during the placement.

SEXUALISED BEHAVIOUR

Many of the young people showed high levels of sexualised behaviour to other children, to adults or to both, as described in Chapter 6. This put them and those to whom they directed their attentions at risk. It has to be remembered that for some of the young people sexual activity had been the principal form of currency in which relationships and other aspects of their lives had been negotiated and that their sexualised behaviour had been systematically rewarded in the past. Sexual contact would therefore have particular meanings for these young people. It could be indissolubly connected with any form of closeness with others, it might have come to be seen as a means of expressing power and control, it could be about the discharge of heightened arousal or be closely connected with feelings of anxiety and fear.

Sexualised behaviour to others was shown by both girls and boys, but girls were by far the larger group to show these behaviours. There were frequent comments that the girls dressed provocatively, that their skirts were near their waists, and that when boys or men were around they would increase the amount of make-up they wore and appear at the door scantily clad. A number of the girls offered themselves sexually to the boys in the children's home or foster care placement where they were staying, and some would get boys to fondle them or would kiss and cuddle the sons of the foster carers with no encouragement to do so. Sometimes this was coupled with similar behaviours outside the placement which were much harder to monitor, such as in the case of one girl of 13 who got fondled in the park by a whole group of 16 and 17-year-old boys.

In addition a considerable number of the girls acted sexually with male and female staff in children's homes and with male foster carers. Staff reported girls "flashing" them by lying naked on the bed, that boys would touch the breasts, hug, kiss and try to suck the necks of female workers or female staff at school and sometimes a boy made women workers the target of his physical and sexual aggression. The impact on male workers and some foster fathers was to make them wary of such sexualised girls and they would become distant and in some cases punitive in their management. However, the issues for female workers who received the sexual attentions of the boys in their care received less recognition and male workers, in particular, minimised the significance of these behaviours. Some of the girls made sexual approaches to any male visitor, undoing their blouses as they went to speak to them or approached men they met in the community, such as attendants at the local swimming baths.

Indeed, the more we became aware of the extent of sexual behaviour shown by some of the girls in the study, the more we became aware of the lack of attention to it in many of the placements which we studied. Residential workers appeared to lack theory or practice ideas to guide them in working with these girls (Hudson, 1989). At the same time, social workers sometimes erroneously judged very sexualised and risky behaviour as normal, even in one case when a 15-year-old was pregnant and could not say which of her many partners was likely to be the father. Social work advice to caregivers tended to be based on the view that sexualised behaviour was a search for emotional support and affection, and sometimes included the rider to caregivers that they could not prevent these girls from doing exactly what they wanted. Their advice was therefore limited because it did not link these sexualised behaviours with the sexual abuse and hyper-sexualised environments many of the girls had experienced previously, which were likely to have played a large part in shaping their behaviours. Nor did it suggest how caregivers could assist in teaching young people to give and receive affection in non-sexualised ways. In addition, by giving the caregivers the message that their power was limited they were inadvertently replicating a situation in which the child's caregivers failed to take steps to make the child safe. Their advice also failed to point out the areas in which the caregivers could usefully intervene, even though the needs of the young people were often far-reaching.

However, there were encouraging examples of good practice when caregivers, sometimes acting in concert with the responsible social worker, had intervened successfully. In so doing they had succeeded in containing and re-shaping children's sexualised behaviours and had also worked on their underlying needs. One girl who was particularly well managed was Alice. Alice had weak interpersonal boundaries, was highly sexualised and sexually touched the male and female staff in her children's home and at school, as well as other adults she met outside the placement. Although she was aged 13 she related at a 7-year-old level and had been entirely rejected by her mother and stepfather. Her behaviour was particularly hard to manage because in her previous placement she had frequently absconded. As a result, an extra residential worker was appointed to shadow her whenever she left the children's home, and this brought results when after a few weeks she stayed in much more.

The message given directly to Alice throughout the placement was that her caregivers cared about her safety, a very important message to girls like Alice who may never have been protected in the past. When her caregivers found that telephone contact with Alice's mother was harmful to her they took steps to limit contact with her mother. (Some young people, like Alice, require active intervention to protect them from damaging associates, who try to encourage them to join in their activities. If this is not achieved then other efforts to work on sexualised behaviour may be actively undermined.) A log was kept of all Alice's activities and staff taught her more appropriate interpersonal boundaries, explaining that she should ask before giving people hugs, that it was not OK to touch people sexually and that she should not tell people that she had had sex with everyone because this led to malicious gossip. She also received a lot of work on acceptable touch with different people, depending on how well she knew them.

As a result of this work and good consistent role modelling Alice became more aware of the effect of her behaviour on others and learned more acceptable boundaries. In addition, staff realised the importance of providing nurturing for Alice, and they put time aside each night to brush her hair and read her a bedtime story. This programme of care and work dealt both with Alice's presenting behaviour and some of her underlying needs.

The staff team in this children's home had high morale and was ably supported by a social worker who had a very clear view of the purpose of the placement and his role in it and connected Alice's current behaviour with her history. At the time of admission the social worker had carried out an extensive review of the 13-year-old girl's background and history of abuse and so was able to tell the residential workers what to expect. He worked hard to establish a relationship of trust with Alice and visited the placement without fail every week at a regular time. Alice's concentration span was very short but despite this he eventually engaged her in a complicated piece of life story work using his knowledge of the dynamics of her relationship with her mother and the difficulties stemming from a confusion about her paternity. Through this piece of work Alice began to establish a chronology of her life that helped to link her fragmented memories and feelings about the past and which would serve as a helpful foundation for later therapeutic intervention.

Some caregivers, however, were less sensitive to the needs of girls like Alice. Another girl, who, like her, was very immature and highly sexualised was, at the age of 13, given freedom more appropriate to a mature 16-year-old. She was allowed to stay out late and frequently left to cross the city alone by bus. The foster carers were used to looking after streetwise adolescents and were slow to realise this girl's immaturity and vulnerability. Inadequately supervised she ended up being sexually assaulted when out one night. No work was provided on her weak interpersonal boundaries or on her underlying needs.

Quite often when inappropriate sexualised behaviour came to light, restrictions would be placed on the child but no work would be undertaken to try to teach the young person more appropriate behaviour. At the same time it must be acknowledged that when caregivers did try to re-shape behaviour, they sometimes found it hard to alter well-entrenched patterns of behaviour particularly at the top end of the age group. The behaviours may in part have delivered some rewards to the young women, who liked the male attention they tried so hard to draw onto themselves. At the broader level, these young people badly needed other non-sexual ways of gaining positive attention and esteem, but few caregivers were actively engaged in trying to involve them in sport, leisure, and other activities or in employment opportunities which could have enhanced their self-esteem in more socially appropriate ways. Those caregivers who put effort into involving young people in leisure activities often got a good response if they were persistent and when they accompanied the young people to events and gave them encouragement. This was particularly evident among foster carers. However, the initial difficulties often discouraged workers and no further efforts were made.

DEALING WITH YOUNG PEOPLE IN THE CONTEXT OF ALLEGATIONS OF ABUSE

Caring for these young people was far from easy. However, the task has been made more difficult by the growing awareness of the possibility of allegations being made by children in care against those who look after them (Nunno and Motz, 1988; Hicks and Nixon, 1989; Rosenthal *et al*, 1991; Cavanagh, 1992; Ryan, McFadden and Weicek, 1992; Verity and Nixon, 1995). How widespread was this awareness among the caregivers with whom we spoke and what impact did it have on the management of the young people in the study?

The risk that an allegation would be made was a real one. Looking at all the placements of the young people about which we had information, 11 allegations had been made by 10 of the children. Thus, a quarter of the young people in the study had made an allegation of mistreatment at some stage during their stay in care. Of the 11 allegations four concerned sexual abuse, four physical abuse and three were either unclear or concerned the child feeling unfairly treated. Three other young people threatened to make an allegation against a caregiver or social worker, including one young man who was always threatening to make allegations when he first arrived in his children's home.

We also asked the residential workers and the foster carers whom we interviewed whether they had ever had an allegation made against them. Seven of the caregivers had had this experience (four foster carers and three residential workers), involving allegations of sexual abuse in two cases, physical abuse in four and of being a drug pusher in one.

Those caregivers who had had allegations made against them described the subsequent investigation as very stressful, a "nightmare" experience, even though all had eventually been cleared:

"It was absolutely appalling. I mean people have committed suicide for less. You know – I mean we are quite strong people, but it affected my husband badly. It still affects him now . . . We're not doing fostering with any kind of ease now . . . If there had been any alternative we would never have fostered again."

These foster carers had only continued to foster in order to clear their name locally as to give up might have seemed an admission of guilt. One foster carer said that making an allegation was the child's ultimate weapon and several commented that the balance between children's rights and those of the caregivers had swung too far in the favour of children:

"I always think in these things the foster carers are the last to be interviewed or spoken to about it . . . I know they have to put the children's needs first but you're the last on the list . . . but it's just got very silly . . . it's taken away all adults' rights."

Another residential worker commented that whilst children could take their concerns to the Advocacy Unit or the complaints section of the local authority, staff had no one to go to:

"They can only take my word. How do I know they're going to believe me?"

The majority of caregivers were aware of the possibility of allegations being made against them and altered their practice accordingly. Among the most careful, of course, were the caregivers against whom allegations had been made in the past. In contrast, nine of the caregivers (five foster carers and four residential workers) had not thought of the possibility of allegations being made against them by the placed child in our study. The foster carers in this group were most at risk because they took no action to keep themselves safe, whereas in three out of the four cases the residential workers were already observing simple rules for keeping safe. The lack of briefing about forestalling allegations in one case was clearly connected with generally poor preparation of the foster carers, because they had not even been told of the child's past abuse or very sexualised behaviour. In another case where foster carers were inadequately prepared, the foster father put himself at risk of allegations by giving a 12-year-old fostered girl hugs on demand. Fortunately, this was observed by the social worker who warned him to desist.

The actions taken by caregivers to lessen their vulnerability to allegations took various forms. Male residential workers and some foster fathers rarely or never touched the girls in their care. One foster father was colder to the adolescent girl they looked after than to other children because of his fears of a repeat allegation. As one residential worker explained it:

"In general, I'll just use my voice. I don't believe it's good to get into physical contact too much with any of the kids. It's just rules I've set myself anyway. It's a lot easier. I mean you could give someone a big hug but in general I don't think it's – it's a lot safer for yourself just not to."

In some establishments playfighting was also avoided in order to protect staff and children. One foster father of a 10-year-old girl never touched her at all because of a comment by the girl in her previous foster home which was construed overhastily as an allegation and led to the breakdown of the placement. Other foster fathers who were aware of the possibility of allegations took the same line. In contrast, one residential school, although highly aware of the possibility of allegations and abuse taking place, put emphasis on showing children that they mattered and this was done by giving gifts, special attention and hugs.

In children's homes care was taken, whenever possible, to have two members of staff with the children, and especially when entering a young person's bedroom. Obviously it was not always possible to adhere to this practice:

"I think you are always wary and let your colleagues know what you're doing, but sometimes you may have a situation where you just don't have time. I suppose you take a chance."

In foster care the option of having two adults is not always available, either because only one carer is present or because the carer has no partner. For foster mothers in households where it had been decided that the foster father would never be alone with a particular child, the burden of care was carried by the foster mother. Some foster carers did involve their partners in difficult situations or when there were arguments, especially if they needed a witness. One couple protected each other, trying to arrange it so that neither of them was ever alone with the child in their care.

Occasionally, children were seen as such a risk that their activities were circumscribed. For example, one girl who frequently touched the genitals of staff and children at school was not taken swimming where it was thought this behaviour could not be supervised. The headmaster and male staff at this school were very worried about the possibility of allegations being made against them. Some workers said that they would be careful to protect themselves when they knew that a young person had been sexually abused, but those who said this had not always known about the histories of abuse of the young people in their care.

Many children's homes and some foster homes kept a log of activities and a record of restraints which could be referred to in the case of an allegation being made. One foster carer, against whom an allegation had been made by a former foster child, also telephoned the social services department immediately if a child threatened to make an allegation in order to get the threat documented.

Multiple Allegations

A few young people posed particular management problems because they made a series of allegations against others while they were looked after. One girl alleged that a residential worker had pushed her downstairs after she had attempted to drown herself in the bath. The worker was subsequently cleared. She also made an allegation of sexual abuse against her previous foster father, which she later withdrew, claiming that she had made the allegation because no one was listening to her real problems which she had not divulged. In addition, she alleged that a woman social worker from the Child and Family Support Centre had made improper suggestions to her. A second girl made an allegation of sexual abuse against her ex-boyfriend before entering care and also alleged that her stepfather had hit her. Once in care, she alleged sexual abuse by a residential worker which she retracted after an internal inquiry had been held and she later alleged rape by a friend's boyfriend when she was out one night.

Male caregivers and social workers involved with these girls became very uneasy and one male social worker became so strained by worries about the possibility of allegations being made against him that he left the case abruptly, without giving Mary, the girl concerned, any explanation. This social worker had adopted the practice of taking another worker with him whenever he saw Mary. On one occasion, he realised too late that he had no escort on a car trip and became very upset when he realised the risk that he had run. Mary also developed strong feelings for her male residential worker and tried to hug him in the "wrong sort of way". The residential worker talked to his manager about it to cover his back but tried to carry on, realising that another change of worker would not be helpful. After Mary left the home a stack of love letters addressed to the residential worker was found in her bedroom.

There was no evidence to suggest that efforts had been made by caregivers to understand the reasons why these young women made multiple allegations, although one might surmise that these girls had felt that their original allegations of sexual abuse had received little attention or had not been believed, and that they had a need either to call attention to the original abuse or to express towards other men the anger that they felt towards an earlier perpetrator. In the absence of any such understanding, and with caregivers and social workers fearful for their reputations and jobs, the girls tended to be handled somewhat punitively. Male workers either left the cases without explanation leaving the girls feeling further rejected, or handled them in as distant a way as they could contrive. The work with the girls was thereby compromised.

CONSENSUAL SEXUAL RELATIONSHIPS WITHIN PLACEMENTS

Five young people were known to have had a consensual sexual relationship with another resident in their children's home, although others may have done so without being discovered. As we have seen, the general rule in both children's homes and foster care was that sexual relationships between the young people living there were not allowed. This was principally in the cause of keeping good order, as it was thought unsuitable for young people to witness physical closeness between two residents, leave alone, as could happen, for children to witness sexual activity when bedrooms were shared. Moreover, frequently one or both of the young people were under the legal age of consent. It will be recalled from Chapter 8 that some placements had instituted methods of surveillance at night which allowed high levels of supervision to take place, whilst in others supervision was much more relaxed.

These higher levels of supervision were not usually in place in ordinary children's homes, even though it was usual for one or two members of staff to be on sleepover duty at night. In the absence of such measures, staff took a fairly resigned attitude to sexual relationships between residents:

"You monitor them as closely as possible, but that's it. You can't stop it."

"You can't stop it. It's like the smoking in the bedrooms. We ask them not to and if we catch them, we'll halt it. But when we're not there, they'll do it."

As we have seen, when a sexual relationship between two residents came to light it was usual for one child to be moved out of the home. Child protection procedures were not invoked in any of the instances of sexual relationships between residents and in one case the social worker was incensed because information about the sexual relationship was not even given to her by the residential worker. In this case, a 14-year-old sexually abused girl with weak interpersonal boundaries had to leave the children's home and this necessitated a return to her sexually abusing father. It was not clear why she and not the boy involved was asked to leave. This case does highlight the vulnerability of young people, especially those who have been sexually abused, when they get involved in sexual relationships within placements in care. The girl's social worker rightly complained about the lack of protection which had been provided for her.

Whilst the usual reaction was to move out one of the residents, there were also cases where such incidents were minimised. One sexual relationship only came to light because the young man, afraid he had made his girlfriend pregnant, told his social worker. Both the young people were under the legal age of consent and the girl was taken for contraceptive advice and counselling about sexuality when their relationship became known, whilst the boy was given some basic sexual information. The main worry in this children's home was of the possibility of the girl becoming pregnant.

The one lesbian relationship which developed in a children's home was dealt with in a similar way to heterosexual relationships, and one of the girls was moved out. In addition, there were concerns that the girl who remained might force herself onto any girl with whom she shared a room. A special meeting was held to discuss this. However, overall there was less worry because pregnancy was not on the agenda:

"I suppose with a lesbian relationship there isn't so much fear – there's less chance of any physical damage being done. There's no chance of having a child as well. There's less worries about that sort of relationship."

Sexual activity in shared rooms was acknowledged to be especially difficult to supervise:

"We had lesbian activity going on, and you can't supervise something like that. Boys molesting each other. If they're in the same room there's no way you can supervise that."

Awareness of the possibility of sexual activity between same-sex young people was higher amongst residential school staff than among residential workers in children's homes. There were no reports of sexual relationships between young people in foster homes and foster carers made a point of emphasising that none was to take place and imposed strict rules to back this up.

MASTURBATION

Four young people masturbated compulsively in public, often in the living room of their care placement. Some rubbed themselves against the carpet or against the furniture. One boy also accompanied night-time masturbation with loud moans which kept the foster family awake.

Masturbation in public was dealt with by the caregivers telling the young people to stop this behaviour in front of others and if they wished to continue, to go to their rooms. This approach was generally successful and the behaviour was extinguished in public. This kind of behaviour emphasises the importance of good preparation for caregivers before placement is made because its emergence could be very disturbing for caregivers. One foster father said that he had not been shocked because he had been prepared for the boy's masturbation but that the initial stages of the placement had, nonetheless, been "horrendous".

At the younger end of the age group there was one girl who used the friction of piggyback rides or sitting on her foster carers' laps to stimulate herself sexually. The foster carers dealt with this by stopping these activities, once they realised on the advice of the girl's previous caregivers, what was happening. A more difficult behaviour to deal with was that of young people who inserted objects into themselves through the vagina or anus, as occurred with two of the children. This behaviour would not be discovered unless its intensity led to bleeding or other signs. There were no examples of such behaviour being addressed directly, although in one such case it may have been thought that the therapeutic work provided for the child would eventually have an impact.

Kelly's research (1988) suggests that some abused children are left with confusing feelings of sexual arousal which they do not understand and compulsive masturbation is one way in which they try to get rid of these feelings. Smith (1995a) comments that children who have become used to the heightened sense of arousal produced by abuse may masturbate or seek sexual contact in order to re-experience it. She suggests that they may need help to give this up and will require other interests to take its place. Other commentators have noted that masturbation may be used for self-comfort and may lessen as children feel more secure. In a similar way Friedrich (1993) considers that the experience of stress may lead to increased sexual behaviour and this could have been the case with some of the masturbatory behaviour in the early stages of placements.

SEXUAL ABUSE TO THE YOUNG PEOPLE IN PLACEMENT

During the period of the index placement one girl alleged sexual abuse by another resident in her children's home and another alleged abuse by a residential worker. The allegation of sexual abuse by a male resident was not substantiated after investigation, but during this period this girl continued to be involved with a group of Schedule One offenders, so it is likely that she was being sexually exploited and abused at this time. The second girl made a series of allegations of sexual abuse both before entering care and thereafter. One was an allegation that a residential worker had rubbed himself against her and, as a result, an internal inquiry was held which did not uphold her complaint.

In addition, two boys, one of whom had moderate learning difficulties, had previously been sexually abused at residential schools by other boys. In one case the abuse was extensive and accompanied by threats of violence and continued up to the age of 14. We noted that another two boys had been placed in a residential home during the time when a paedophile ring was operating there and staff have since been convicted of sexual offences against the children in their care. In the case of one of these boys the social services department was also investigating sexual abuse by a foster father with whom the boy in our study had been placed at the age of three, at which time he was soiling and bedwetting.

When reviewing this evidence about the management of sexual behaviours within placements it is clear that caregivers lack frameworks for understanding and managing these behaviours effectively (National Children's Home, 1992). Part of the reason for this is that adolescence is a time of sexual exploration and it can be difficult to differentiate between what is normal and acceptable behaviour and what is not. Moreover, sexuality is a sensitive area which raises deep feelings for everyone. For these and other reasons, we found that there was little discussion about the links between the young people's earlier experiences and current behaviours, a lack of work on the behaviours themselves, on teaching young people how to keep themselves safe and on how to give and receive affection in non-sexualised ways. The difficulty of providing physical affection and nurturing to children who tended to sexualise physical contact had been given insufficient attention, although, as we have seen, there were examples of good practice. With these older children the focus was on *what* the children were doing and not on *why* they were doing it or what they were communicating by their behaviour. The sexualised behaviour of girls was a particularly neglected area, and their behaviour excited rejection by some male workers and only a passive stance by many caregivers who failed to act proactively to make the placements as safe as possible for these vulnerable girls. They were viewed as troublesome rather than troubled.

SUMMARY

1. Seven young people sexually abused other children while in the index placement, but incidents of sexually abusing behaviour were

rarely referred for investigation or to a child protection case conference. The low levels of investigation and prosecution even for serious sexual offences meant that the young people avoided facing up to their actions and subsequent attempts to offer them counselling were undermined, since denial had proved so effective.

2. The guidance in *Working Together* (Home Office *et al*, 1991) recommends that a comprehensive assessment should be undertaken in respect of any child who sexually abuses another. However, very few assessments appeared on the files and only two involved child psychiatrists. Moreover, only five of the 22 abusing children received a referral for therapeutic intervention and in only one of these cases did it lead to ongoing work in relation to the abusing behaviour.

3. The study did reveal some examples of good practice in managing sexually abusing behaviour. In most cases, once such behaviour came to light, caregivers fashioned ways to provide intensive supervision. Caregivers rarely discussed the behaviour itself with the child or addressed the children's own experiences of victimisation.

    The placements of particular concern were those where caregivers were given no information about the child's background of sexual abuse or abusing behaviour and so could not plan to keep other children safe.

4. Many of the young people showed high levels of sexualised behaviour to other children, to adults or to both. Sexualised behaviour by girls within placements elicited most concern and often made male caregivers wary of contact, for fear of an allegation of abuse being made against them.

    Residential staff, foster carers and social workers lacked theory and practice ideas to guide them in working with these girls. Little work was directed at teaching them more appropriate behaviour or in encouraging them to find non-sexual ways to gain esteem.

5. The majority of caregivers were aware of the likelihood of allegations being made against them and altered their practice accordingly. However, just under one in four had not considered this possibility. Caregivers, particularly men, devised a variety of strategies to lessen their vulnerability to allegations. In foster care, if it had been decided that a foster father would never be alone with a child the additional burden was carried by the foster mother.

6. A few of the girls had made a series of allegations while in care. There was little evidence to suggest that caregivers or social workers developed an understanding of why these girls made multiple allegations. In the absence of such understanding, and with caregivers and social workers fearful for their reputations and jobs, the girls tended to be handled somewhat punitively.

7. During the index placement one girl alleged sexual abuse by a boy in her children's home and another sexual abuse by a residential worker. Neither allegation was substantiated. Two other boys had previously been sexually abused at residential schools by other boys.

8. Consensual sexual relationships between residents in children's home were also a cause for concern and occurred in five cases. When this happened one child was usually moved out of the home but child protection procedures were not invoked. There were no reports of any sexual relationships between young people in foster care and foster carers usually imposed very strict rules to prevent this from happening.

9. Four young people in the study masturbated compulsively in front of other people. Consistent management led to these behaviours being extinguished but such behaviour was disturbing for caregivers.

10. In general, there was little discussion about the links between the young people's earlier experiences of sexual abuse and their current behaviours, a lack of work on the behaviours themselves, on teaching young people how to keep themselves safe and on how to give and receive affection in non-sexualised ways.

10

MANAGEMENT OF SEXUAL BEHAVIOUR OUTSIDE PLACEMENTS

Sexual behaviours which occur within placements are not easy to manage, but those which take place away from placements pose particular challenges to caregivers. As we saw in Chapter 6 some young people show sexual behaviours only within their care settings, others only outside, whilst still others show such behaviours both within and away from their placements. This simple division is not entirely straightforward as some young people involve other children from their placements in sexual behaviours outside substitute care and sometimes adults outside placements manipulate one young person in a placement to involve other children in their sexual activities.

The amount of responsibility taken by caregivers for young people when they were outside placements was extremely variable. In general, staff in children's homes did not see their responsibility as extending beyond the four walls of the home. Even when they knew that young people were going out to engage in highly risky behaviour, staff would counsel them to desist but would not attempt to stop them. If young people did not return on time the police were routinely called. This gave children the message that staff were powerless to contain them and inadvertently repeated the situation with their parents who had often been unable to control their behaviour. Not surprisingly, parents were often vehemently critical about these low levels of supervision, which allowed the behaviours that had led to admission to care to continue unabated thereafter (see also Fisher *et al*, 1986). Two children's homes were the exception: in them staff expected to exercise high levels of supervision and succeeded in doing so.

Some foster carers worked on a very similar model to children's homes, but most saw their responsibility for the children in their care as extending to their activities outside the placement, as ordinary parents in the community do. Some gave children lifts to their evening engagements, especially if they thought the activities planned might hold risks for the young people. Others intervened if relationships were made which might prove harmful or exploitative to the young people and some would go out to look for children who did not return home on time. What then were the sexual activities which took place outside substitute care that caused caregivers concern and how did they manage them? As in Chapter 9 we will describe not only the behaviours which occurred in the index placement, but also where we have the information, the behaviours in previous care settings.

SEXUAL ACTIVITY OTHER THAN PROSTITUTION

As previously mentioned, concerns about sexual activity outside placement centred on girls. Eight girls were the subject of professional concern about such behaviour in the index placement. It was rare for anxiety to be expressed about the sexual lives of boys unless they were sexually involved with girls who were clearly under the legal age of consent. In one such case the foster mother became worried about a sexual relationship between the 14-year-old boy in her care and a 13-year-old girl and took this up with the social worker. In another case where a 15-year-old sexually abusing boy in a residential school became involved with a 12-year-old girl, the residential worker contacted the girl's parents to let them know where he was living and by implication to indicate that the relationship was unsuitable.

However, it was predominantly girls whose sexual behaviour attracted attention. There were concerns about girls who had a large number of partners or who had sexual relationships which appeared to be exploitative. The sexual double standard ensured that boys who were involved in similar levels of sexual activity escaped attention (Cawson, 1987). Since the majority of girls and boys were under 16, the issue of unlawful sexual intercourse and under-age pregnancy was present but the police were never involved for this reason.

When girls made relationships with undesirable partners, caregivers varied as to whether they saw this as an area in which they could intervene. One 12-year-old girl, Irene, was regularly picked up outside her children's home by known Schedule One offenders whom she had met through her sister before she entered care. There were also concerns about involvement with drugs through these contacts. The children's home staff took no action, beyond trying to persuade her not to go out with them. Irene would sometimes telephone the children's home in distress after going out with the men. The only record of any action by staff was when she was taken to see a GP after she stayed out overnight with one of the men. Yet when Irene was living at home a police protection order was taken out after she stayed the night with them. However, as the placement progressed, Irene became attached to her keyworker who was a mother figure for her and she gradually gave up these associates.

In contrast, another girl, Annie, who was 13 and in another children's home was much more closely supervised. She was at risk of being drawn into prostitution through contact with a relative, but the staff who had formed very good and trusting relationships with her were able to help her to see the dangers of so doing. She also formed a relationship with an older man who gave her money and lifts in his car and the staff intervened quickly to end this relationship.

Another area of concern was when girls were involved with a number of sexual partners at the same time or made indiscriminate sexual relationships. Young people who have been sexually abused may become more sexually active than their peers and this may be a coping mechanism for surviving sexual abuse (Friedrich, 1988; Smith, 1995a). Caregivers often commented that the girls craved attention from men and sought such attention at every opportunity. For example, Trudy who was aged 15 when taken on a caravan holiday by her foster carers got picked up by different men every night and the foster carers would eventually find her in a man's caravan in the early hours of the morning. They decided that they could not ever take Trudy on holiday again. She would go to the local club with her foster family and within half an hour of meeting a man would go out in the car with him. The foster mother saw her as "a danger to herself" because she had no idea of how to keep herself safe. However, the social worker did not judge Trudy's sexual behaviour as unusual for her age and apparently did not connect it to her former abuse. She therefore failed to provide any useful advice for the foster carers. Trudy had received no counselling about her past abuse. Girls like Trudy gained, as we have seen, a reputation as an "easy lay".

Malicious gossip could then make attendance at school painful for them, and as in Trudy's case, become a contributory factor in non-attendance. At the top end of the age range these sexual behaviours were sometimes well established and difficult to change. Trudy's foster mother often talked to her about contraception and the struggles of bringing up a baby, but none of this advice had any impact and she became pregnant when only 15.

Another foster mother who found that the 15-year-old girl in her charge refused to respond to her efforts to supervise her behaviour outside the home commented in despair:

"That's been the biggest impact, not being able to control where she goes, who she's with, what she does and how she turns out."

This girl, Stacey, would stay out late at night and bring men back to the house who tried to involve her in taking drugs. When the foster mother discovered, after many attempts, that she could not exercise supervision over the times when Stacey came home or over her activities when out, she decided to allow the girl to have her boyfriend to stay and a separate bed was provided in an annexe to the girl's room. The message which the foster mother tried to convey to the girl was that it was a shame that she was sexually active so early, but that she did not have to sleep with her boyfriend in her house, that she had a choice. This action was supported by the social worker.

Difficult as it was to supervise these girls or to bring about a change in their behaviour, there was one case in which change did occur. Zoe at the age of 13 was seen as "on the slippery slope" because of her sexual promiscuity and involvement in drug use. She had become known locally as the "Townsville Bike". However, when she moved in with a friend's family who were approved as Regulation 11 foster carers, her behaviour changed. She had no sexual relationship for a time until she became involved with a steady boyfriend. Zoe shared the bedroom with her friend and it appears that a family who cared about her and provided strong alternative models of adolescent female behaviour provided the context for this positive change.

One difficulty in caring for these girls was that not only had they been sexually abused but often they had never had the experience of being safely looked after. As a result, they had no idea about keeping themselves safe. They placed themselves in risky situations with little thought of the consequences, such as getting into cars with men they had just met. Indeed, some of them spoke to their caregivers about situations which they had entered willingly, but which quickly got out of control, leaving them open to coerced sex and other forms of exploitation. When they stayed out they often stayed with men they met who took advantage of them.

YOUNG PEOPLE WHO INVOLVED OTHERS IN SEXUAL ACTIVITY

There were examples of older more sexually experienced girls leading younger girls into situations which put them at risk. One girl of 16 regularly involved younger girls from her foster placement in her sexual activities. She took a 12-year-old girl from her placement out to her boyfriend's flat and while she had sex with him, left the younger girl with another boy who expected the same favour from her. The girl was "scared half to death". On another occasion the older girl had sex in the back of the car while the younger girl sat in the front. The older girl may have been used to an audience for her sexual activities or may have been involved by others in their sexual contacts, but no analysis of her behaviour was offered which would have led to greater understanding and no one talked to her about it. Her foster carers tried to stop other children going out with her without giving her any reason. The caregiver also wisely decided that she could not foster younger girls whilst this girl lived with her.

Another 15-year-old girl took an immature, sexualised and multiply sexually abused younger girl from her foster placement out with her one evening, where they met two young men, one of whom raped the younger girl. These examples demonstrate the risks of placing sexualised girls together where the older girls may endanger younger ones, by setting up meetings with predatory men and not foreseeing the risks they run. At the very least caregivers need to be more aware of these risks and actively to teach young people about how to keep themselves safe.

ABSCONDING AND SEXUAL ACTIVITY

One fundamental challenge to the effective management of the young people was their tendency to abscond. Ten of them were persistent absconders (five boys and five girls), so much so in four cases that no placement ever held them. This was particularly so in the case of those who worked as prostitutes and those boys who had never separated from their mothers and could not cope with being apart from them. At least six of the young people who ran away regularly took other young people with them, often leading them into situations of high physical or sexual risk.

Absconding also carried the risk that the young people would exchange sex for shelter or be sexually abused while on the run (Stein, Rees and Frost, 1994). Indeed, for 14 young people this was what happened (seven boys and seven girls). The young people who worked as prostitutes returned to those pursuits while on the run and one girl regularly took refuge with a local "madam" when she absconded, which hastened her return to work on the streets and to involvement with drugs and alcohol. Other young people stayed with boyfriends or men with whom they had sexual relationships while they were on the run or they ran off with men they hardly knew. A few young people ran away under the influence of another child from the placement and stayed with this child's boyfriend in situations where they came under pressure to provide sex for his friends. A few probably exchanged sex for money when they were absconding in order to provide a means of survival, and others got involved in criminal activities with their associates when on the run.

Four young people had previously been sexually abused while on the run. One was only 7 years old when he accepted shelter with an older man who lived in a caravan in exchange for sexual favours and another absconded with a girl from his foster placement who often worked as a prostitute. She took him to a house where he was indecently assaulted in front of the girl and four adults. The third young person alleged that he had been sexually assaulted while he had absconded from a residential unit and the fourth was raped by her neighbour's son when she ran away from the physical abuse she suffered at home.

PROSTITUTION

An even more worrying problem than young people who absconded was that of prostitution. There are particular risks that sexually abused young people will become involved in prostitution, especially if they run away (Silbert and Pines, 1981; Finkelhor, 1986; Widom and Ames, 1994), and some feel that for the first time they are actively in control of their own bodies, as they make men pay for that which was previously taken (Jesson, 1993). Five young people (two girls and three boys) had been involved in prostitution either in the index or other placements, during periods of absconding or after leaving care. There were worries that another three young people (all boys) were on the fringes of involvement. It is worth noting that at least four of these children had themselves been initiated into prostititution or encouraged to enter it by members of their families. Others had been initiated by friends within or outside the care system.

There was no evidence that social workers or caregivers routinely screened children before admission in relation to their involvement in prostitution. In one case, a foster mother who was already looking after one young man who had worked as a prostitute took on another. She was the only person who was aware of the situation and had assumed that the rules of confidentiality meant that she could not tell the second young person's social worker about the first boy. The more experienced newly fostered young man soon ran away with the other boy to clients of his.

The risks attendant on placing a young person who works as a prostitute are far-reaching. There are not only the risks related to sexual disease and exploitation for the young prostitutes and the likelihood that they will become involved in drug use, but also there are high risks that they will involve a number of young people from their placement in their activities. Three of the young people (two girls and one boy) procured other children from their placements for the purposes of prostitution or involvement in activities such as the making of pornographic videos. Sometimes this was done while on the run together and was a way of making money or finding shelter. For some, initiating others seemed to be a compulsive activity, a replay of their own experience of being initiated, and on occasions young people procured others for their clients, at the request of those adults. This was one way in which paedophiles in the community could gain access to new children and it is known that some pimps target particular children's homes (Shaw *et al*, 1996). One young woman involved at least seven other young people whom she met in children's homes in prostitution.

Ben at the age of 13 was an attractive boy of mixed race who had been on the fringes of the rent scene before he began to be looked after. Three weeks after he arrived at the children's home he began his activities as a prostitute. He had gained the confidence to embark on a long career as a prostitute from other young people in his children's home, including a young woman with considerable experience of prostitution:

"When I first went into care. Hanging around down the Bus Station. I did that before I went into care, but I never knew the ropes or whatever. But when I went into care, I got to know people and know their background and I just started doing it, I suppose. That's what started it all off."

Staff quickly became aware of Ben's activities and saw him being picked up and later dropped off at the children's home late at night by men in expensive cars. He would return to the home under the influence of drugs. He also made arrangements to meet his clients from the telephone at the children's home and involved other young people from the children's home in prostitution. Ben's keyworker tried to get him to join in the children's home activities and sought medical attention and advice but no one actually restricted his activities:

"At one time at Field Place I was escaping every day. What I would do was go out in the night, come back, have dinner, say sorry, get shouted at, go out and sleep out three or four nights in a row, come home, say sorry, get shouted at, have something to eat, run off and so on."

He felt, in retrospect, that more could have been done to control his behaviour:

"They could have restrained me, but they can't do that. They could have put me in a secure unit, because they knew I was getting worse and worse and worse. But they weren't taking any notice."

His stepfather certainly considered that to be the case and would pick Ben up from the bus station where he was soliciting for clients.

The social worker said that his local authority considered Ben to be "the most at risk teenager" in the county and the residential care staff were out of their depth. It took five months for the local authority to react to this situation and Ben was then assigned a support worker. He helped to arrange a move to an out-of-county foster placement to try to break the pattern of prostitution and drug abuse. This placement achieved some success. Ben, who, under the influence of other young people at the children's home, had stopped attending school, began to attend again and he only absconded once back to a pimp in his home town. Sadly, the placement was temporary and Ben was moved on in spite of the pleas of his parents and social worker. In view of the fact that no later placement held Ben and he continued to work on the streets, the decision to end this placement was in retrospect unfortunate.

Ben's support worker spent a great deal of time with him, focusing in particular on the question of his sexual identity. However, although this involvement took some pressure off his placements in care and at home, it did not contribute to controlling his risk-taking behaviour and did not succeed in involving him in education or in any other activities that would have given him other interests and involvement with his peer group. The support worker's action to get Ben banned from the gay clubs he frequented was a helpful one and he introduced him to an outreach health worker at the local hospital who could advise him on HIV/AIDs testing and counsel him about his sexual safety.

During all this time Ben's involvement in prostitution became entrenched. Some aspects of the lifestyle were reinforcing:

"I like money, that's one thing I like. I like to have it in my hand, like. And getting paid for doing it just makes you want to do it more and more and more. And you just get so used to it. It's like doing a normal job really."

This argues for as swift a response as possible when young people become involved in prostitution and great care in the choice of placements for them. Eventually, since Ben's prostitution was unaffected by these interventions, he was placed in a secure unit.

Amy, who had a background of sexual abuse and had been gang-raped, was introduced to prostitution at the age of 12 by a girl, Fiona, whom she had met through her brother. She frequently absconded from placements and when on the run found shelter at the home of Fiona's mother, who was a "madam" and who would involve her in drink, drugs and prostitution. Amy's mother and the social worker wanted action taken to stop her going to this house. The place was well known to the police for prostitution and drug-taking. However, no such action was taken and a care order was never sought on Amy. She involved other young people in prostitution when she was in residential care and in a later foster placement the foster mother tried to protect her from Fiona's influence by shielding her from telephone calls. The foster mother knew when Amy was going out on the game, but was unable to stop her:

"Oh, bless her heart, we knew when she was going out to work because she had a big bag, fair enough, she has condoms galore, and when that bag and the condoms were missing . . ."

Amy was placed in two out-of-county foster placements but absconded from both. She too ended up in a secure unit, the only place which contained her behaviour.

Fiona began to work as a prostitute at the age of 12. It was well known that she inducted other young people into prostitution, often when they reached the age at which she herself had become involved. This may have been simply a repetition of her own experience or her mother, who acted as her pimp, may have encouraged her to do so. One foster carer commented that "Fiona was corrupted, so Fiona goes for the young ones" and corrupts them. She presented a high risk to other children with whom she was accommodated because she would procure them for her adult clients. When she absconded she would take other girls with her whom she would introduce to prostitution. In one foster placement, Fiona started to settle down until her youth justice worker told her that the foster carers could not keep her in. She then started to abscond and returned to the streets. A series of subsequent placements were unable to hold her and eventually she was returned home because she could not be contained in care.

After her return home, Fiona seriously injured a man and received a custodial sentence. It seemed likely that her past sexual abuse and her prostitution were linked to her offence. However, no therapeutic intervention had been provided after almost a one year stay in a secure unit. Fiona herself made it clear that she had been unable to come to terms with her sexual abuse and linked her subsequent behaviour with it:

"I just gone off the rails. I didn't care about nothing, what I have done, no respect for myself."

One young man was nearly evicted from the hostel, to which he went when he left care, for inviting other young people to his room for the purposes of prostitution. However, he was unwilling to take any advice from his social worker about minimising the risks of infection. Another young man spent a lot of time at the bus station where young prostitutes met their clients, partly as a result of contacts he had made in care. His foster father actively tried to discourage inappropriate contacts and when someone unknown rang to suggest a meeting he would offer to give the boy a lift there and back, which generally led to the idea of the meeting being dropped. Two of these boys had also been involved in the making of pornographic videos.

All the young people who worked as prostitutes had been in children's homes and as concerns about them mounted, attempts were made to find them placements in foster care. However, as we have seen, only one young person was briefly contained in an out-of-county foster home. However, there was little evidence of practice of any kind which had made a contribution to moving these young people away from their involvement in prostitution and none of them was contained in either foster care or in an ordinary residential home. This was no doubt, in part, because the young people often became part of a sub-culture of prostitution involving pimps or minders. Pimps did search out and threaten young people who wished to cease their activities and some had to be placed out-of-county for their protection. Even then they frequently absconded back to the city to continue their involvement in prostitution. Boys who worked as prostitutes sometimes had contact with pimps, but they were more likely to have associations with well-to-do older men who offered them a seductive lifestyle and good money in return for sex. The attraction of the money and this lifestyle were considerable. When absconding, these boys would often link up with such men for shelter and material rewards.

As a last resort the young people who persistently worked as prostitutes were often placed in secure accommodation to remove them from the immediate network which drew them back into prostitution. However, although this temporarily stopped their activities, none of them was offered any interventions within the secure institutions which were relevant to assisting them to leave prostitution. Since the placements were short term their behaviour was temporarily contained but not altered. In addition, it should be noted that some commentators have suggested that confining prostitutes in such institutions can have the effect of reinforcing them in the deviant role (Davis, 1978).

There was some evidence that the care system not only introduced some young people to prostitution but also reinforced them in it. One girl, who had herself been in care, worked as a pimp and provided refuge for children who had run away from care. In exchange for drugs she sent them out to earn money by working on the streets. It was also evident that some young people found company among the children who gathered at the bus station soliciting for business (Lowman, 1987), and that the search for physical closeness and the illusion of affection drew them to prostitution (Shaw *et al*, 1996). Indeed, some sexually abused children have been taught to get their basic needs for touching met through sexual activity (Jesson, 1993). Other young people in the study became involved in prostitution after leaving care, no doubt partly as a means of survival because of financial difficulties, their lack of access to the benefit system and housing and their detachment from education, training and employment opportunities (Stein, Rees and Frost, 1994; O'Neill, Goode and Hopkins, 1995). The networks which young people formed in care also had an impact. The Assessment and Action records (Parker *et al*, 1991; Ward, 1995) showed that more of the young people in our study who were in residential care had *many* friends whom they had known for more than six months from within the care system (41%) as compared with those in foster care (13%). These networks, whilst providing company and some friendship, also introduced them to high risk behaviours such as prostitution, particularly when they met up with former care associates when on the run or after leaving care.

There has been little research on young people in care and prostitution and there is an accompanying absence of an agreed professional practice in this area (Jesson, 1993). Most of the published work on practice describes outreach projects for young people who are living independently and making a living by means of prostitution. These projects are usually based on models of empowerment and risk reduction (Kjeldsen, 1991; Lee and O'Brien, 1995; Barnardo's, 1996). Ideas about more general service developments which are needed are now starting to emerge (Barrett, 1997a; Shaw and Butler, 1998) but there is little guidance about how to work with young people in substitute care who become involved in prostitution. Whilst in the second half of the 19th century a considerable proportion of girls were committed to care to rescue them *from* prostitution (Parker, 1990; Lee and O'Brien, 1995) the evidence from our research is that more young people these days may be initiated *into* prostitution as a result of their stay in care than are admitted for this reason. Such a situation requires clearer policies about the placement of young people involved in prostitution and the development of a range of interventions to assist them. This shortfall has been recognised and the Department of Health is working on inter-departmental guidance on intervening in situations where children become involved in prostitution.

There is room for debate about whether children involved in prostitution should be subject to child protection procedures. The guidance in *Working Together* (Home Office *et al*, 1991) is unclear. The guidance suggests that abuse by an adult who was previously unknown to the child may not require the application of child protection procedures, although organised abuse does. However, if all incidents of children involved in prostitution attracted the full attention of the child protection system, as recommended in the Utting Review of the Safeguards for Children Living Away from Home (1997), then it would be made clear both to the children, and to the men who buy their sexual services, that such activities were taken extremely seriously. It would also act as a counterbalance to the current rather passive attitude of residential staff and provide a forum for inter-agency planning (Barrett, 1997b). It would require a shift of viewpoint to one in which men who purchase sex from young people were placed in the category of child sex abusers and the children who supply those services were viewed as victims of exploitation. This would run counter to the response of the criminal justice system which treats children who solicit as offenders but fails to prosecute the adults who use their services. It has been argued that the criminalisation of young people serves to marginalise them further and to keep them on the streets and some return to prostitution to pay the fines which result from prosecution. Unfortunately there is evidence that social services departments do not view young people involved in prostitution as a high priority for services (Aldgate and Tunstill, 1995).

SEXUAL ABUSE TO THE YOUNG PEOPLE OUTSIDE PLACEMENT

Looking at all the placements of our young people, not just the index placement, five children alleged that they were raped or indecently assaulted while outside their placements. Four other young people were at risk of sexual abuse from close relatives during contact visits. The 13-year-old, Tracey, has already been mentioned. She naively went off with a 20-year-old man she met in a pub garden minutes after meeting him, while out for the evening with an older girl from her foster placement. She had no idea of the risk she ran and ended up being raped both vaginally and anally. The girl who had led her into this risky situation was moved from the placement. Tracey was not offered any counselling after the rape because the counsellor whom she had seen previously, had by that time left and no other referral was made. This was a worrying gap because Tracey was unable to make sense of what had happened to her and her background included sexual abuse by a number of perpetrators. Revictimisation in these circumstances was likely to have had a particularly negative impact. No work on how to protect herself was provided for her, which in view of her background and naiveté was a serious omission.

A girl of 15 alleged that she had been raped by her friend's boyfriend as she was walking back to her children's home one night but there was insufficient evidence to lead to a prosecution. Her key worker believed that this girl probably did have sex with the boy in question and was left drunk in a field, but wondered if it was rape. A boy of 13 alleged that he had been mugged and raped while absconding from a secure unit. A police investigation revealed that his account was not consistent with those of others involved and the residential worker in his subsequent secure placement considered that he had "got off on" the sexual contact of the incident. Another boy at the age of 13 was indecently assaulted by a man he met while on the run from his foster home with a girl from his placement. A boy who regularly worked as a male prostitute while in a children's home, was sometimes forced into sexual activities by his clients and saw this as abuse to him.

In addition, one girl, Mary, used to pay regular visits to her grandfather who was in an old people's home. He would pay her for her used under-wear and talked "dirty" to her. Mary told her foster mother about these visits and disclosed that her grandfather had sexually harassed her since she was young. The foster mother persuaded Mary not to go to see him any more, since in her view he was "waiting to abuse her" and found Mary other ways to make money. Two boys had regular contact with their mothers whom the residential workers saw as having incestuous relation-ships with them. A third boy made regular visits to a relative who was a Schedule One offender and who had probably abused him in the past. The social services department had only recently become aware of the man's record but had taken no action to make the boy safe at weekends.

SEXUALLY ABUSING BEHAVIOUR OUTSIDE PLACEMENT

During the index or another placement, one boy sexually assaulted some girls he met in a park, another was suspected of having raped a girl he met in the street when he was visiting his mother, and a third boy sex-ually abused a boy he met in foster care when the two of them were on the run. None of these incidents resulted in a prosecution.

PREGNANCY

Given the extent of sexual activity of these young people and the gaps in their knowledge about contraception it was not surprising that four of the 22 girls became pregnant. Three were under 16 when they conceived and the fourth was aged 17 and six months pregnant with her second baby. Three of the four became pregnant by their steady boyfriends, but the fourth had so many partners she did not know who the father was. It was not uncommon to find that the foster carers had tried to offer advice on contraception and the girls had resisted it. In one case the foster mother confronted the girl's boyfriend with the question of whether or not they were having a sexual relationship just too late. When she found that they were doing so, she took the girl to the family planning clinic only to find that she was already pregnant.

The findings from this chapter show that whilst monitoring the activities of young people outside their placements was not easy, caregivers who saw this as an important part of their role had some success. Clearly more work was needed to help the young people learn how to keep themselves safe and recognise situations of potential risk to them. However, persistent absconding was a pattern which was hard to change and it was often linked with the exchange of sex for shelter and with sexual abuse.

Prostitution was the behaviour which proved hardest of all to alter. It brought the young people rewards and involved them in networks which reinforced the behaviour, sometimes involving pimps. This suggests that a rapid response is required to this high risk behaviour and the careful choice of placements. Geographical distance from the networks within which they work the streets may be necessary. There is also a need for the development of new ideas about ways to engage and contain young people involved in prostitution.

The extent to which children act out their inner distress by engaging in sexualised behaviours or exploitative sexual relationships may relate, in part, to their ability to process and integrate past traumatic events. We turn next to look at the therapeutic interventions which had been provided for the young people in our sample.

SUMMARY

1. Professional concerns about sexual activity outside placements centred on girls. Boys were rarely the subject of such concern, unless they were involved with girls who were known to be under the legal age of consent or were involved in prostitution. This double standard ensured that most of the boys who were involved in high levels of sexual activity escaped attention.
2. Attempts by caregivers to protect the young people once they were outside their placements met with varying success. Not all caregivers accepted that they had responsibility for the young people beyond the four walls of the home. This was particularly true of the staff in most of the children's homes.
3. Older sexually abused girls sometimes led younger abused and immature girls into situations of high risk which they could not manage. In one such case the younger girl ended up being the victim of a rape.
4. Children who absconded were at even greater risk. Clearly, running away made the management of their sexual behaviour very difficult. It also exposed them to further abuse because they might exchange sex for shelter, become involved in prostitution or be sexually abused. Altogether 10 of the young people persistently absconded, so much so

that in four cases no placement ever held them. Six of the young people who ran away regularly took other young people with them, often leading them into situations of considerable risk.

5. Altogether eight of the young people at some stage worked as prostitutes with all of the associated risks. Once involved it was difficult to leave prostitution which became a way of life. Social services departments had little success in containing these boys and girls in any placement. Some limited success was achieved in out-of-county placements which isolated them from their exploitative networks.

6. Those working as prostitutes posed a danger to other children they lived with, particularly through their activities in procuring their fellow residents for their clients. There was one young person who had involved in prostitution at least seven other children whom she had met in children's homes.

7. Many sexually abused children had never had the experience of being protected and safely looked after and they often had no idea of how to keep themselves safe. This made them particularly vulnerable to being coerced into sex or other forms of exploitation. Five young people had allegedly been raped or indecently assaulted while outside their placement. Four young people were at risk from sexual abuse from close relatives during contact visits.

8. Three of the young people sexually abused one or more young people outside their placement. Two boys assaulted girls who were strangers to them and the third boy abused a boy he met in foster care while on the run with him.

9. Many of the young people were engaging in high levels of sexual activity and were reluctant to accept advice about contraception. It was therefore not surprising to learn that four of the 22 girls became pregnant, three of whom were under 16 when they conceived.

11

THERAPEUTIC INTERVENTIONS

In this chapter we describe the ways in which the young people were helped to come to terms with their experiences of sexual abuse or the difficulties connected with their abusing behaviour. The interventions which focused directly on these experiences and behaviours both in the index placement and in the past will be examined. The less formal interventions by caregivers, social workers and other professionals, that may nevertheless have had important therapeutic effects, will also be described. We will also explore the children's part in the process, their capacity and readiness to make use of the help which was offered and how successful it appears to have been.

FORMAL THERAPEUTIC INTERVENTIONS IN THE PAST

Taking into account any kind of specialist intervention offered in the past, at least 24 of the children (60%) had previously had contact with health or social services professionals who provided therapeutic work. Seven of these referrals were made at the time of the original disclosure of abuse and it can be inferred that the work focused on the abuse itself. Only one referral was made after the initial discovery of abusing behaviour. These figures are higher than Macaskill's estimate (1991) of 11% of fostered or adopted children who had attended individual or group therapy sessions but for both samples the figures may be underestimates as often there was little information about past interventions.

This previous work had been provided for two thirds of the children (16) by psychiatrists, psychologists and social workers in psychiatric settings and took the form of extended assessments, individual counselling or family therapy. The young people's views of these health services inputs were generally negative and for at least six of the children the sessions had ended prematurely leaving the young people feeling that they had not been properly listened to, or that they had been unable to talk in what were often described as very formal or "cold and uncaring" settings.

Nina, for example, saw a psychiatrist shortly after she had to leave home following the disclosure of her stepfather's sexual abuse:

"I did get counselling but the lady I had I couldn't really say anything to. She seemed really cold. She didn't feel comforting. She'd just stick a box of tissues in front of me and say 'If you're going to cry use them'. She'd be tapping her fingers or twisting her fingers waiting for me to stop crying if she made me cry over what she said. She was impatient and it just made me worse . . . I had her for about six sessions which was once a week and then after those six sessions she said 'Do you want to see me any more?' and I said 'No'''.

In a considerable number of cases girls who had been sexually abused by men were assigned to male counsellors to whom the girls felt unable to talk. The impact of these difficult or unsatisfying experiences was felt later when re-referral was suggested by social workers but refused by the young people, closing the door on much needed help.

Specialist therapeutic services provided by the social services departments themselves were offered to a third of the children who received assistance (8) and tended to have lasted longer and to have been seen as more helpful. Young people who had had these positive therapeutic experiences were more willing to consider further help when it was offered later.

Thus it can be seen that these referrals had mixed consequences for the young people either forestalling or paving the way for future therapeutic intervention. This suggests that the way in which early referrals are handled is more important than may initially be apparent. Failure to engage young people or their families in work which was experienced as accessible and relevant to their concerns could lead to a generalised loss of confidence in the possibility of any therapeutic help. Conversely initial good experiences could provide a solid foundation for recovery, and if necessary, for further work later if it was needed.

FORMAL INTERVENTIONS IN THE PAST OR PRESENT WHICH FOCUSED ON THE SEXUAL ABUSE TO THE YOUNG PEOPLE OR ON THEIR ABUSING BEHAVIOUR

Although 24 of the young people had previously been the subject of direct work, rather fewer appeared to have received any counselling in relation to the sexual abuse which they had experienced. Four of the children had not, as far as we knew, been abused. Of the remainder it appeared that 16 of the children had been provided, either in the past or during the index placement, with some direct work about the abuse and its impact.

However, it was not always possible to tell if a brief involvement with a service had covered issues connected with children's abuse, and for some who did receive intervention the work was brief and not in depth. It appears then that over half of the young people had had no such help. The finding that 44% (16) of the young people had been offered direct work which focused on their abuse compares with the figure of 20% of all the abused children in the case file sample who were recorded as having received any counselling. It may be that the difference is accounted for by the older age group, the greater severity of problems in the interview sample or that the interviews had yielded further information. These percentages compare with figures of three fifths of sexually abused children on the child protection register who had received any direct work in Farmer and Owen's study (1995) and 29% of children referred for reasons of sexual abuse in a study by Sharland and her colleagues (1996).

The position of the young people who had shown sexually abusing behaviour was far worse. Only five of the 22 children who had abused others received a referral for therapeutic intervention in relation to their abusing behaviour at any stage, but in only one case did this lead to ongoing work. The proportion who were referred for intervention is similar to that found in our case file sample for abusing children.

What do we know about the referrals for help with the young people's abusing behaviour? In the case of a 10-year-old who had regularly sexually abused his brother a psychologist saw him twice and then advised the foster mother that "further sessions would only draw attention to it" and a behavioural approach was recommended to the foster carers. The boy concerned went on to re-abuse his younger brother. In another worrying case sexually abusing behaviour from the past emerged as the reason a boy could not return home. Instead of offering some work with the boy as the parents desperately wanted, the clinic said that no work could be offered until the boy's future was resolved and thus reinforced the pre-existing stalemate on this case. One boy was seen twice at the department of psychology at the local hospital and the resulting assessment opined that he needed a placement with no younger children and that his many sexual assaults were not planned attacks, without commenting on the implications of this view. This added nothing of assistance to the professionals with responsibility for him.

A very disappointing response was given to a foster mother after the girl she was fostering had sexually abused her 6-year-old son. The clinic made two appointments with a male social worker who proved most unsuitable for the girl whose original abuse was by a man. The worker suggested that she was reacting to a change of environment and gave advice on management. There was a general hope, unfortunately not borne out by experience, that the abusing behaviour would remit spontaneously. One residential worker who described a 12-year-old boy's "unhealthy and un-usual" wish to share showers with older learning disabled boys said:

". . . the attitude is that he will grow out of it and it will fade away."

Even where the abusing behaviour very clearly needed to be on the agenda for work, therapeutic intervention was scanty. Neither of the two seriously abusing older adolescent boys in specialist therapeutic residen-tial establishments were offered effective direct input on their abusing behaviour. In one case, work on the boy's victimisation took precedence and the residential carer in this well-resourced specialist unit "hoped" that someone else would pick up the work on offending behaviour after he had left on the expiry of his secure order. The chances of this boy taking up such a service after leaving were minimal. In the other case the boy's violent behaviour escalated so dramatically when his abusive be-haviour was addressed that it was agreed by social services management not to continue with the work. Both of these young men were still con-sidered to be likely to be extremely dangerous when the time came for their discharge from care. In the one case where work was provided a residential worker involved an adolescent girl in a series of planned sessions on appropriate touching.

These findings suggest that therapeutic services are not well geared up to work with children who sexually abuse others and their caregivers, or possibly that they are not very willing to offer such work when the young people are in substitute care. Indeed, there appeared to be a general lack of clarity about what therapeutic interventions could be used with the abusing children, other than advice about how to extinguish these be-haviours. In view of the risks posed by the young abusers this lack of direct work on their abusing behaviour was a disturbing gap.

INFORMATION ABOUT PAST INTERVENTIONS

Although, as we saw in Chapter 7, two fifths of the young people had been formally assessed at some stage, these assessments had rarely influenced the services which were offered to them. Social workers were often either uncertain of the nature of the recommendations in the reports or felt that what they had to say was not new. In one case the psychiatrist recom-mended that the child should not go home because of the level of risk, but she was returned to an abusive parent a few days later.

Uncertainty about the contents of these reports was part of a more general picture of lack of information about what therapeutic help had previously been offered, particularly if the abuse had occurred several years before or there had been several changes of placement, social worker or keyworker. The caregivers in our sample, like the foster carers in Macaskill's study (1991), rarely knew any details of the content or purpose of the sessions which had taken place in the past. It was worrying that the social workers seemed to be equally unclear about any previous help to the young people. In some cases this meant that there was a false assumption that the young person had been helped to work through the emotional consequences of the abuse, particularly if their behaviour was unproblematic or if they currently demonstrated no obvious need to talk about their difficult experiences.

In one such case a 15-year-old girl had been severely sexually assaulted 10 years before by an elderly relative who had served a prison term for the offence and died of a heart attack shortly after his release, causing an unresolved schism in the family. This young person revealed in our interview that apart from a brief and unsatisfactory contact with a psychiatrist she had never spoken of these events since the time of the court case. Her social worker assumed that she had been engaged in counselling somewhere along the line in her long care career. Becky herself said:

"I do not show I need to talk about it . . . I can forget about it when I want to but when I get 'down' it comes back again and I just remember everything. I do not let it take over me, I push it to the back of my mind."

Her keyworker felt that she might need to talk at some time but felt unqualified to open up such a discussion:

"At the moment we're progressing nicely so I'm not sure if there's any need to rake up her past . . . I don't feel qualified to do that sort of work . . . I don't want to open a can of worms that I can't put the lid back on. It may be going over old ground and I don't want to dig it all up again."

In her placement she was offered direct work aimed at increasing her assertiveness and confidence. When she attributed these difficulties to her abuse her keyworker told her not to "blame" her abuse for her current problems.

FORMAL THERAPEUTIC INTERVENTIONS DURING THE INDEX PLACEMENT

During the index placement the young people were offered a wide range of direct work broadly focused on helping them to deal with their emotional or behavioural difficulties, their relationships with their families and their entry into the care system. Sometimes the work was directed at the consequences of the abuse itself or the events surrounding it. Involvement in specific pieces of professional work did not depend on the type of placement or whether children were only abused or both abused and abusing. Of the 40 young people 22 were engaged in such work while in the index placement. Some of them had help from more than one source. The work could be broadly categorised into individual counselling (20), family therapy (2), behaviour modification (4), groupwork (2), life story work (5) and psychiatric treatment (1). Again, these figures are higher than Macaskill's report (1991) of 31% of children in her sample who received individual counselling while in placement.

The focus of this direct work was not always easy to discover and it was equally difficult to know whether and in what detail the abuse itself had been discussed. However, it seemed clear that fewer than a third of those who had been abused (11) were working directly on the abuse itself. Other counselling was focused on issues such as bullying, aggression, sexual identity, phobic anxiety and difficulties with assertiveness which may have touched more indirectly on issues connected with the abuse. It will be remembered that these young people frequently came from backgrounds of severe adversity and the abuse itself was often only one of a range of difficulties with which they needed assistance.

As shown in Chapter 9, therapeutic work which addressed the young people's abusing behaviour was absent except in one case, despite the fact that there is a growing practice literature on models of intervention for young abusers (see for example Becker, 1990; O'Callaghan and Print, 1994; Smith and Bentovim, 1994; Vizard, Monck and Misch, 1995; Vizard *et al*, 1996). Where the abusing behaviour was not known about by the social worker or caregiver or was not manifest in the placement it was easily ignored or minimised and not dealt with in any way. Where sexually abusive behaviour *did* occur in placement caregivers tended to respond to incidents as they happened and either talked to the young people about acceptable and unacceptable behaviour or took steps to tighten their supervision.

The reasons that 18 of the young people were not involved in direct work were either because the necessary resources were unavailable (4), such work was not thought to be necessary or appropriate (12) or they had refused the offer of such help (2). For some young people referral was not thought to be necessary because the link between past abuse and current difficult behaviour had not been made, although chronologically a link was clearly likely. The emphasis here was on behaviour management, addressing current problems rather than a therapeutic approach which linked past experiences to current behaviour.

Refusal to accept a referral to a psychiatrist or psychologist was linked in some cases to a young person's fear of being labelled as "mad". In addition, treatment at psychiatric units could be felt to be stigmatising in the more public context of a children's home where it was difficult for young people to be discreet about their movements. As we have seen, some young women were inappropriately referred to male counsellors with whom they felt unable talk. For these reasons, there may be considerable value in the provision of self-referral resources, for instance in schools or leisure centres, where young people can initiate help when they feel they need it.

The majority of the therapeutic interventions during the index placement were provided by psychiatrists and psychologists from departments of Child and Family Psychiatry (36% of children). The next most commonly used resource was Child and Family Support Centres (18% of children) and voluntary organisations – particularly Barnardo's and the NSPCC (18% of children). Twenty eight per cent of this assistance was provided by caregivers (mainly residential workers) or by social workers.

Five caregivers were involved in direct work with the young people. Of these, two were keyworkers in specialist residential placements working with severely disturbed abused and abusing adolescent boys, one was the key worker in a residential unit who did work with a young person on inappropriate touching, one was a residential worker who did life story work with a young person and the other was the foster carer of a highly disturbed abused and abusing girl who worked collaboratively with a specialist therapist. Other caregivers offered valuable but more informal interventions which will be discussed later. Six social workers offered direct work to the young people but for others there seemed to be considerable resistance to providing such assistance, even when it was clearly seen as necessary.

In four cases a collaborative model of work was used in which an outside professional worked with the main caregiver. These ranged from fortnightly intensive "holding" therapy sessions over a two-year period involving a therapist from a specialist agency who worked closely with the child and foster mother to a foster carer seeking advice from a psychologist about a child's sexually inappropriate behaviour and working to a behavioural control model suggested by him.

CAREGIVERS' ATTITUDES TO EXTERNAL HELP

While the majority of young people (35/40) had been offered some specialist input either during the current placement or at some time in the past, as has been shown, only 44% of the abused children had ever been offered help that specifically focused on their abuse. There was a general feeling among foster carers and residential workers that they did not have the training to offer skilled therapeutic work and that the children whom they looked after would benefit from professional intervention to help with their emotional or behavioural problems. At the time of the interviews 78% of the caregivers felt that such input would have been helpful. This included some cases where help was being provided but was thought to fall short of what the child needed. A further 13% felt that such help would be necessary in the future. At least six social workers were criticised for failing to find appropriate resources and make the necessary referrals.

When intervention was offered, however, some caregivers complained that they did not know what was going on in the therapeutic sessions (see also Macaskill, 1991) but were left to pick up the pieces when a young person returned to the placement in an unpredictable or unhappy mood. Additionally, caregivers sometimes felt that information disclosed by young people in the course of their sessions with other professionals should be shared with them and the workers' insistence on confidentiality was felt as an exclusion. In some cases caregivers effectively discouraged referral for fear of what might be stirred up by counselling or showed resistance to outside help by trivialising its importance. One Child and Family Support Centre worker described the foster carers' attitude to the weekly counselling sessions which she was providing:

"I felt they were not very keen on our involvement, that they were suspicious of it even though I did sit down with them and go through what we were doing. I think they saw it as quite trivial."

This worker went on to make the point that this attitude was potentially undermining of her work

"I felt it wasn't good for David to be hearing [this] because he got quite a lot out of our sessions and needed to know that they were respected by everybody."

It was clear that sometimes discussion of the abuse was encapsulated within the counselling sessions without being more fully integrated in other parts of the child's life. For example, Margaret had been able to establish an apparently open and trusting rapport with a female psychiatrist whom she had been seeing weekly for several months, but was completely unable to talk to her keyworker or social worker, who were both male. Neither the keyworker nor the social worker had any idea of what had been discussed in her therapeutic sessions and were in no position to continue the work informally in the placement. Her behaviour in the residential unit continued to be extremely disturbed and disruptive. She showed no sign of having made sense of any of her past experiences. This suggests that for professional therapeutic intervention to be effective it needs to be consolidated elsewhere in the young person's day-to-day life to allow for a gradual and manageable integration of disturbing and difficult feelings and memories. In practice this would argue for more sharing of information between the professionals involved in the young people's care so that a more creative balance between therapeutic confidentiality and teamwork could be forged. Like Macaskill (1991) we would argue that caregivers may need more information about what happens in therapeutic sessions in order to complement a therapist's work.

INFORMAL INTERVENTIONS IN PLACEMENT: TALKING TO CAREGIVERS AND SOCIAL WORKERS

Despite the patchy provision of specialist input to the young people, caregivers and social workers sometimes provided an invaluable *informal* context for recovery in which the opportunity to talk about distressing experiences was combined with ongoing daily care, security and affection, which at its best offered a highly reparative emotional environment. At the other extreme, placements sometimes reinforced aspects of the original abusing circumstances making it difficult for the young people to feel safe and move forward.

In this context we first consider what the caregivers and social workers offered to the young people in the way of informal attention, concern and support. We then relate the quality of the caregivers' engagement with the young people to whether the young people had been able to communicate openly with them about their difficult past experiences. Finally we look at whether being able to talk openly was related to behavioural improvement as a measure of outcome.

Eighteen of the young people had been able to talk about their abuse or the events connected with it to their caregivers or social workers while in the index placement. Of these, half had been able to talk fully about what had happened to them and half had begun to talk openly. Only one young person had talked in placement about her own abusing behaviour and this was in a limited way.

Permission to Talk About the Abuse

Secrecy about sexual abuse is almost invariably a part of the abusive experience itself. Following disclosure sexually abused children are often caught in the trap of not knowing who knows about their abuse. It can either seem as if *everyone* knows, particularly if there has been a well-publicised court case, or conversely it may feel as if *no one* knows or has been able to remember the distressing secret, particularly if the disclosure has taken place some time before or in a different setting.

These uncertainties can lead to various difficulties in talking about the abuse. As we have seen, for some children in the study there was a marked lack of boundaries in relation to whom they talked. People at bus stops, in the street and in shops, as well as other young people in school and placement were given intimate details indiscriminately and caregivers had to work hard to set appropriate boundaries to the disclosures.

On the other hand a continuation of the secrecy about the abuse was reinforced where caregivers and social workers either genuinely did not know about a past disclosure because of a failure in history taking or transfer or did not tell the child clearly that they knew about the abuse. Children were sometimes placed in the centre of a complicated guessing game in which silence was the preferred, if costly, option.

Philip's foster mother displayed extreme ambivalence about hearing about his abuse:

"Philip knows that I know about the abuse because the meeting about his father's court case was held at my house. Before this he could pretend that I didn't know and though I stayed out in the kitchen during the meeting he now has to admit that I know whereas before he could pretend that I didn't."

However, she said that she was not confident about talking about sexual matters and so had done nothing to clarify the situation for Philip. This had led to a continuation of the uncomfortable conspiracy of silence between them, a repetition of Philip's earlier family life.

For other children however, being able to talk openly about their abuse in placement started with being given clear permission to do so. Sharon's foster mother told her early on in the placement that she knew that "certain things" had happened to her in the past and that if she ever wanted to talk about them she was always there to listen. Despite the fact that this caregiver had been given relatively little information about Sharon's abused and abusing background she was able to draw on her previous experience of working with sexually abused girls and understood the importance of establishing open lines of communication at the outset. Shortly after this Sharon was able to open up and talk in detail about her past abuse. She started talking to her foster mother in the middle of the night after waking up after a nightmare.

"We sat and talked about the incidents surrounding the abuse for hours and from then on she talked about it more and more."

While a clear statement of permission to talk about the abuse did not of itself necessarily lead to an open discussion, where it *was* given it established an invaluable ground rule for an honest dialogue between caregiver and child and as such should be a routine part of every new admission of sexually abused or abusing children to substitute care.

Caregivers' capacity to talk about young people's distressing experiences sometimes depended on whether they touched on painful issues of their own and if so, whether these had been adequately resolved. Two of the caregivers alluded to the fact that they themselves had been sexually abused and another 12 caregivers mentioned abusive and violent relationships, deaths and separations in their own past, memories of which had been stirred up by their care of these children. Where the caregivers had come to terms with these experiences they had enhanced their understanding and concern. However, for others there was a clear sense of maintaining an emotional distance from the young people's distressing accounts or an over-involvement which may have felt intrusive.

If caregivers are to be able to give clear permission to the young people to talk openly about their experiences they have to be able to contain not only the young person's potential distress, but also their own. The need for effective selection, support and supervision is clear.

New Disclosures of Abuse

Among those who talked about their abuse were young people who disclosed abuse for the first time in substitute care. During the care period five children made new disclosures of abuse, three of these in the index placement. Four of these were connected with sexual abuse and one with sadistic physical abuse with sexual overtones. In three of the cases the initial disclosure was to the foster carer's child rather than to the carer directly. These "fostering" children all had significant relationships with the young person and while two managed the disclosure process well, one, a boy of eight, was put under considerable pressure for several weeks not to repeat the revelation to his mother, which proved to be a harrowing experience. In the two cases of disclosure where the caregivers were not closely engaged with the young people there was no further discussion of the abuse in the placement. The young person refused to say any more. However, where the caregivers were fairly or highly involved with the children these disclosures were not one-off events and the young people continued over time to reveal more details of what had happened. In one other case a girl of 13 in a residential unit talked indirectly about an abusive situation involving a Schedule One offender and a "friend" but this was not pursued at the time as a potential personal disclosure.

Young People's Capacity to Talk

While there was sometimes a reluctance to explore difficult feelings on the part of the caregivers, some of the young people also found it difficult to be open about their inner worlds. These were children who had often been profoundly silenced during their upbringing, either by their abusers or because there had been no trusted, reliable and concerned adults to listen to them when things were going wrong. In addition, a significant number of children (11) had learning difficulties. Three had moderate or severe speech problems, one of whom was profoundly deaf and did not use sign language. There was often an impression that these young people had no words to express their inner experiences and no sense that putting words to feelings might offer relief.

The children had often developed elaborate defensive strategies to avoid thinking and talking about painful issues. These defensive strategies fell broadly into four overlapping areas; emotional detachment, behavioural diversion, outright refusal to talk and indiscriminate disclosure.

At the extreme end of the emotionally detached group were three children who demonstrated dissociative behaviour and were described by their caregivers as sometimes isolated, as if they were in a bubble or another world. One of these young people regularly responded to voices in his head rather than the outside world. Other young people in this group gave the superficial impression of talking openly but caregivers described a confusing sense of not getting through to the real person, as if their feelings were not engaged in the communication. These children would talk but not communicate and listen but not hear. Behavioural diversions ranged from absconding from placement whenever there were difficult emotional issues to be addressed (see also Farmer and Parker, 1991) to hyperactive, aggressive or restless behaviour and a short attention span when difficult issues were raised. These were children who were hard to pin down for more than a few minutes. Sustained dialogue was virtually impossible.

Outright refusal to talk about difficult issues was demonstrated by a variety of obstructive behaviours. One boy would put his head on the table and refuse to talk, another lay curled up on the floor sucking his thumb. "Clamming up" or changing the subject were common, often resulting in a sense of intense frustration on the part of caregivers. Indiscriminate disclosure was described in relation to five young people. Although these children seemed to be talking openly about abusive experiences, it was as if there was no one listening. The sense was of a discharge of words rather than a communication between two people. Like the young people in the detached group, there was no appropriate emotional affect associated with the words, as if the feelings were buried elsewhere.

Where relationships of trust developed in placement, these defensive strategies often lessened, although they might not disappear, and the young people were described as becoming more emotionally open and rewarding. Where the defensive strategies were deep-seated it was often difficult for relationships with caregivers to deepen and for appropriate and trusting attachments to form. As a result open discussion of difficult and painful issues was precluded.

INTERVENTIONS AND BEHAVIOURAL OUTCOMES

We now explore whether the twin dimensions of formal and informal help were related to discussion of the abuse by the young people in placement and improvements in behaviour.

It will be remembered that nine of the children had been able to talk fully and openly about their abuse and other difficult experiences and another nine had been able to begin to talk in this way with an appropriate caregiving adult during the index placement. Of these 18 children, 10 had also been able to talk to a professional therapist. Twenty two of the children in the sample had not been able to talk about their abuse during the placement.

Talking About the Abuse and Behavioural Improvement

We looked to see whether those children who had been able to talk about difficult experiences in their past had shown an improvement in behaviour during the course of their placement.

Nearly three quarters of all the young people were reported by their caregivers to have demonstrated a clear improvement in behaviour since the start of the placement. As can be seen in Table 1, all of the children who had talked fully during their placement showed clear improvements in behaviour, as compared with behavioural gains for just under two

Table 1   Talking about abuse and behavioural improvement

Behavioural improvement	Talked fully in placement	Talked partially in placement	Did not talk in placement	Total
Behaviour improved	9	6	14	29
Behaviour not improved	0	3	8	11
Total	9	9	22	40

thirds of children who had not talked at all about their past experiences during the placement. When the young people who had talked fully or partially in placement were combined, over four fifths showed behavioural improvement.

We were therefore interested to explore whether any aspects of the placements were related to the young people's ability to talk about their past. One factor which emerged as important was the extent to which caregivers were closely engaged with the children.

CAREGIVER ENGAGEMENT

Placements differed markedly on a dimension that we defined as "caregiver engagement", a global measure that included both the caregiver's attitude towards their role and their physical and emotional availability for a particular child. We divided the placements into high, medium and low caregiver engagement and two raters scored them independently, with a high level of agreement (initially only three were rated differently and only one of these was by more than one scale point).

Where the caregiver engagement was high there was a general atmosphere of unconditional acceptance, support and concern for the child and a degree of understanding of the significance of the child's inner emotional world. The importance of open communication about difficult feelings and issues, particularly about past abuse or family difficulties was acknowledged, and where possible such communication was encouraged and validated. More specifically, "high" caregiver engagement meant that there were either regular keywork sessions or the caregiver made him or herself available for the child, there was a committed relationship of trust and acceptance, there was an extended view of the caring role in which the caregiver defined his or her role in terms of the individual child's emotional and material needs and there was a general concern for the child's long-term welfare. A quarter of the placements (10) fell into this category.

Medium caregiver engagement was characterised by a more managerial approach to the caring role. In this category were caregivers who demonstrated acceptance of and commitment to the child and a concern for the child's welfare but who showed a limited capacity to understand or address the child's underlying emotional needs. The focus of work tended to be on the management of present behaviour. Such placements often offered a high degree of security and adaptability to the child's current needs but a lower sense of warmth. There might still be regular keywork sessions or caregiver availability but the focus of the sessions or exchanges between caregiver and child tended to be limited, sometimes by design, where the caregiver felt unable to handle more emotionally demanding material. Just under half of the placements (19) fell into this category.

In placements with low caregiver engagement the caregiver's role was clearly limited to day-to-day management of behaviour and basic care-taking. There was often no sense that a relationship had been established between the child and caregiver. Where a relationship had been established it was often characterised by frustration, hopelessness, hostility or negativity on the caregiver's part. Where the young person's behaviour was difficult it was often considered to be mystifying and not felt to be redeemed by more positive attributes. There was little emphasis on the importance of communication and discussion and the caregivers were felt to be emotionally unavailable. There were 11 such placements.

Foster placements tended to offer slightly higher caregiver engagement than residential placements, although the numbers are not large. For example, just under a third (6/19) of the foster placements provided high caregiver engagement as compared with less than a fifth of the residential placements (4/21).

There was a marked difference in the level of caregiver engagement between the children in the abused only and the abusing categories. Those young people who had demonstrated some sexually abusing behaviour were significantly more likely than the abused children to be in a placement offering high caregiver engagement. Almost half of the abusing young people fell into the high caregiver engagement category but *none* of the abused only children did so. Only one in seven (three children) of the abusers fell into the low caregiver engagement category compared with almost half of the abused only children. This finding is partly explained by the fact that most of the abusing children were placed with experienced foster carers or were in specialist residential care.

Caregiver Engagement and Talking about the Abuse

We found that levels of caregiver engagement were significantly associated with the young people having been able to talk either fully or partially about their experiences of abuse and the associated difficulties which they had experienced. Over two thirds of the young people in high caregiver engagement placements had been able to do so, compared with only one in eleven (one child) in low engagement placements. Just over half the children in medium engagement placements had been able to begin to talk openly.

This finding suggests that children will talk about painful feelings only when they feel safe in a supportive environment and when they believe that what they say will be listened to, accepted and understood. Some children will choose not to talk in this way at this time whatever the quality of the caring environment. For instance, Jason maintained a loyal silence about his schizophrenic mother's part in his abuse despite being able to talk about other current problems to his "high engagement" foster mother.

Therapeutic Help During the Placement and Talking About the Abuse

Receiving therapeutic help during placement was also related to an increased likelihood of young people talking about their past experiences to their caregivers (nearly two thirds of such children talked fully or partially), but it was not always a sufficient reason for a young person to open up during the placement. More than a third of the children who received counselling or other help during the placement did not talk openly about their past in their placement. However, the majority of the young people (four fifths) who were not offered therapeutic help while in placement did not talk about their abusive or difficult experiences in placement and of the four who did, two had previously had good experiences of counselling and one was in a very supportive placement.

Caregiver Engagement, Therapeutic Help and Talking About the Abuse

While both the level of caregiver engagement and the provision of specialist therapeutic intervention during placement appeared to have had independent effects on the likelihood of young people talking in placement, when we looked at them together it seemed that they also had a cumulative or possibly interactive effect.

Those children who had *both* high caregiver engagement *and* specialist intervention were most likely to have been able to start to explore and make sense of their difficult experiences. Of the seven children who had these high levels of support and intervention six had been able to talk either fully or partially in their care setting. On the other hand, none of the five children who had low caregiver engagement and no other intervention had been able to discuss their emotional problems.

Past Therapeutic Intervention

Therapeutic counselling in the past could also have a positive impact. As Table 2 shows, 25 of the 29 children whose behaviour improved had

Table 2 Behavioural improvement and therapeutic intervention

	Behaviour improved	Behaviour did not improve	Total
Talked in placement and current/ past therapeutic intervention	15	2	17
Talked in placement and *no* current/past therapeutic intervention	0	1	1
Did not talk in placement and current/past therapeutic intervention	10	8	18
Did not talk in placement and *no* current/past therapeutic intervention	4	0	4
Total	29	11	40

received some therapeutic help, either during this placement or in the past. For the four children whose behaviour improved with no such help other factors such as more general support in placement were important.

A majority of the young people whose behaviour had improved in placement but who were not talking about their abuse in placement *despite* having had therapeutic help had received this help at some time *in the past*. This suggests that the behavioural effects of previous therapeutic help could be enduring where the caregiver engagement was adequate to meet the young people's other current needs. These young people may have had no further need to talk about their abusive experiences at this time.

Current Therapeutic Intervention and Low Engagement Caregivers

The behaviour of five children who were *currently* receiving therapeutic help had not improved. These were children like Margaret, described above, whose caregivers were not closely engaged with them and who seemed to have been unable to integrate the therapeutic help into other aspects of their daily lives. In their unsupportive environments they may, in fact, have been acting out some of the emotional disturbance generated in their counselling. While Macaskill (1991) emphasised the problems arising out of poor communication between therapist and foster carer, these data suggest that such lack of communication may at times be complicated by an unwillingness or inability on the part of the caregiver to take the therapeutic work forward.

While therapeutic intervention clearly had a beneficial effect on behaviour for some young people, the *context* in which therapeutic help was
offered seemed to be of considerable importance. *The best outcomes in terms
of behaviour were for those young people who had been helped to explore their
difficult experiences and feelings **both** in a therapeutic relationship **and** in their
everyday lives in care.* For other young people where past help had been
sufficient to allow a degree of acceptance and understanding of difficult
experiences the current placement only needed to be "good enough" for
behavioural improvement to be sustained. However, where the young
person was unable to talk about difficult experiences, even partially, in
their placement, concurrent therapeutic intervention could lead to an
escalation of behaviour problems and placement difficulties. Other young
people might simply not have been ready to talk and might for the time
being simply have needed a safe and secure environment in which to rest.

Just over half the children in the study had received therapeutic work
while in the index placement, and of these just under two thirds had been
able to talk fully or partially to their carer or another significant adult
about their past abuse. Therapeutic intervention did not of itself ensure
good behavioural outcomes, particularly where it was offered in the context of a low level of caregiver support, but where such input was complemented by high levels of caregiver engagement, the young people
were enabled to talk more openly about their past and their behaviour
improved. The impact of caregiver engagement on the capacity to talk in
placement appears to be the single most important factor in predicting
behavioural outcome. Unsurprisingly, low caregiver engagement and an
absence of therapeutic input were associated with young people not talking and there was a sense that these children might never have the opportunity to come to terms with their past.

Young people who had histories which included abusing behaviour as
well as sexual abuse were more likely to be placed in high caregiver
engagement placements, often in foster care. However, the emphasis
there was on the young person's own victimisation and there was little
work on these young people's abusing behaviour.

In their efforts to manage these young people, and in some cases to
provide direct therapeutic help, the caregivers needed support. How far
they received such assistance is the subject of the next chapter.

SUMMARY

1. At least 60% of the children had previously had contact with health or
   social services professionals who had provided therapeutic work. Two

thirds of these referrals were to psychiatrists, psychologists or social workers in psychiatric settings. The young people's view of this work was generally negative, and in some cases this led them to refuse later offers of further therapeutic help. Therapeutic services provided by social services departments had been offered to a third of the young people and this work had lasted longer and was seen by the young people as having been more helpful.

2. There was often little information on file about past therapeutic intervention. This made it difficult to assess what help had previously been offered and sometimes led to a false assumption that the young person had already been helped to work through the emotional consequences of the abuse. It appeared that 44% of the sexually abused children had been offered therapeutic help at some time that directly addressed the sexual abuse and the issues surrounding it. This meant that over half of the children had never received such help.

3. Only five of the 22 children who had shown sexually abusing behaviour had received a referral for therapeutic intervention in relation to this behaviour and in only one case did this lead to ongoing work.

4. Fewer than a third (11) of those who had been sexually abused received any therapeutic intervention during the index placement which addressed the abuse itself.

5. Caregivers and social workers sometimes offered a valuable informal context for recovery in which the opportunity to talk about distressing experiences was combined with ongoing daily care, security and affection. At the other extreme, placements sometimes reinforced aspects of the original abusing environment making it difficult for the young people to feel safe and move forward.

6. Eighteen of the young people had been able to talk about the abuse or the events connected with it to their caregivers or social workers while in the index placement. Only one young person had talked in placement about her own abusing behaviour and this was in a limited way. Where caregivers were able to give the young person clear permission to talk about the abuse it established that open discussion of painful issues could take place between the caregiver and child, and as such should be a routine part of every new admission to substitute care.

7. Placements differed markedly on the dimension of "caregiver engagement". High levels of caregiver engagement were significantly associated with the young person having been able to talk about their past experiences of abuse and the associated difficulties for them. Being in receipt of specialist help during the placement also increased the likelihood that they had been able to talk about past abuse in the placement. Those children who had *both* high caregiver engagement *and* specialist

help during placement were most likely to have been able to explore
and make sense of their earlier difficult experiences.

8. Being able to talk about past experiences of abuse during placement
was associated with behavioural improvement. More than four fifths
of the children who had been able to talk fully or partially in placement
about their past abuse showed behavioural improvement compared
with under two thirds of the children who had not talked about their
abuse in placement.

9. The best outcomes in terms of behaviour were for those young people
who had been helped to explore their difficult experiences and feelings
both in a therapeutic relationship *and* in their everyday lives in care. For
other young people where past help had been sufficient to allow a
degree of acceptance and understanding of difficult experiences the
current placement only needed to be "good enough" for behavioural
improvement to be sustained. However, where the young person was
unable to talk about difficult experiences, even partially, in their placement, concurrent therapeutic intervention could lead to an escalation
of behaviour problems and placement difficulties.

12

SUPPORTS PROVIDED
FOR THE CAREGIVERS

Having examined the behaviours and the management of the young people, as well as the therapeutic interventions provided for them, we now turn to explore the impact which they had on their caregivers, the stresses experienced by both foster carers and residential workers and the supports which were available to assist them in managing the adolescents in their care.

THE IMPACT OF THE SEXUALLY ABUSED AND ABUSING YOUNG PEOPLE ON THE CAREGIVERS

The caregivers who had the greatest adjustments to make were those who had had no warning about what to expect before the young people arrived in placement. But even for those who had been given relevant information the reality could put them to the test. As we have seen, for several caregivers issues from the past were stirred up by looking after the young people. These included for a few, sexual abuse in their own backgrounds. Whilst two of the caregivers were involved in counselling training and were able to make good use of issues from their past to assist the young people, for others they created extra difficulties. In the most worrying cases such memories affected the management of the young people in adverse ways and this was not dealt with by the other professionals. For example, one foster mother could not handle the information that the boy in her care had been sexually abused by his father. Her reaction was to hate the abusing father and to tell the boy that he should put the abuse behind him. In contrast, for two foster families the advent of a sexualised child led to more open family discussions or to a growing together of the couple as they worked out ways to handle the child.

Sometimes an initial disclosure in substitute care led to the emergence of further information. Caregivers, social workers or both were often then furnished with long accounts of these events. One boy disclosed distressing details of physical abuse to him, which were very hard for the foster mother to listen to and the social worker of one girl was profoundly affected by listening to the statements she made "day in and day out" about her experience of sexual abuse.

As we have seen, fear of the possibility of allegations by sexualised girls bedevilled the care offered by some male caregivers, so that such girls were sometimes dealt with coldly or distantly. This brought into relief the question of how such deprived and needy children could be adequately parented at a distance when they were so hungry for physical contact, contact which they tended to sexualise. On the whole the response was to avoid physical contact with these girls. Foster families often had to revise their family arrangements, for example, by ensuring that the foster father was never left alone with any of the girls.

At least 16 of the young people showed behaviours which the caregivers found hard to manage. Quite a few of the boys were highly distractible and attention-seeking and found it hard to concentrate, others were verbally abusive to their caregivers, some of the girls had very poor hygiene and a high number of both boys and girls harmed themselves (nine in the index placement), a behaviour which was especially difficult to manage without outside advice and support. Young people who did not respond to their caregivers' attempt to exercise supervision, who indulged in high risk sexual behaviour, or were intimidating and threatening to other children or adults quickly drained their resources. A large number of the young people were not attending school, and this put added strain on the placements, especially those in foster care. Sexual advances to other children and inappropriate sexual touching of adults were difficult and disturbing behaviours to manage. The highly sexualised girls had a particularly strong impact on their caregivers. One put it this way:

"She'd make you feel quite extreme. She would actually bring up in you, and I'd think 'I don't want anything to do with you. Just stay away from me'. She could bring up very extreme emotions in you."

Given the difficulties presented by these young people it is not surprising to find that at least five of the caregivers and one of the social workers commented on having feelings of failure in relation to the way that they had managed them and a large number of caregivers, especially the foster carers, commented on the constant need for vigilance whilst the young people were with them.

FOSTER CARERS

The Stress Experienced by Foster Carers

Eight of the 17 foster carers whom we interviewed spoke of the stress that they had experienced in looking after the young people in the interview sample. This was often caused by their unsociable behaviour. In one case the foster mother was brought to a low ebb by her foster daughter's thieving and the fact that she was leading the other children in her care into trouble. In this case the social worker was very helpful in alleviating the stress by talking things over with the carer. In another case where an out-of-control fostered teenager caused anguish for the carer, the support worker was credited with providing help.

A single carer whose foster son was harming himself said that his actions, plus her unsuccessful attempts to get social services to take the problem seriously, had made life difficult for her. For another carer, looking after a teenager who did not attend school was "the hardest thing" she had coped with in her fostering role. When a subsequent foster child did attend school regularly she said it was a relief, "because you're given your days back".

Three carers suffered particularly high levels of stress. In one case this had been brought about by a false allegation of sexual abuse made against the foster father. The allegation was made by a previous foster child 17 months before our interview, but the repercussions were still strongly felt. This foster mother found that her reaction affected the other children in her care: "I shout and I rant and slap them." She also found that having to keep confidential the knowledge that her foster child was a young abuser caused her stress. She felt that the other parents "had a right to know what happened . . . I know that I can't tell them".

A second carer said that the placement was causing a great deal of stress in the family. It started with the "emotional blackmail" to which she felt she had been subjected, to provide an emergency placement for an abused and abusing boy. His subsequent disclosure to her of distressing details of his abuse thrust her into a counselling role. In addition, his intimidating and aggressive behaviour towards her own children and other foster children meant a need for constant vigilance, including secret surveillance of play activities. The household was greatly disrupted. At the time of the interview the carer was finding the placement so stressful that she was looking towards his removal to another placement.

The third carer who found the fostering role extremely stressful laid the blame on social services, not the young people he was looking after:

"I say I'm here to use my energy to battle with the kids and not to battle with social services . . . Most of the stress comes from my relationship with social services."

However, other carers had devised various means of relieving their stress which included discussing matters with social workers, support workers and their own families, and seeking support from other carers.

Difficulties for Foster Carers Caused by Social Services Departments

The foster carers voiced a range of issues concerned with social services departments which had made fostering difficult for them. Seven carers were concerned at the refusal of social services to give them information on the child's background, including their abuse. In one case the carers said that they would have been prepared for the false allegations made by the girl against the foster father if they had known her history. Another carer was very angry that she had not been told that her new foster child would not be attending school. Had she known she would have refused the placement.

Other complaints made by foster carers were about the lack of service provided by the social services department. These included a refusal to provide counselling for a boy; resistance to a request that ineffective art therapy be replaced by another form of therapy; and no progress being made in finding a school placement or permanent foster home. The carer of a special needs child found that social services were full of promises but did not come up with the goods:

"They say if there's any special needs the child wants, like a computer or what-ever, just let us know. There's absolutely zero chance of getting it. There's not just a remote chance, it's no chance – zero."

This same carer found that other things, including payments, took a very long time to come through. He was still awaiting mileage expenses after a year and was threatening social services with the small claims court. He summed up social services as follows:

"This big machine that goes at about half-a-mile an hour, that's oblivious to everything and everybody. [It] takes on board all these new ideas which are totally alien for fostering and it just grinds on at this pace . . . They go through the motions of listening to people and all the rest, but they don't.*"*

A carer who had been told that he was "overstepping the boundaries" when he tried to get things done for the child, including finding him a school placement, had been sent letters to that effect and had clashed over it with the placement officer. He complained of "too much red tape" and added:

"But it's so frustrating when you know that it will affect someone living with you . . . you should be allowed to go ahead but no, you can't do that . . . A lot of the time we feel that some of the problems we've had with the boys could have been solved here and now – quicker, you know, rather than waiting for social services to come along and sort it all out. So we're always having this argument."

A few fosters carers felt that the Children Act had made the fostering task more difficult. Such carers felt that children had too much power:

"Oh they know what they can do and they tell you . . . This is about getting holidays free and they get this free and that free, and they think, 'Oh, if I offend I can do that'."

This couple also felt that the input to a girl from her juvenile justice worker had been unhelpful. The efforts of the foster mother, who was trying to encourage the girl to stay in at night for her own protection, were undermined by the worker who told the girl she could come and go as she pleased. The foster carer had challenged the juvenile justice worker about this and been told that it was "the law".

One couple were upset that they were not allowed to operate a no-smoking rule. They found it embarrassing when the youngsters in their care smoked at the meal table whilst in public with them. The foster mother said that she felt she should wear a T-shirt with "They don't belong to me" emblazoned across it.

The Supports Used by Foster Carers

Of the 17 foster carers just over half (nine) felt that their needs for support from social services were not being met. Dissatisfied carers commented on the low esteem in which they felt that they were held by social services (see also Berridge and Cleaver, 1987):

". . . very much undervalued, very, very, very much . . . We don't feel our efforts are recognised in any way."

"I don't think social services value their carers enough and that is the view of most carers."

"They don't support you enough and they don't seem to realise that you're a person in your own right and that you need time out as well . . . Just to have time that you can relax and you haven't got all that pressure."

One couple suggested that the status of foster carers would be improved if they received a proper wage on which they were taxed.

Support by Linkworkers

Some of the foster carers, including all those in special schemes, had a linkworker assigned to them who was responsible for a group of foster carers. Their remit was to provide support for the carers. However, as already mentioned, in one of our authorities the foster carers who were not in special schemes had no linkworker and in both authorities linkworkers were not provided for the Regulation 11 carers.

A carer who derived a great deal of support from her linkworker described her as "wonderful – always on the end of a phone". She had had this linkworker for two years and said that the continuity had enabled them to develop a friendship, which in turn led to the carer being well resourced:

"If I have any problems she is always ready to listen . . . If things get out of hand she is here . . . She knows every move that is made in this house really, because I feel it is important that she knows what is going on. I think if you've got a good worker then you don't need any more support."

Another carer who singled out her linkworker for praise said:

"It's a brilliant support service. I can phone any time of the day and most of the night and she'd be there."

She said that she would approach the linkworker before the child's social worker if there were problems and she would not disturb the emergency duty team as they were considered to be very busy and "tend not to have time to talk". Another foster carer who had moved from a neighbouring authority told us that her old linkworker still liaised by phone with her "very supportive" new social worker, which she found advantageous.

One carer praised a link worker who had visited her every second week and would have done so more often if she had requested it. This officer was available 24 hours a day and could be reached by mobile phone on days off. Another couple, where the father was the main carer, had appreciated the placement officer sending them a thank-you letter for coping with "the worst behaved kids" they had ever had.

Support by the Child's Social Worker or Support Worker

In addition to a social worker, a child was sometimes assigned a support worker who had a special remit to do intensive work with the child. Some carers found that the support which they received from the social worker was more effective than that received from the child's support worker, or vice-versa.

In eight of the 17 cases carers expressed particular dissatisfaction with the support offered by either the social worker or support worker. Two carers described this as extremely unsatisfactory. In the first of these cases complaints centred on the failure of the young person's social worker to visit when requested, even when the placement was in danger of breaking down, the worker's lack of involvement in the young person's education, his failure to listen to the carers and his frequent lack of availability.

In the second case of extreme dissatisfaction with the social worker, the main grievance centred around the withholding of information concerning the child, including the minutes of a planning meeting and the child's file. They described the social worker as "unreliable and insensitive to the child's needs," particularly for failing to make arrangements for residential schooling. When a placement was eventually found she broke the news to the child over the telephone, which was "very upsetting for him". This social worker was also difficult to contact. In contrast, this carer said that she found the child's support worker "very good".

One foster mother praised the black worker who was assigned to her mixed-race foster son because he discussed race issues with him and was a good role model. The white worker who was still responsible for his case, was deemed to be of little assistance however, particularly because of inactivity in finding a school placement and also because of failure to pass on information to the carer.

Three foster carers were not satisfied with the support they received from the child's support worker. One of these carers had two support workers, one male, one female, and he contrasted the work of each, praising the female, a "wonderful support worker" but denigrating the male for not visiting often enough (three-weekly intervals instead of the agreed weekly visits), and not discussing sexual issues and behaviours with the boy as had been intended.

Other shortcomings by social workers included pressing a carer to take a teenager when the preferred age range was 0–5 years, which had very negative effects on the foster family; failing to clarify a young person's future, leading to deteriorating behaviour; failing to work directly with the child, or to visit; a lack of emotional support for the foster mother; and lack of feedback about a child's visit to a medical centre.

It was not unusual to find that carers thought that the social worker could have done more to secure a school placement for a foster child but one foster carer said: "You're all afraid to speak your minds because you're all afraid of losing your jobs." She said it was known that if a carer "caused a rumpus" social services would fail to find them another placement "and then you don't get your income". In addition, the failure of social workers to keep promises made to children about holidays and outings, resulted in foster carers having to "pick up the pieces". One commented after a cancelled go-karting session:

"She'd just tell him and we took the consequences . . . The kid was gutted. He was broken that day and he'd been building up to that."

When carers were happy with social work support they were enthusiastic in their praise of the social worker. This was so with 11 social workers, five of whom were rated by carers as *very* good. Even where they felt unsupported by social services generally, carers singled out particular workers as having helped them. One carer said that she had received more help in one year from her child's social worker than she had done in eight years from her previous foster child's worker. The carer who said of her social worker: "We work very closely together. I think she is brilliant," said that they perceived each other as mutually supportive. One carer who expressed satisfaction with her social worker said: "I found that since this social worker took over, that it's made my job easier".

The social worker in one case was especially good at sharing information and he visited the carer before placement to "share his thoughts". She said: "He's marvellous . . . he does all that is expected of him." This social worker's superior was also involved, taking the young person out at least once a week, which the carer found a great help to her.

Support by Other Professionals

A child's therapist merited special mention by one carer. The child had been receiving art therapy which was proving "useless". The girl was very disturbed and the social worker had offered the carers false reassurance that she would be all right in two or three months. They were in despair until, as a result of a great deal of pressure on their part, a therapist was assigned to work with the girl. The therapist involved the foster mother in collaborative work with the girl and there was a great improvement in the child's behaviour. This therapist also informed the couple that they could claim extra payments for their foster child's difficult behaviour. In another case, good counselling was provided for the young person and in a third instance, a special needs teacher and an educational psychologist had given a lot of support to one foster mother.

This contrasted with the experience of other foster carers who, as already described, were excluded by their foster child's counsellor. One foster carer said that the child's therapist had felt that the work she did was "nothing to do with [the foster carers] whatsoever," although they had been the ones to persuade the child to see the counsellor. This therapist had neither explained to them what he was doing nor written a report. They concluded: "It was just a waste of time."

In contrast, two carers had asked for counselling to be provided for the children in their care but none had been forthcoming.

Foster Carer Support Groups and Informal Networks

Foster carer support groups were discussed in 15 of our 17 foster carer interviews. In seven cases the carers attended regularly, usually monthly, and found them very useful.

"It is always nice to know they are there . . . I am still quite new . . . It gives you a chance to meet people from the other support groups . . . Somebody to sound off to, shout at."

Of this group of seven, two said that this was their main source of support, more so than that given by social services. However, couples were not always in agreement about the usefulness of the groups. One foster father attended regularly but his wife thought they were a waste of time. She said that two particular sets of community parents had dominated the group giving no chance to share experiences.

A further four carers did not attend foster carer groups for various reasons. One said that her other supports were quite sufficient. Two couples were constrained by babysitting difficulties, because of the very challenging behaviour of their foster children. The fourth carer, a lone male, had attended the group for foster carers in his area but it had folded after just two meetings. However, he said that he would not have gone back anyway because it was of no practical help, but merely "a platform for other carers to blow their own trumpets".

Four other carers said that there was no foster carer support group in their area but that they would attend if one were formed. One wanted the group to be specifically for the carers of teenagers, whilst another said that she would be happy just to be put in touch with other foster carers for the purposes of gaining reassurance.

Half of those attending foster carer groups on a regular basis said that family, friends and neighbours still played an important part in their support. Overall, these informal supports were important in nine cases. The help received included babysitting and talking things over, especially with other carers in informal networks or with the extended family. When fostering threw up issues from one carer's past, her own counsellor was invaluable. This single carer also received support from her church, especially the minister who respected her confidences.

One set of foster carers who had a 14-year-old daughter of their own said that she was "brilliant – she sees it from a totally different angle". They found her a great help in their fostering role, together with their extended family and a foster carer, with whom they would "talk for ages" whenever they met. The lone male foster carer also had a friend who had been approved by social services to stand in when the foster carer wanted a holiday for up to four weeks each year.

A disabled foster mother who had expressed dissatisfaction with the support given by social services had found a voluntary organisation which gave her a lot of practical help, such as cleaning and home hair-dressing. The birth mother of one girl was credited with easing the fostering task for a carer because she saw the foster mother as the "boss" and gave her leverage to exercise full discretion over what constituted good guidance for the child. Support sometimes came from the wider community. One couple described how they were helped by local publicans who prevented their under-aged foster children from obtaining alcohol.

Time Off from Caregiving

Seven of the 17 carers mentioned that they wanted more respite or time to themselves. In one case the plea was for at least three weekends away each year. There was also a need for a break between placements. Some carers with abusing foster children were unable to visit friends with them, nor could they go out together and leave them at home as they felt that no one else was vigilant enough to look after them. One fostering couple made the point that payments for babysitting had to come out of their foster care allowance. On the other hand, two carers said that although respite was available to them they had not needed it because of support from their parents and the extended family.

RESIDENTIAL WORKERS

The Stress Experienced by Residential Workers

Eight, or just under half of the 17 residential workers whom we interviewed, said that their jobs caused them stress. One head of home felt that this was due to the "uncomfortable environment" in which the staff had

to work, with the ever-present possibility of young people making allegations against them. Complaints, often malicious, were made "on a daily
basis" at her children's home, and she had to judge which were serious
enough to refer for investigation, along with the suspension of the member of staff concerned.

An African-Caribbean residential worker blamed the stress she suffered on racist remarks made to her by the young people. Another residential worker who, together with her husband, looked after a boy with
moderate learning difficulties in a flat, described this young person as the
most stress-inducing person she had ever looked after because he was
constantly seeking attention. Strain for another worker was caused by the
unpredictability of the children in the home, which meant that staff had to
be on their guard at all times.

One residential worker told us that she, like her colleagues, found
one-to-one work with a very sexualised girl very stressful: "At first
people used to tear their hair out." This adolescent girl brought out
extremes of emotion in the residential workers who looked after her.
One was sometimes under so much stress that she would stay on shift
to make sure that she had dealt sufficiently with her feelings to be able
to continue the next day. The emotional aspect of her work with a very
sexually active girl caused another residential worker considerable
stress. "I used to go home feeling so exhausted. I didn't enjoy the job at
all really, I've got to say". She felt constantly drained by the child's
situation, became depressed because of the issues from her background which work with this child raised, and at the time of our
interview was having counselling "related to the job, but not directly
because of it".

Another residential worker found that demanding shift work with very
aggressive young people left him unable to devote sufficient time and
energy to his own family. Another worker was concerned by the attraction felt towards him by a girl in his care.

Two workers who found their employment stressful were able to
cope by participating in sporting and other outdoor activities. Others
who were free of stress said that it was their attitudes to their jobs
which made this possible. A worker who said that she enjoyed working with young people and loved the lack of routine added: "The more
you put into it the more you get out of it." She spent half-an-hour
winding down after each shift before she went home. Similarly, another worker said:

*"At the end of the day, after my feet go through the door to go home, I leave it all
behind."*

The Supervision Provided for Residential Workers

Only four of the 17 residential workers whom we interviewed received formal supervision on at least a monthly basis. One whose supervision was provided by the manager of the children's home found the sessions extremely helpful, as did another whose supervisor was a senior staff member from her unit. A senior worker at a specialist secure unit received his supervision from a forensic psychiatrist and he said that he was "guided by his professional expertise and training". The psychiatrist also gave him debriefing sessions and supervised his clinical work with young people. This worker said that it was essential for the staff at his unit to work as a team, and meetings and discussions played an important part in this:

"The one tool that we can share with each other is consistency, and that is a key issue with the teams, and that is part of what the planning and meeting and discussing problems is about – making sure we can share consistency."

Although one worker had regular, formal, individual supervision which she thought was very important, she stressed that the weekly staff meetings held to discuss each child living in the independent unit were also essential. This was also the opinion of another worker in an independent living unit. She did not receive individual supervision but the weekly meetings with the two accommodation officers enabled her to "go through everything". Two other workers, who did not receive supervision, also mentioned that their weekly staff meetings were helpful in sorting out problems.

The head of home whom we interviewed formally supervised her staff on a monthly basis, and in addition was available for informal discussions. She herself had fortnightly supervision from a Principal Social Services Officer but this dealt with management matters and did not cover her personal growth and professional development, a situation which she found unsatisfactory. At a meeting in her authority she had argued that time should be built in to allow senior managers sufficient time to supervise officers-in-charge about such issues.

In spite of some shortcomings these levels of supervision were considerably greater than those offered in residential schools. In one residential school the Head of Care met up with care staff just once a term to discuss the children's progress. It took the form of a discussion lasting about 40 minutes. Where informal links were strong, as in the case of one worker in a residential school who could talk with his unit manager at any time, this lack of formal supervision posed less of a problem.

Five residential workers had neither formal supervision nor regular meetings with other members of staff. One said that the staff in her unit felt isolated. Similarly, a worker in a residential school with no supervision was excluded from participation in formal meetings. This precluded her from decision-making related to planning and caseloads. She had had no contact with, nor did she know the name of, the child's social worker. She presumed that the school liaised with the social worker but she was not informed.

A worker who had in the past received infrequent supervision told us that it had now stopped altogether. She did not know the reason for this and the lack of supervision had left her feeling depressed. She commented on the previous high turnover of supervisors:

"I had so many supervisors over a period of time. Something like eight supervisors. By the time you've established a regime et cetera, I had another one. I found it very difficult."

Two other unsupervised workers both wanted supervision sessions in order to give them guidance in dealing with the confidences of the sexually abused children in their care. One residential worker told us that no one in his children's home received regular supervision, and what supervision there was, was very informal. If their rotas happened to coincide with the officer-in-charge, then "conversations" took place. A male residential worker who was unsupervised wanted the opportunity to discuss his fear of unfounded sexual allegations being made against him by the girl in his care. The absence of formal supervision and the dismissive attitude of his manager when he had broached the subject had led him to turn for help to the manager of a unit in which he had previously worked.

The majority of residential workers saw a need for supervision in order to reinforce their confidence, and where this was not forthcoming they often felt left to cope alone, although this feeling decreased where regular staff meetings were a feature of their routine.

The Supports Used by Residential Workers

Assessing the overall level of support which residential workers received from social services including from their colleagues, 11 of the 17 workers whom we interviewed considered it to be good or satisfactory. Another five carers were less happy with their support system, and we had no information in one case.

The Support Provided by Managers

Four residential workers found their officers-in-charge very helpful in terms of support, although one of these workers said that she would turn to her other colleagues in the first instance. One of the managers was on 24-hour call to help with any problems that arose in the children's home and would give advice over the phone or come in person at a moment's notice if necessary. On the other hand, two keyworkers criticised their managers. One felt that he was not being protected against the possibility of false abuse allegations being made against him. The other residential worker mentioned the lack of support from the officer-in-charge when he was under pressure.

Support by the Child's Social Worker

Of the 17 residential carers interviewed, seven said that they were very satisfied with the support that they received from the child's social worker, six did not rate them as very helpful and there was no specific information concerning the child's social worker in four cases.

When discussing reasons for their satisfaction, five residential workers mentioned the excellent contact that the social worker maintained with the children's home and stressed the good working relationship that existed. One social worker was praised for keeping the home well informed and another for the "wonderful" communication and clear role divisions for her and the residential worker, where the social worker's research into the child's family history had alerted the residential worker to the mother's inclination to fight authority and threaten to sue. This knowledge enabled the residential staff not to be intimidated by the mother's threats and abuse. The residential worker was able to phone the social worker to access resources for areas of work she felt unable to do herself.

Two of the social workers had obtained therapeutic help for the young people, which in one case involved a private psychiatrist treating a girl with an eating disorder. A keyworker was impressed by the manner in which one social worker discussed plans for the young person with the children's home staff, and was prepared to listen to their views, "take them on board willingly and act on them". This social worker was also willing to accept the residential worker's help when it came to introducing the girl to her new foster parents, a move not normally adopted by fieldworkers. She was also available to the keyworker 24 hours a day, which the latter found "very useful".

Where residential workers had found the social workers unhelpful their reasons included a lack of visits to the child in two cases, and a lack of direct work with the child in three others. One residential worker complained that the social worker often broke promises made to the young person to take her on outings, and left this keyworker to do the work that she should have undertaken, such as accompanying the young person to meetings and court hearings. She said: "It's like they dump them here and run. They put a lot of their duties on us."

One worker criticised the social worker for not doing enough to arrange a foster placement and another was frustrated by the lack of consultation over decisions made by the social worker about the child:

"We are the ones that are living with this young person. We are the ones that know this young person."

One male keyworker objected to the way in which the male social worker insisted that he be accompanied when he was with the girl, for example when taking her to view her new placement. The keyworker pointed out that residential workers did not have this protection but "put themselves on the line" regarding the possibility of sexual abuse allegations. The same worker said that the social worker never sent him copies of the letters which the young person received when, for example, she was told that she was moving to another placement. This information would have explained the girl's behaviour and subsequent suicide attempt. Another social worker was criticised for supplying only practical assistance, such as transport or shoes for the child, and for failing to provide any advice to the keyworker.

Support from Others

The availability of a psychologist to assist with advice on behaviour modification was an important support in three cases, and a visiting psychiatrist was available to help with major problems affecting young people at one residential school. One senior residential worker said that he would not hesitate to have counselling for himself because:

"You can't push on on your own in the dark without realising this work is going to have an effect. Whether it is beneficial or detrimental, it will have some effect."

In one case the staff at a local school were praised for "excellent links" with the children's home which enabled a young person to maintain her school placement. One residential worker was thankful that the home could call on the specialist fieldwork team for adolescents with difficult behaviour, and although they did so infrequently, the help that the team were able to provide meant that children rarely had to be removed because of their unmanageable behaviour.

An area where one worker felt unsupported concerned the Crown Prosecution Service's refusal to prosecute a young person's alleged abuser because they thought that she would make a poor witness. This resulted in the girl exhibiting angry and depressed behaviour. One key-worker said that the lack of support from parents who refused all contact with their daughter had impeded work with the girl.

Support from Colleagues

The opportunity to discuss problems with other staff members and receive informal advice and support was highly rated by eight of the residential workers, five of whom said this was their main form of support. Good working relationships and a "team spirit" enabled them to help each other in practical ways such as "doubling-up" on outings with young people, and their friendships led to a sharing of problems, as indicated by the following quotations:

"It's nice to know when you've had a particularly bad shift you can off-load onto another member of staff. Or you can always ring them up."

"You see someone else having problems then you know you can discuss it and say, 'Well, I tried this and it worked for me. It may not for you but it's worth a try'."

"I get the encouragement and the support from all the staff . . . The staff group was very good because they all know that I've taken a difficult girl."

Support from Friends and Relatives

Only two workers said that they would turn to their friends for support and one of them had friends who also worked in the care system. Three workers said that they could off-load their worries to their partners, one of whom also worked for social services, and another turned to her mother to talk over her work problems.

Overall then, just under half of the foster carers reported that they were experiencing considerable stress in looking after the young people in our study and just over half felt that their needs for support from social services were not being met. Similarly, just under half of the residential workers said that their jobs were causing them stress but when the support they received from their colleagues was added to that from other professionals, rather fewer – only a third – felt that their support was unsatisfactory.

The stresses on the caregivers and the supports which they used in looking after the young people in the study provide a background against which the placement and management patterns of the young people can be considered. That is the subject of the next chapter.

SUMMARY

1. Almost half of the foster carers had found looking after the young person in their care very stressful. The causes of this stress sometimes lay in the difficult behaviour of the children. Other causes of stress included the fear of allegations of abuse being made against a foster carer and listening to the young people recount details of the abuse which they had suffered.

2. Just over half of the foster carers felt that their needs for support from social services were not being met. There were a range of reasons for this dissatisfaction. A number felt undervalued by the department and two fifths complained about the lack of information given to them about the children before they arrived. Carers felt particularly undermined when their efforts to arrange a school placement or invoke a particular house rule were vetoed by the social worker.

3. Two out of five of the carers attended foster carer support groups and found them a valuable source of support. Just over half of the foster carers received support from family, friends and neighbours. However, two fifths of the carers wanted more respite or time to themselves both during and between placements. This need was heightened for carers who looked after abusing children whom they often felt could not safely be left with other adults.

4. Just under half of the residential workers found that their jobs caused them stress. Causes of such stress included unpredictable and aggressive behaviour, complaints and allegations by children and the emotional burden of looking after very sexualised girls.

5. Fewer than a quarter of the residential workers received formal supervision on at least a monthly basis. Some found staff meetings helpful. However, 29% had neither supervision nor regular staff meetings. Unsupervised workers sometimes spoke of needing guidance on how to deal with the confidences of sexually abused children or advice on dealing with their fears of allegations being made against them.

6. Two thirds of the residential workers considered that the support that they received from social services, including from their colleagues, was good or satisfactory. However only two fifths were satisfied with the support that they received from the child's social worker.

7. The availability of a psychologist to assist with advice on behaviour modification was a support to residential workers in three placements. In addition, a third of the staff interviewed turned to friends, relatives or partners for support.

8. Overall, just under half of both the foster carers and residential workers reported that they were experiencing considerable stress in looking after the young people in our study. Whereas just over half of

the foster carers felt that their needs for support from social services were not being met, fewer residential workers (a third) felt unsupported by the department, principally because of the assistance that they received from their colleagues.

13

PLACEMENT AND MANAGEMENT PATTERNS OF THE YOUNG PEOPLE

When the all the sexually abused and/or abusing young people in the sample were looked at together six distinct groups of young people and placements emerged. These groupings were based principally on the sexual behaviours which the young people displayed in substitute care and the behaviours in each category were sufficiently different to require a distinctive type of management and often also of placement. Of course, the behaviours shown are not independent of the management provided. They may, in some cases, have been influenced by the adequacy and appropriateness of the way in which the young people were handled. In this chapter these six categories of young people will be described along with the strengths and weaknesses of the management provided for them.

We rated the children's management firstly in terms of the levels of supervision exercised in the placements, using a rating of high, medium or low supervision. Placements were rated as providing high levels of supervision when children were closely supervised and monitored within the homes and they were asked to account for their movements outside the placement. This applied to 38% (15) of the placements. Medium levels of supervision were considered to be in place when caregivers placed emphasis on monitoring but there were areas of the children's lives which were not subject to scrutiny and this was the case in 10% (4) of the settings. Low levels of supervision obtained in 52% (21) of placements, where caregivers did not exercise full supervision of the children's activities within or outside the settings. Low levels of supervision were slightly more often a feature of residential care where they applied in 57% of placements than in foster care where it was true in 47% of the placements.

The second area of management which we rated was how far the caregivers had succesfully modified or re-shaped the young people's general or sexual behaviour during the index placement. In 53% (21) of placements behaviour was successfully modified. Whilst, as shown in Chapters 11 and 14, a larger proportion of children showed improved behaviour overall, this was not always as a result of the specific efforts of the caregivers to change the children's behaviour. Successful attempts to modify children's behaviour were apparent in similar proportions of residential and foster placements. The third management issue which we rated was whether the young people had any outstanding needs which had not been met, apart from any need for counselling. Almost two thirds (65%) of the children (26) did so. Fewer young people in residential care had their needs well met (29%) than was the case for the children in foster care (42%). Finally, we looked to see whether the young people had had any formal therapeutic intervention from any source to help them with their behavioural or emotional difficulties during the index placement. Fifty five per cent (22) had received such help and the proportion who received this work was similar in the two care sectors.

CATEGORY 1: NO PROBLEMATIC SEXUAL BEHAVIOUR IN PLACEMENT

A third of the group (13) fell into the first category of young people who showed no problematic sexual behaviours while they were being looked after in the index placement. Seven were boys and six girls. Six of the 13 young people had shown sexually abusive behaviour previously. About half were in foster care and half in children's homes, with one child in residential school. The management provided for the 13 young people in this category is shown in Tables 1 and 2.

Table 1   Levels of supervision in Category 1

High	Medium	Low
4	4	5

Table 2   Management provided for children in Category 1

	Yes	No
Modification of behaviour	5	8
The child's outstanding needs were met	4	9
The child received formal therapeutic intervention	6	7

As can be seen, varying levels of supervision were provided for the young people in our first category with nearly two fifths receiving only low levels of supervision. Successful attempts were made to modify the general behaviour of almost two fifths of them but fewer than a third had their outstanding needs met. Fewer than half of the children received some formal therapeutic intervention during the course of the placement.

The fact that these young people were not symptomatic in the index placement did not, of course, mean that their problems were resolved. But their lack of problematic behaviour led some caregivers to sweep the children's past under the carpet and assume that it would be best if no reference was made to it. Caregivers of non-symptomatic children needed to be alert to the triggers which elicited distress in them and to be ready to provide opportunities for the young people to talk to them or to a counsellor outside the placement if they wished to do so. There were children in this group who were clearly ready to do some direct work on their past abuse, but in the absence of difficulties in the here and now, such help was not always forthcoming. Supervision of the young people needed to be maintained at high levels because abusing behaviour could emerge.

The wider needs of the young people in this group were often ignored because they were not causing any difficulties for the professionals or for their caregivers. Yet many of them had significant gaps in their education and deep unresolved feelings of loss and rejection with which they needed assistance.

CATEGORY 2: BEHAVIOURALLY DISTURBED YOUNG PEOPLE WHOSE BEHAVIOUR INCLUDED SEXUAL SELF-HARM
Risk to Self

Category 2 covers two children, one boy and one girl, who had clear behavioural disturbance, in which genital self-harm figured. They were placed in a separate category from other children because their behavioural disturbance seemed unlikely to be affected simply by ordinary good parenting and firm boundaries. It seemed highly likely that without work on the underlying issues for them no progress would be made. These two children were at the younger end of our age group and both had suffered prolonged sexual abuse at a very young age, which they may well have been quite unable to process. One was in foster and the other in residential care. One had abused another child before the placement and both abused other children in this placement.

Both of these children were subject to high levels of supervision in placement and attempts to modify their behaviour. In one case but not the other the child was receiving direct work and her outstanding needs were being met.

The range of disturbed behaviour exhibited by these children was difficult for caregivers to handle. Their masturbatory behaviour was compulsive and included insertion of objects into the vagina or anus which sometimes led to bleeding. Because the behaviours shown by the children were disturbing for their caregivers they needed intensive support and one placement was given much-needed back-up in the form of direct work and consultancy by an experienced therapist. Monitoring and supervision of these children was not easy because much of their disturbed behaviour took place in private, was hidden or was difficult to understand. One child destroyed everything in her bedroom and the caregivers resorted to removing everything from the room to prevent this. Another child was an isolate and withdrawn. When he started sexually to target other boys the careworker at his residential school tried to divert him, but did not understand the significance of his behaviour.

It was clear that to be effective the management of these children's behaviours needed to be linked with therapeutic work with the child and this was provided in one placement. Even with this help the foster carers were often at a loss as to how to manage such a disturbed child. Ideally the behaviours needed to be named and addressed and an attempt made to understand what needs the behaviour was expressing, in the hope that the pain which fuelled the behaviour would itself eventually emerge. Work on the children's underlying problems and the range of their unmet needs for nurture and parenting was also required. Because of the depth of these children's difficulties they needed either a specialist placement such as a therapeutic community or, if they were in an ordinary placement, an intensive package of support to sustain it. Without this there was a risk that they would have many placement breakdowns, as had been the case for one of the young people. The child in the residential school was a new admission to care. He was being contained but because the school had no specialist expertise with sexually abused and very disturbed children there seemed every possibility that his early problems would remain unresolved and might surface at a later date.

CATEGORY 3: YOUNG PEOPLE WITH WEAK INTERPERSONAL BOUNDARIES WHO SHOWED SEXUALISED BEHAVIOUR
High Risk to Self/Some Risk to Others

Category 3 consisted of thirteen young people (33%) who had been prematurely sexualised and lacked appropriate personal boundaries. They sexualised most forms of contact with other young people and adults and some but not all were also very sexually active. Five of them had previously sexually abused another child. Nine of the 13 young people in this category were girls and just over half of them were in residential care. Many had had very little ordinary good enough parenting and some were markedly emotionally immature with a pronounced disparity between their emotional and chronological age. As we have seen, when the very immature children in this group were placed with more mature adolescents they were sometimes exposed by them to high risk situations which they did not know how to manage. This included being drawn into situations where they met sexually predatory young men. The mix of young people in placements was therefore very important.

The lack of personal boundaries of these young people put them at risk from others with whom they initiated sexual contact or who sensed their vulnerability and targeted them. They also placed others at risk through their sexual advances. The management provided for the 13 young people in this category is shown in Tables 3 and 4.

As can be seen, for the majority of the young people in this group the levels of supervision provided were very low. As a result they put themselves at risk outside the placements without any boundaries being provided. Attempts were made to modify the general behaviour of fewer than a third of them and the needs of only three of the children were met, although a higher proportion (over two thirds) received some direct work.

The management provided for the majority of these young people fell far short of what was needed by them. However, there were examples of good practice with such children which served to illustrate that effective management could be provided for them. The lessons from these good practice examples were, first, that it was important to reduce the risks to the children by providing clear boundaries for their behaviour and

Table 3   Levels of supervision in Category 3

High	Medium	Low
2	0	11

Table 4   Management provided for children in Category 3

	Yes	No
Modification of behaviour	4	9
The child's outstanding needs were met	3	10
The child received formal therapeutic intervention	9	4

effective supervision, including rules about the times the young people were to be home and some monitoring of their contacts. These simple rules needed to be accompanied by the direct message to the young people that their safety mattered to the caregivers and they would do what they could to ensure it, since most of the children had not had the experience of being protected by parent figures. Second, caregivers had to work at helping the young people to modify their sexualised behaviour and to learn to separate physical touch and affection from sexual contact. The young people needed to learn what was and was not appropriate touch and what were safe personal boundaries. Third, the underlying problems of the young people needed to be addressed and often they needed to be reparented in a non-sexual way. Often these children were desperately in need of nurture appropriate to a much younger child and ways could be found to meet that need, for example through simple routines like bedtime stories and brushing a girl's hair. The provision of active nurture was also important in forestalling the young people acting out this need through sexual contacts.

CATEGORY 4: YOUNG PEOPLE WHO WERE INVOLVED IN EXPLOITATIVE SEXUAL ACTIVITY INCLUDING PROSTITUTION

High Risk to Self/High Risk to Others

Category 4 covers three young people who were actively involved in exploitative sexual activity during their placement and one other young woman was also included who had been working actively as a prostitute during this care episode, although she was contained in a secure unit during the index placement. Whilst, as we saw in Chapter 10, there were other children (most of them boys) who had some involvement in prostitution at one stage or another, for example while absconding or after leaving care, the young people in this category were regularly involved with sexually exploitative adults for most of their placements or were placed in secure accommodation for this reason. Of the four, three (two girls and a boy) worked as prostitutes and one other girl was involved with a number of Schedule One offenders. Three were in residential care and one in a foster home. One had shown sexually abusing behaviour. They were themselves at high risk because of the nature of their sexual activity and, as we have seen, they put other children at risk by involving them in prostitution and procuring them for their clients. Some were also involved in the making of pornographic material and all had become involved in drug and alcohol misuse. The management provided for the four young people in this category is shown in Tables 5 and 6.

Table 5 Levels of supervision in Category 4

High	Medium	Low
1	0	3

Table 6 Management provided for children in Category 4

	Yes	No
Modification of behaviour	0	4
The child's outstanding needs were met	0	4
The child received formal therapeutic intervention	2	2

As can be seen, the levels of supervision provided for all but the one young person in a secure unit were very low. As a result they put themselves and others at risk outside the placements. Caregivers were unable to intervene effectively to modify their general behaviour and the young people's outstanding needs were not met, although two out of the four did receive some therapeutic help.

All but the young person in secure accommodation frequently absconded from their placements which made them especially difficult for the local authorities to manage. Nonetheless it was essential for local authorities to act quickly once their involvement in sexually exploitative activity became known, both because it quickly became entrenched behaviour and because of the risks they posed to other children. Careful recording of all the young people's activities and absconding was important as was a log of all the contacts which staff observed between the young people and their adult associates. Information held by the local authority and the police needed to be co-ordinated and the parents involved in the strategies devised to contain the young people.

The most effective placements were out-of-county because it was only in this way that young people could be separated from the networks of pimps and clients which reinforced their behaviour and sometimes maintained it through threats and other forms of coercion. It was difficult, if not impossible, to modify the children's behaviour until it was no longer being strongly reinforced elsewhere. Occasionally, when other interventions had failed, a secure placement could be the only way in which the behaviours could be temporarily halted but this was only of assistance if it was offered as part of a wider plan for change. In the long run the young people would require work on the problems underlying their behaviour and active assistance to develop other activities, including school attendance and work experience, which could bring them rewards and involvement with a positive peer group.

CATEGORY 5: YOUNG PEOPLE WHO SEXUALLY ABUSED OTHERS IN PLACEMENT (for whom sex and aggression were not linked)

High Risk to Others

The fifth category excludes young abusers for whom sex and aggression were closely linked, who will be described in Category 6. Four children, three girls and one boy are in this grouping because they sexually abused other children in the index placement, which was foster care in three instances and a children's home in the other. One had sexually abused a child in a previous care setting. Clearly they presented risks to other children. (Because of their particular features, two other children who abused others in the index placement are in Category 2 and one in Category 6). The management provided for the four young people in this category is shown in Tables 7 and 8.

As can be seen, half of these children were very well supervised and half less so. Considerable attempts were made to modify their general behaviour and for three quarters their outstanding needs were met. Two out of the four received some formal therapeutic intervention. Overall, the management provided for these young people was better than that provided for the children in the other categories described so far, except Category 2.

As we saw in Chapter 6 there are few clear predictors of which young people who have been sexually abused or who have sexually abused other children will abuse a child in placement. The young people in this group and others with these backgrounds therefore require careful attention to mix at the time of placement, close supervision and the opportunity to talk about their experiences. Since the sexually abusive behaviour may well be connected to their own experience of being abused they ideally need some counselling about their abuse. They would also be likely to benefit from counselling about their abusing behaviour although only one of the young people in this group had received such help.

Table 7   Levels of supervision in Category 5

High	Medium	Low
2	0	2

Table 8   Management provided for children in Category 5

	Yes	No
Modification of behaviour	3	1
The child's outstanding needs were met	3	1
The child received formal therapeutic intervention	2	2

CATEGORY 6: YOUNG PERPETRATORS FOR WHOM SEX AND AGGRESSION WERE LINKED
Very High Risk to Others

Category 6 covers young perpetrators for whom sex and aggression were closely linked (10%). These young people are in a separate category because the nature of their past abusive acts and the very high risks that they presented to others meant that they were often placed in specialist provision. Where no further abusing behaviour re-emerged it appeared to have been connected to the high levels of supervision in placements and because they were well contained, not because of any change in the young people themselves.

Four of the young people were in this group and all were boys. The sexually abusing behaviour previously shown by these boys had involved coercion and aggression to their victims and they were considered to be at high risk of committing further acts of aggressive coerced sexual assault. One of them raped a girl when he was sent home from his placement for misbehaviour. Three were in specialist placements designed to contain their abusing behaviour: one was alone in a supervised flat, one was at a specialist secure unit and one was in a residential school. The fourth boy was in foster care awaiting placement in a residential school. The management provided for young people in this category is shown in Tables 9 and 10.

As can be seen, all these children were very well supervised and attempts were made in most cases to modify their general behaviour, whilst half of them had their outstanding needs met. Half of them also received some focused therapeutic work. Their management was similar to that of the young people in Category 5 but with higher levels of supervision.

The young people in this category required very structured placements which could provide consistently high levels of supervision both within and outside the placement. The one young person who had been

Table 9 Levels of supervision in Category 6

High	Medium	Low
4	0	0

Table 10 Management provided for the children in Category 6

	Yes	No
Modification of behaviour	3	1
The child's outstanding needs were met	2	2
The child received formal therapeutic intervention	2	2

prosecuted was placed in secure provision. The focus in the structured regimes in which they lived was on controlling their behaviours but none of
the young people had received any direct work on their abusing or violent
behaviour, in spite of the services which were available in the probation
service and elsewhere on work with abusing adults (Barker and Morgan,
1993; Morrison, Erooga and Beckett, 1994). There was very little work on the
extensive problems in their backgrounds and in only one case was a psychiatrist involved. These boys were difficult to engage because they were restless
and often had a short concentration span and a low tolerance for frustration.
They all had enmeshed relationships with their mothers which raised concerns amongst the professionals about the possibility of incest.

Clearly boys in this category are in urgent need of interventions which
do address their abusing behaviour (O'Callaghan and Print, 1994; Vizard,
Monck and Misch, 1995; Monck and New, 1996) and they require constant
challenge to their misogynist views. Until such interventions are provided
the risks posed by these young people are highly likely to reappear when
they leave care. Attention also needs to be paid to the severe disruptions,
parenting deficits and traumatising experiences in their backgrounds
(Skuse et al, 1996) and to the fact that they had often had little exposure to
normal family life and non-exploitative relationships. The placements
which take them would also benefit from consultancy from experienced
professionals for their staff and greater involvement by psychiatrists, probation officers or others with a specialist knowledge of the field.

This analysis shows the importance of making a thorough assessment of
young people entering care so that the best possible placements are found
for them. Some young people can be well managed in ordinary placements but the young people in Category 6 require specialist placements
as do some children in Category 2. The caregivers of children in these two
groups also require more support and consultancy if they are to manage
them satisfactorily and reduce the risks which they pose to others. In
addition, it is clear that at present satisfactory frameworks for practice are
lacking with young people in Categories 3 and 4, the young people who
show sexualised behaviour and those who work as prostitutes, although
the ideas to develop some of these frameworks do exist. The large numbers of young people whose outstanding needs were not met and the
gaps in therapeutic work meant that a basis for recovery had not always
been provided for them. Even more worrying, only one of the young
people who had sexually abused others had received any work directed
at her abusing behaviour.

Now that we have looked at the groups into which the young people
fell in terms of their behaviour and management in placement, we turn to
examine the outcomes for the young people in the study.

SUMMARY

1. The young people in the study were placed in six categories based principally on the sexual behaviours which they displayed in substitute care. Each category required a distinctive type of management and often also of placement.
2. The management of the children was rated on four dimensions. First, it was rated in terms of the supervision they received (high, medium or low) and second, in terms of whether caregivers had successfully modified the young people's general or sexual behaviour during the index placement. The third area of management was whether the young people had any outstanding needs which were not being met, apart from any need for counselling. Finally, we looked to see whether the young people had received any formal therapeutic intervention during the placement.
3. A third (13) of the young people fell into in Category 1 (no problematic sexual behaviours while in the index placement). The management they received was variable. The wider needs of the young people in this group were often ignored because they were not causing any difficulties for professionals or caregivers. Yet many had significant gaps in their education and deep unresolved feelings of loss and rejection with which they needed assistance.
4. Two young people fell into Category 2 (children who were behaviourally disturbed, where the behaviours included sexual self-harm). Both had suffered prolonged sexual abuse at a very young age and were subject to high levels of supervision and attempts to modify their behaviour. In order to be effective, the behaviour management of these children needed to be linked to intensive therapeutic work. Without this there was a high risk of placement breakdown.
5. The 13 young people in Category 3 were prematurely sexualised and lacked appropriate interpersonal boundaries. These children posed a high risk to themselves and some risk to others because they sexualised most forms of contact with other young people and adults and, in some cases, were very sexually active. Nine were girls and over half were in residential care.

   For most of the young people in this category the levels of supervision provided were very low and as a result they were at risk outside placement. Attempts were made to modify the behaviour of fewer than a third of them and under a quarter had their needs met, although some examples of good practice were found. These young people needed to learn how to keep themselves safe, to separate physical affection from sexual contact and to be nurtured in non-sexual ways.

6. Four children were placed in the fourth category of young people who were involved in exploitative sexual activity, three of whom worked as prostitutes during the index placement. As well as the dangers to themselves, they placed others at risk through procuring children from placements for their clients.

    Very low levels of supervision were provided for these young people, interventions to modify their behaviour were unsuccessful and their outstanding needs were not met. All of them absconded frequently.

7. The four young people in Category 5 had sexually abused others in placement. Clearly, these children posed a high risk to others. Three were in foster care and one in a children's home. Considerable attempts had been made to modify their behaviour and three quarters had their outstanding needs met. Overall, the management provided for these young people was better than that provided for the children in Categories 1, 3 and 4.

8. Children in Category 6 were young perpetrators for whom sex and aggression were linked. All four of the young people in this group were boys. Three were in specialist placements with structured regimes designed to contain their abusive behaviour, and one was in foster care. They all received high levels of supervision, for most there was some success in modifying their behaviour and half had their outstanding needs met. However, none of them received any work which focused on their abusing or violent behaviour. Without such interventions the risks they posed to others were likely to reappear when they left care.

9. This analysis shows the importance of making a thorough assessment of young people entering care so that the best possible placements are found for them. Some young people can be well managed in ordinary placements but the young people in Category 6 require specialist placements as do some children in Category 2. The caregivers of children in these two categories also require more support and consultancy if they are to manage them satisfactorily and reduce the risks which they pose to others.

14

OUTCOMES FOR THE
YOUNG PEOPLE

In this chapter the outcomes for the young people in the study are considered on a number of dimensions. Using these dimensions the states of affairs of the young people at the time of interview are analysed in order to compare first, the outcomes of the young people in residential and foster care; second, those of the sexually abused and abusing children; and third, those of the six groupings described in Chapter 13. Overall outcomes, with a division of the sample into the young people with "good", "fair" and "poor" outcomes, were also constructed and these are also used to make this set of comparisons.

At the time of the interviews, as we have seen, a third of the young people had been in the index placement for less than six months, over a third (38%) between six months and a year and the remainder for over one year. The average age at the time of interview was 15 years 5 months for those in residential care and 14 years for the children in foster care. At that point the outcomes, or more accurately the "states of affairs", of the young people in the index placements in the sample were considered in relation to seven dimensions, which were considered to be particularly relevant to assessing outcomes for sexually abused and abusing young people in substitute care. The outcome dimensions which were used include direct outcomes for the children, descriptions of the young people's behaviours, areas of management which were considered instrumental to good outcomes and, in addition, the young people's impact on others. The latter was included to ensure that the outcome patterns would reflect not only the child's progress but also the extent to which they had caused harm to other children in the placement.

The first outcome dimension was the child's sexual safety in the index placement. Young people were not considered to have been safe if they had been sexually abused, if they had been working regularly as prostitutes or if their sexualised behaviour or high levels of sexual activity had made them vulnerable to sexual exploitation by others, had involved them with multiple partners or if they became pregnant under the age of 16. Looked at this way a third of the sample had not been safe (12 girls and one boy). The second dimension concerned whether the young person had sexually abused others during the period of the index placement. As we have already seen, seven of the young people in the sample did so (four girls and three boys).

The third dimension was whether the young person had had an adverse impact on other children in the placement, apart from that caused by sexually abusing behaviour. More than a third of the young people (14) did have such an adverse impact for a variety of reasons. The reasons included procuring young people for the purposes of prostitution, placing other children in situations of high sexual risk, assaults by the young person and gang reprisals. The fourth dimension of outcome, which was referred to in Chapter 13, was whether the young people had any outstanding needs which had not been met, apart from any need for counselling about their past abuse. Almost two thirds of the young people (26) did so. Such needs included help with enuresis, with unresolved grief about the early death of a mother and for containment in placement. For a worryingly high number of the young people (14) the outstanding gap identified was for a basic education. This meant that only just over a third of the children (35%) had had their needs reasonably well met in the index placement.

The fifth dimension was whether the young people's behaviour improved in placement. The behaviour of 29 of the young people did improve while in the index placement. The sixth area considered was whether the young people's sexual behaviours, if any, were well managed. Thirteen children showed no sexual behaviours during the placement. The sexual behaviours of 12 of the remaining 27 children were well dealt with, leaving more than half where the management in this area was inadequate. The seventh and final dimension was the level of engagement established by the caregiver with the child, as described in Chapter 11. In the case of 29 young people, their caregivers had established a high (10) or medium (19) level of engagement with them. Thus, high or medium levels of engagement were experienced by 73% of the children in the study.

The outcome dimensions for the whole sample are shown in Table 1

RELATIONSHIPS BETWEEN THE OUTCOME DIMENSIONS

Of course the outcome dimensions do not simply stand alone. Some are interrelated. Using two-tailed Fisher's Exact tests a number of the dimensions were found to be statistically significantly related, where $p<0.05$. There was a significant relationship between improvement in the young people's general behaviour and four other dimensions. When children

Table 1   Outcomes for the young people in the interview sample

During the index placement	Yes		No	
	No.	%	No.	%
1. The child was safe from sexual risks	27	67	13	33
2. The child did not sexually abuse others	33	82	7	18
3. The child did not have an adverse impact on other children in placement	26	65	14	35
4. The child's outstanding needs were met	14	35	26	65
5. The child's behaviour improved	29	73	11	27
6. The child's sexual behaviour was well managed	12/27	44	15/27	56
7. High or medium caregiver engagement	29	73	11	27

showed improved behaviour there was an increased likelihood that their needs had been met, their sexual behaviour well managed, that they had not had an adverse impact on other young people and had themselves been safe.

Those young people who had enjoyed high to medium levels of engagement by their caregivers were significantly more likely than others to have had their sexual behaviours well managed and to have had their major needs met in placement. Two further findings about significant correlations between the dimensions concerned children who sexually abused others. The young abusers were likely to have had their needs met and for their sexual behaviour to have been well managed. These connections signal that on the whole the care and management of the abusing children was of a high standard. Indeed, as we shall see later, it was better than that provided for those who had only been abused.

OUTCOMES FOR THE YOUNG PEOPLE IN RESIDENTIAL AS COMPARED TO FOSTER CARE

Using these dimensions we can explore whether there were any differences in outcome for the young people according to the type of substitute care provided. In making these comparisons it must be emphasised that there was considerable diversity within the foster and more particularly the residential care placements in the sample, since in the latter case we have grouped together ordinary children's homes, secure accommodation and specialised facilities. In addition, as we have seen, the young people in residential care in our study were older and more behaviourally and emotionally disturbed than those in foster care. Bearing these caveats in mind a number of differences did emerge. A higher proportion of the children in residential care (71%) as compared to foster care (58%) had outstanding needs which were not met while they were in placement. Also, whilst 84% of the young people in foster care showed improved behaviour, the corresponding proportion of children in residential care was lower at 62%. Similarly, the sexual behaviour of a higher proportion of the children in foster care (over half) was well managed than was the case in residential care (over a third). High to medium levels of engagement on the part of the caregiver were a feature of the experiences of slightly more of the children in foster homes than of those in residential care. Interestingly, slightly more of the young people in residential care were safe from sexual risks as compared with those in foster care. Finally, a higher proportion of fostered young people sexually abused others, but this is to be expected because foster care was the placement of choice for abusing children, whilst the abusers who were placed in residential care were mostly in settings which provided high levels of monitoring. These differences are shown in Table 2.

Using the Looking After Children Assessment and Action records (Parker *et al*, 1991; Ward, 1995) with 33 of the 40 young people in the sample a number of other differences emerged between the care provided in residential and foster settings, which may have a bearing on the differences in outcomes for these children. Whilst the educational disruption already suffered by children in each sector was similar (over half of all the children had had five or more unscheduled changes of school) we found

Table 2 Outcomes for the young people in residential and foster care

During the index placement	Foster care (N=19)		Residential care (N=21)	
	No.	%	No.	%
1. The child was safe from sexual risks	12	63	15	71
2. The child did not sexually abuse others	2	9	5	26
3. The child did not have an adverse impact on other children in placement	8	38	6	32
4. The child's outstanding needs were met	8	42	6	29
5. The child's behaviour improved	16	84	13	62
6. The child's sexual behaviour was well managed	7/13	54	5/14	36
7. High or medium caregiver engagement	15	79	14	67

particular educational disadvantage among the children in residential care, with most of the exclusions and poor school attendance occurring in this sector. This was despite the high number of abusing children with learning difficulties, most of whom were in foster care. It was also the young people in residential care who were most likely to say that there was no adult who discussed their school progress with their teachers. The adolescents in residential care also took more risks with their health in terms of drug use and smoking than those in foster care, they had fewer hearing and sight tests and recommendations by their doctors had more often been ignored. Sex education and the provision of information about contraception was also given a lower priority in residential than in foster care.

The children in foster care were much more likely to say that they got on well with other young people in the placement (50%) when compared with those in residential care (19%), but on the other hand those in children's homes had more friends in the care system than did fostered young people. Children in residential care had the advantage of more contact with family members when compared with those in foster homes, but the children in residential care were less likely to be attached to their caregivers and missed out on physical affection from them. Finally, more children in residential than foster care described themselves as having serious emotional or behavioural problems.

OUTCOMES FOR THE SEXUALLY ABUSED CHILDREN COMPARED TO THOSE FOR THE SEXUALLY ABUSING CHILDREN

Using our outcome dimensions the states of affairs of the 18 young people who had only been sexually abused were compared with those for the 22 children who had sexually abused other children at any stage, all but four of whom had also been sexually abused. Similar proportions were safe in placement, and by definition none of the children in the abused only group had sexually abused another child, whilst almost a third of the abusers had done so in the index placement. On the other hand it is interesting to note that a considerably greater proportion of the sexually abused young people (44%) had an adverse impact on others in their placement as compared with the abusing children (27%). Account needs to be taken of this broader risk to other children when sexually abused young people are placed.

As many as four fifths of the sexually abused children had outstanding needs which were not met in placement as compared with half of the abusing young people. General behavioural improvement was only slightly more evident among the abusing children but good management of sexual behaviour was considerably more often a feature of the placements of the abusing children (64%) than of the abused young people (23%). Similarly, a noticeably higher proportion of the abusing children had caregivers who were well engaged with them (86%) than was the case with the abused young people (56%). These differences are shown in Table 3.

OUTCOMES OF THE YOUNG PEOPLE BY CATEGORY

The outcomes of the young people were also analysed in relation to the six categories of young people described in Chapter 13 to see if any major differences emerged. Fairly high proportions of young people in Categories 3, 4 and 5 were not safe sexually, that is the young people who showed sexualised behaviour, those involved in exploitative sexual activity, including prostitution, and those who sexually abused others in placement. The young people who sexually abused others were from Category 2 (the behaviourally disturbed young people) and Categories 5 and 6 which contained the sexual abusers and young perpetrators. The children who had an adverse impact on other young people came especially from Category 4, the young people involved in prostitution (who not infrequently procured other children from their placements), Category 6, the young perpetrators (who often displayed aggressive and violent behaviour to other young people) and the first category of non-symptomatic children.

Table 3 Outcomes for the sexually abused and the abusing young people

During the index placement	Sexually abused children (N=18)		Sexually abusing children (N=22)	
	No.	%	No.	%
1. The child was safe from sexual risks	11	61	15	68
2. The child did not sexually abuse others	7	32	0	0
3. The child did not have an adverse impact on other children in placement	6	27	8	44
4. The child's outstanding needs were met	3	17	11	50
5. The child's behaviour improved	12	67	17	77
6. The child's sexual behaviour was well managed	3/13	23	9/14	64
7. High or medium caregiver engagement	10	56	19	86

The highest proportions of children whose needs had not been met were those in Category 4 (prostitutes) and 3 (young people showing sexualised behaviour), closely followed by the non-symptomatic children (Category 1). (It is also interesting to note that the young people who had least been able to talk about the abuse or other painful events were the young people involved in prostitution and the adolescents showing sexualised behaviour.) On the other hand, behavioural improvements were most evident among the abusing children followed by the non-symptomatic children and the young perpetrators. Good management of sexual behaviour was particularly a feature of the placements of the young perpetrators and the abusing children. Finally, high levels of caregiver engagement with the young people were particularly evident in the placements of groups 5 and 6, the sexually abusing children and young perpetrators, who were often in specialised foster or residential settings, and to a lesser extent with the non-symptomatic children.

OVERALL OUTCOMES

Overall outcomes for the young people were also constructed. Criteria for a division of the sample into "good", "fair" and "poor" were established using the first six dimensions described. The criteria for inclusion in the "good" outcome group was that the child had been safe and had not sexually abused other children or that the placement had helped to make the child safe or reduce any abusing behaviour; that the child's needs were met and that, aside from sexually abusing behaviour, the child had not had an adverse impact on other children. The young people whose outcomes were considered to be "fair" had either been safe or if at some point not safe the placement had helped to make them safer; any incident of sexually abusing behaviour had been well managed; and either their behaviour had improved although some needs were unmet or whilst their main needs were met their behaviour did not improve. Children in the "poor" outcome group had not been safe in placement or had sexually abused others, and/ or their behaviour had not improved and their needs had not been met.

Of the whole sample a quarter were in the good outcome group, 42% in the fair outcome group whilst a third had poor outcomes. A case from each group will be described to illustrate the differences between the groups.

Case Example from the Good Outcome Group

Roy and his brother were brought up by their single mother until he was 9 years old when his mother, who had mental health difficulties, was no longer able to manage them both. Roy had witnessed his mother's sexual activity and possibly been involved by her in it. He said that his grand-mother had sexually abused him. What was clear was that he had been prematurely sexualised. At the age of 7 years there were three incidents where Roy had sexually abused girls in his school and when placed in foster care with his younger brother it was evident that sexual activity between them was commonplace. By the age of 10 Roy had had a number of placement breakdowns and his very sexualised behaviour made him a difficult child to place. The social services department were running out of ideas when they asked one of their experienced foster carers to take him for a time-limited assessment. In this index placement the carers supervised his behaviour closely and the risks to others were reduced because all the other children in the family were considerably older than Roy. He settled so well that the family agreed to take him long-term. His behaviour im-proved, he attended school regularly, made good progress and got in-volved in local activities. There was only one further incident of abusing behaviour when Roy was staying with another family in which the adults did not offer the close supervision exercised by Roy's foster carers.

Case Example from the Fair Outcome Group

Peter had been sexually abused by his father from at least the age of 7 years. The abuse included anal penetration. He also witnessed a great deal of violence to his mother by his father. By the time he was 12 he was beyond control, not attending school and setting fires. He was also bulimic. He settled very well in his first foster placement where the foster mother was sensitive to his high need for nurture appropriate to his immature stage of emotional development. In this family Peter first dis-closed his sexual abuse. Unfortunately, this was only a short-term place-ment and he moved to the index placement with another foster carer where his needs were not well met. He was given a lot of freedom but little warmth and his foster mother had real difficulty in facing his back-ground of abuse. She made it clear that this was something he would need to get over but should not talk about. His behaviour did improve in foster care although in school his difficult behaviour escalated. After one incident in which Peter and another boy damaged some park benches the foster mother requested his removal.

Case Example from the Poor Outcome Group

Lucy witnessed violence between her parents and was aged 5 years when her father left the family. She was rejected and scapegoated by her mother

who saw her as being like her father. At the age of 13 she was sexually
abused by a babysitter who was a boy of 15. She was suspended several
times from school for violence and verbal abuse and later excluded. After
her mother beat her with a stick she was accommodated first in a foster
family and then in a children's home, which was the index placement.
Lucy made two suicide attempts in the home, on one occasion drinking
washing-up liquid. She was also subject to vicious bullying by two boys
who tried to set light to her clothes. She would dress provocatively and lie
in wait for any new boy joining the home. Her basic need for safety was
not met in this placement and nor was her need for an understanding
relationship with a member of staff and for reasonable peer relationships.
Not surprisingly her behaviour did not improve. Indeed, her mother was
sufficiently concerned about Lucy being bullied to remove her from the
children's home.

Now that some case examples have been given of children in each of the
outcome groups, we can examine whether there were any differences between the overall outcomes for young people in residential and foster care.
This comparison showed that more of the children in foster care than
residential settings had good outcomes and fewer (half as many) had poor
outcomes. The better performance of foster care is particularly interesting
when we remember that the majority of the abusing children were placed
in this sector and these were the young people who might have been
expected to display most problems. On the other hand, account needs to be
taken of the fact that the young people in residential care showed higher
levels of disturbance and their average age at interview was higher than the
children in foster care. These findings are shown in Table 4.

A comparison of overall outcomes for the sexually abused and the
sexually abusing young people showed that three times as many of the
sexually abusing children had good outcomes and slightly fewer had
poor outcomes than was the case with sexually abused young people.
Part of this difference may be related to the slightly higher use of foster
care for sexually abusing young people, 59% of whom were in foster
placements as compared to 48% in the interview sample as a whole. The
small number of children in the sexually abused group with good

Table 4 Overall outcomes by placement type

	Foster care (N=19)		Residential care (N=21)	
	No.	%	No.	%
Good	6	32	4	19
Fair	9	47	8	38
Poor	4	21	9	43

outcomes and the large number with poor outcomes suggests that the management and placements currently offered to abused young people fall far short of meeting their needs. The overall outcomes are shown in Table 5.

When the overall outcomes were looked at in relation to the six categories of young people some interesting differences emerged. The best outcomes were found in Category 5 which contained the children who sexually abused others. The worst outcomes, as might be expected from our previous discussion, were in Category 4 (young people who worked as prostitutes) but more than half of the adolescents showing sexualised behaviour also had poor outcomes. These differences are shown in Table 6.

Better overall outcomes were also found to be significantly related to those placements where there was a high or medium level of caregiver engagement with the young people ($p<0.03$). A relationship also emerged, which did not quite reach statistical significance ($p<0.11$), between the provision of therapeutic help and overall outcomes. The young people who had received some therapeutic intervention had a higher proportion of good outcomes (32%) when compared with the children who had no such help (17%) but they also had more poor outcomes. Of those who had received such help 41% had a poor outcome as compared with 22% of the other children. This may be because the more difficult young people were more often referred for help. A more straightforward relationship, which again did not quite reach the level of significance

Table 5 Overall outcomes by background of abuse or abusing behaviour

| | Sexually abused (N=18) | | Sexually abusing (N=22) | |
	No.	%	No.	%
Good	2	11	8	36
Fair	9	50	8	36
Poor	7	39	6	28

Table 6 Overall outcomes by category of child

| | Category 1. Non-symptomatic (N=13) | | Category 2. Disturbed (N=2) | | Category 3. Sexualised (N=13) | | Category 4. Prostitutes (N=4) | | Category 5. Sexually abusing (N=4) | | Category 6. Young Perpetrators (N=4) | |
	No.	%	No.	%	No.	%	No.	%	No.	%	No.	%
Good	3	23	1	50	2	15	0	0	3	75	1	25
Fair	9	69	0	0	4	31	1	25	1	25	2	50
Poor	1	8	1	50	7	54	3	75	0	0	1	25

(p<0.18), was found in respect of whether children had talked about their abuse or associated events to their caregiver or social worker. Of those who had been able to talk about important past events 39% had good overall outcomes, as compared with only 14% of those who had not spoken. Fewer of those who had been able to talk in this way (22%) had poor outcomes when compared with those who had not been able to share details of the past (41%).

THE YOUNG PEOPLE'S VIEWS OF THE PLACEMENTS

In addition to considering outcomes from the point of view of the care-givers and the social workers whose accounts informed the ratings just described, we asked the young people themselves how satisfied they had been with the index placement. Half of them said that they were very satisfied and almost a third (32%) that they were satisfied, whilst 9% each reported that they were unsatisfied or very unsatisfied. Thus four fifths were satisfied or very satisfied and only a fifth unsatisfied or very un-satisfied. When we divided these responses according to the type of place-ment higher satisfaction rates were found for children in foster care, with 64% of the young people very satisfied with these placements as compared with only 39% in residential care. More dissatisfaction was shown by the young people in residential care, 28% of whom were unsatisfied or very unsatisfied as compared with only 7% in foster care. The responses of the young people were in line with those which emerged from our overall outcome ratings. Their views of the placements are shown in the Table 7.

This analysis shows that better overall outcomes were achieved by the young people who were in foster placements rather than in residential care and that better overall outcomes were achieved when caregivers displayed high to medium levels of engagement with the young people whom they looked after. In addition, more of the sexually abusing chil-dren had good outcomes than was the case with the abused young people, probably partly because more were placed in foster homes or in specialist residential care where the caregivers were well engaged with

Table 7 Child satisfaction by type of placement

	Foster care (%)	Residential care (%)
Very satisfied	64	39
Satisfied	29	33
Unsatisfied	0	17
Very unsatisfied	7	11

them and their difficulties were recognised and addressed. The worst outcomes were evident in relation to the young people who were involved in prostitution and those who displayed sexualised behaviour.

SUMMARY

1. The outcomes of the young people in the index placements in the sample were considered in relation to seven dimensions. The first was the child's safety from sexual risks, the second was whether the children had sexually abused others, and the third whether the young person had had an adverse impact on other children, apart from any sexual abuse by them. The fourth dimension was whether the children had any outstanding unmet needs, apart from counselling about the abuse. The fifth dimension was improvement in behaviour and the sixth considered whether the young people's sexual behaviour (if any) was well managed. The level of engagement shown by the caregivers to the children was the final dimension.

2. Using these dimensions we found that more children in foster than in residential care had their outstanding needs met, showed behavioural improvement and received good management of their sexual behaviour. In addition, slightly more of the children in foster care experienced high to medium levels of caregiver engagement than did those in residential care, although safety from sexual risks was slightly higher in residential than foster care.

3. More of the abusers than the sexually abused children had their outstanding needs met, were provided with good management of their sexual behaviour and had caregivers who were well engaged with them. Similar proportions of both groups of children were safe in placement but more of the abused young people had an adverse impact on others as compared with the abusers.

4. Outcomes were examined according to the six categories devised for the sample. The children who were not safe from sexual risks were predominantly the adolescents showing sexualised behaviour, the young people who were involved in prostitution and the abusers. The young people who had had a negative impact on other children, not involving abusing behaviour, were the young people who worked as prostitutes, the young perpetrators and the non-symptomatic children. The highest proportions of children whose needs had not been met were the young people with sexualised behaviour, those involved in prostitution and the non-symptomatic children.

    Good management of sexual behaviour and high levels of caregiver engagement were features of the placements of the abusers and the young perpetrators. Finally, behaviour improvements were most evident among the abusers, the young perpetrators and the non-symptomatic children.

5. Using the first six dimensions, overall outcomes for the young people were also constructed. Of the sample, a quarter had good outcomes, 42% fair and a third had poor outcomes. A comparison of children in the two major care sectors showed that more of the children in foster than residential care had good outcomes (32% as compared with 19%) and fewer had poor outcomes (21% as compared with 43%). The better performance of foster care is interesting in view of the fact that many of the abusing children, who might have been expected to display most problems, had been placed in this sector.

6. Three times as many of the sexually abusing children had good outcomes and slightly fewer had poor outcomes than was the case with the sexually abused young people.

7. When these overall outcomes were analysed according to the categories of young people in the sample, the best outcomes were found for the young abusers. The worst outcomes were evident among the young people who were involved in prostitution and those who showed sexualised behaviour.

8. Better overall outcomes were found to be significantly related to those placements where caregivers were well engaged with the young people whom they looked after. Good outcomes were also particularly evident among children who had received therapeutic help during the placement and who had talked about their abuse or associated events, and these latter relationships approached statistical significance.

9. Four fifths of the young people said that they were satisfied or very satisfied with their placements and a fifth were unsatisfied or very unsatisfied. Higher satisfaction rates were found for children in foster care, with 64% of the young people very satisfied with these placements as compared with only 39% in residential care.

15

CONCLUSIONS

This research project was undertaken to provide reliable and valid information about an extremely vulnerable group of young people. The subjects of our study had not only aroused concern because of sexual abuse or sexual behaviour that endangered others, they had also had to be removed from their own families and looked after in state care. By studying the records of a large sample of such young people and through more intensive interviews with a smaller number of them and their caregivers, we hoped to shed light on their needs and how these needs were met in the care system. The study focused most closely on the issues of how sexual behaviour was manifested and managed and to what extent vulnerable children were protected and their wider needs addressed. This involved examining the mix of children within placements and the interventions provided for them. We were also concerned with the needs of caregivers for support and training.

In reviewing the results of our research, a number of themes stand out. Of particular importance for policy and practice are the differences between the looked after sexually abused or abusing children and other children in care; issues about the placement, management and mix of child abusers and sexually abused children, including the provision of therapeutic intervention; and the need to distinguish between different sub-groups of sexually abused and abusing young people in substitute care. These themes and issues are discussed below.

DEFINITIONAL AMBIGUITIES

Sexual behaviours generally occur outside the public gaze and those which come to attention are subject to variable interpretations. Similar behaviour may be defined as normal adolescent sexual exploration, problematic sexual behaviour or pathological activity depending on the viewpoint of the adult who discovers it. There are also complex definitional issues about what is interpreted as sexual abuse and, even more so, sexually abusing behaviour. Throughout this study we have grappled with these definitional issues and the classifications which we made for some behaviours might be open to dispute. There can be a fine line, for example, between overtly sexualised behaviour and sexually abusing activity. These definitional difficulties bring home the complexity of the task facing caregivers and social workers who deal with sexualised behaviour in substitute care.

Overall, there was a tendency for social workers and some caregivers to normalise the sexual behaviours of young people who put themselves at risk and to develop rather high thresholds for taking action in relation to them. Sexually abusing behaviour in placements was seen as problematic and received a rapid response. In contrast, the behaviours which occurred *outside the care setting*, such as indiscriminate sexual activity and prostitution, were less visible and received correspondingly less attention.

SEXUALLY ABUSED AND ABUSING CHILDREN ARE MORE DISADVANTAGED THAN OTHERS IN STATE CARE

Notwithstanding such definitional dilemmas, records are kept on the numbers of children on the child protection register for reasons of sexual abuse. No such records are kept by local authorities on the numbers of sexually abused and/or abusing children who are looked after by them. It was therefore interesting to find from our case file data that 38% of a large group of newly admitted children had experienced an incident of sexual abuse and/or had shown abusing behaviour at some stage, and that in the over 10 age group this rose to 47%. However, information such as this is only useful if its implications are understood.

As would be expected, girls and older children were over-represented amongst those who had been sexually abused. Over and above this, using tests of statistical significance, we found that the abused/abusing children were more disadvantaged than other looked after children in a number of ways. They were significantly more likely to have been placed on the child protection register (under any category), to have had a previous care experience and to have spent longer in care than their non-abused counterparts. In addition, tests of statistical significance showed that the sexually abused/abusing children were more likely than the others to have had severe educational problems, (that is serious behaviour problems at school, being bullied, non-attendance and school exclusion) and to have experienced rejection and disrupted parenting (that is multiple separations from their main parent, a parent who had multiple partners and care which adversely affected their emotional development) and to have been seen as troublesome (that is serious behaviour problems and being beyond control at home). In addition, the abused and/or abusing girls were more likely than others to have become pregnant.

These findings suggest that sexual abuse to or by children when combined with placement in care may often be a marker for family situations which in a variety of ways fall far short of those which are optimal for children's development. The disadvantages in the backgrounds of the sexually abused and/or abusing children would indicate that they will have particular needs when they enter care. Such needs, however, may be missed since fewer than one in five will be looked after because of the sexual abuse to them or the abusing behaviour which they have shown. Most will enter care for other reasons.

Were the experiences in care of sexually abused or abusing children any different from those of other residents? Although the information on the files was somewhat limited, differences did emerge. More of the sexually abused and/or abusing children than the others were on care orders and fewer were placed with a sibling. The abused and/or abusing children had more moves in care in the first six months after admission, were more often moved between the residential and foster care sectors and had slightly higher rates of placement breakdown than the other looked after children. Once in care significantly more of the abused and/or abusing children showed new behaviour problems when compared with their non-abused peers. In addition, there were risks which were specific to the sexually abused and/or abusing children. A considerable proportion showed sexualised behaviour, were involved in prostitution, sexually abused another child or were themselves re-abused.

CHILDREN WHO SEXUALLY ABUSE OTHERS HAVE THE MOST DIFFICULT BACKGROUNDS

It is clear that the looked after sexually abused and abusing children emerge as an especially disadvantaged and behaviourally demanding group when compared with other children in care. What then of the differences between those known only to have been victims of abuse and those who had abused others, whether or not they had themselves been abused? As expected, boys predominated among the child abusers and girls were in the majority among abused children. Overall, the child abusers were found to have more difficult backgrounds than the children who had only been abused. This is not entirely surprising when it is considered that most of the child abusers had been sexually abused in addition to showing abusing behaviour.

The child abusers had experienced more adversities in the past than the abused children. They were significantly more likely than the abused children to have witnessed the sexual activity of their parents and to have shown inappropriate sexualised behaviour. The parents of the child abusers had also had significantly more psychiatric problems than those of the sexually abused children. Moreover, twice as many of the abusers had learning difficulties as compared with the victimised children.

Overall, more professional concern was expressed about the child abusers than about the victimised children, with a higher proportion of the abusers having been subject to statutory proceedings and to child protection registration than the sexually abused children. In keeping with this more pessimistic assessment of the problems facing the child abusers, they had been moved more often than the abused children in the first four months of care, either because they were more difficult to place or because they became so as a result of their abusing behaviour. Plans for long-term care or adoption were also made in relation to more of the abusers than the abused children.

The standardised measures of children's emotional and behavioural problems showed that whilst almost two thirds of the abused children in the interview sample were in the clinical or borderline clinical range as many as 94% of the child abusers were in this range. The child abusers also demonstrated significantly higher levels of social problems, attention deficits and aggressive behaviour than the victims. Both groups were therefore highly disturbed, but the levels of disturbance were higher among the child abusers.

These data show that children in care who have sexually abused others stand out as children who come from especially highly sexualised backgrounds and who have been exposed to a variety of sexual activities. They excite high levels of professional concern and their future is more likely to be envisaged in terms of long-term care than the abused children. However, as will be shown, because of the extent of their difficulties they are directed into the more specialised placements with highly skilled caregivers.

FAILURE TO USE CHILD PROTECTION PROCEDURES AND THE CRIMINAL JUSTICE SYSTEM

Our scrutiny of the casefiles revealed the large number of incidents of sexual abuse or abusing behaviour which came to the attention of social services departments but which were not dealt with under child protection procedures. Child protection procedures were enacted much less vigorously when sexual abuse *by a child* came to light than when abuse by an adult was uncovered. Twice as many incidents of sexual abuse by an adult had been subject to an investigation as compared with those by children. These low levels of investigation were reflected in relatively low levels of case conferences. Whereas a child protection case conference was held in respect of 45% of incidents of sexual abuse by an adult, the equivalent proportion of conferences held after the discovery of sexual abuse by a child was only 29%. The discovery of children's abusing behaviour very rarely led to registration.

In line with the evidence from other studies (Department of Health, 1994, 1995; Farmer and Owen, 1995; Gibbons *et al*, 1995; Sharland *et al*, 1996) we found that very few of the adult perpetrators were prosecuted and just 7% were found guilty. Although more of the child abusers acknowledged their actions than did their adult counterparts, there was only one prosecution. The low level of prosecutions undertaken with children shows that diversion from the criminal justice system was widely practised. It was interesting that in residential homes incidents of physical assault or damage to property were routinely reported to the police. As a result, young people were rapidly criminalised for assault or damage to property but those who had committed even aggressive sexual assaults were left with no criminal record. This allowed young people involved in serious offences to continue to deny the significance of their abusive behaviour and to avoid treatment.

KEEPING CHILDREN SAFE IN PLACEMENTS

When a new admission to care was being considered, little attention was given to assessing whether the child would be a good match with other children already in the placement or whether the child or other young people would be safe. Indeed, there was no reliable mechanism to ensure that these issues were fully deliberated. The placing social worker would often have an incomplete knowledge of other children in the setting, and the head of home or foster carers who did have this knowledge would not always refuse an unsuitable new admission, either because in the case of some heads of home they did not have the power to refuse, or because they felt constrained by concerns about the consequences of refusal. In contrast, some specialist residential placements had admissions panels which gave extended consideration to the suitability of any new applicant before agreeing to placement. In spite of these gaps in placing procedures, it was clear that child abusers were generally placed in foster care or specialist residential facilities because of the risks which they posed to others. Clearly, there was less concern about protecting the sexually abused young people from other children since most were placed in residential homes.

However, such placement planning was vitiated by the extensive gaps in the information passed on to the caregivers. Information about sexual abuse in the backgrounds of more than two fifths of the abused children was not conveyed to caregivers and the fact that young people had sexually abused others was not passed on in over half of the relevant cases. Indeed, information was lost at each stage of the process. The paucity of investigations meant that not all files provided good quality information. In addition, when files were not fully read by social workers the information which was in them was not available for use. This was particularly an issue when there was a change of worker. At times social workers did not pass on information about children's backgrounds of sexual abuse, either because of a mistaken view about confidentiality, a lack of appreciation of the risks involved or to secure placements. Further to this, social workers sometimes minimised the facts which they did know, so that caregivers received bland accounts of serious events. In addition, even when incidents of abuse were recorded there was a lack of detail on file about these events. For example, there was no information on file about the nature of the abuse suffered by almost half of the victimised children in the case file sample or about its duration in over two thirds of the cases.

This study shows that half of the sexually abused young people abused another child at some stage, so the experience of sexual abuse can be taken as an important risk factor in the later development of sexually abusing behaviour. In addition, most of the abuse was of other children in care. It is therefore essential that information about sexual abuse or sexually abusing behaviour is passed on to caregivers. Indeed, the decision as to whether to place a victimised child or a young abuser should depend on the feasibility of providing full supervision and ensuring that high risk children are not left alone with others. Moreover, young perpetrators for whom sex and aggression are linked require controlled settings in which they can be subject to high levels of monitoring.

If fuller information is to be provided to caregivers when children are placed, case files will need to be ordered in a way which makes the retrieval of vital facts easier than at present. It would help if full details of the child's history were kept at the front of the file and regularly updated (see also Monck and New, 1996). Such a history should include an incident checklist, which obliges the social worker to make a note of all allegations of sexual abuse to or by the child, the action taken and whether the child has been involved in prostitution. Other adversities might also be included in any such list. In addition, clearer policies are required which spell out the priority to be given to passing information about children's backgrounds to caregivers in all kinds of settings, including those in residential school and short-term placements. The policies should also clarify that foster carers as well as residential workers are allowed access to the child's case file. It is likely that social services departments will in future face legal challenges from aggrieved caregivers or parents if they have failed to share such vital information.

One important finding about mix was the impact which young people who worked as prostitutes could have on other children in their placements. They initiated others into prostitution and procured other resident children for their clients. Whilst in the second half of the 19th century a considerable proportion of girls were committed to care to rescue them from prostitution, it is possible that more young people are now initiated into prostitution as a result of their stay in care, especially residential care, than are admitted for this reason. In addition, we found that older sexually abused adolescent girls sometimes led younger or more immature abused girls from their placements into situations of high sexual risk, in which the younger children did not have the skills to keep themselves safe. Children were particularly at risk when they absconded with other children from their placements.

The mix of young people in a facility is, in practice, constantly changing. A very large influx of young people at one time can unsettle a stable child group as can a lot of coming and going. There were examples in our study of children who had been making good progress until a major change in the child composition of a children's home occurred, after which their behaviour deteriorated rapidly. However, there were also young people, who after leaving one residential home where they had been out of control, made good progress in another unit where they were no longer the oldest child and the group leader, and where the rules were sufficiently strict to contain them.

Three groups of children who present high risks to others in placement stood out. Two have already been mentioned. The first are young people with a background of sexual abuse or abusing behaviour. As we have seen, they require careful placement planning, full information to the caregivers and high levels of monitoring. The second group are young people who become involved in prostitution. They require a rapid response and a placement which will isolate them from their networks of contacts. The third category are sibling groups when one or more children have been sexually abused over a period of time, because in this situation there will be a high risk of continuing sexual activity between the siblings in placement.

Were there any lessons about how young people's safety while in care settings could be maximised? The principal messages from the study have just been rehearsed: more thought is needed at the time of placement about the match between the needs of the child to be placed and others already in the setting, and the risks which each will pose to the other. At the same time, caregivers require full information about children's backgrounds if they are to be able to decide about the suitability of a placement and plan to keep children safe. More use could also be made of foster care placements where there are no other children or only much older children, and occasionally a single foster mother or same sex residential placement may be needed. In addition, more assistance could be given to foster carers in planning how best to provide high levels of supervision; and practice needs to be developed in children's homes which will enable residential workers to provide higher levels of monitoring and supervision of young people's activities when outside the home. Ideally, all children need some way to communicate their worries if they are placed at risk within care and it was clear that sometimes bullying and sexual harassment had gone unrecognised. The provision of a phone line to an independent agent or to a Children's Rights Officer or regular interviews with children by experienced independent workers designed to discover such difficulties could be of assistance.

THERAPEUTIC INTERVENTIONS

Although three fifths of the children had received some therapeutic work in the past, caregivers and social workers rarely knew any details about the interventions which had been provided. It was of concern to find that at least a quarter of these sessions had ended prematurely because of dissatisfactions occasioned either by an unsympathetic approach or by the allocation of male counsellors to girls abused by men. In general, therapeutic services provided by social services departments were seen as more helpful than those offered in psychiatric settings. Negative experiences of such help made an enduring impact and often led to refusal of later offers of therapeutic assistance.

Over half of the children had never had the opportunity to talk in a therapeutic setting about their experience of sexual abuse and to develop a perspective on it which could form the basis for their recovery. It was clear from our interviews that some young people battled alone with intrusive and painful memories of their victimisation. The situation was even worse for sexually abusing children, only one of whom had ever been offered any work on the behaviour itself. However, there was little evidence in care planning that information about past interventions, or from assessments on the children, were used to assess children's needs for therapeutic interventions.

During the index placement, fewer than a third of the abused young people were provided with work on the abuse itself, whether from specialist counsellors or social workers. Even then, caregivers were not informed about what occurred in the therapeutic sessions, although they were sometimes left to pick up the pieces when children returned to the placement feeling angry or distressed. This was unfortunate because it weakened the ability of young people to integrate the gains from the therapeutic work into their everyday lives.

Forty five per cent of the young people talked to their caregivers or social workers either fully or partially about the abuse or about events connected to it. Only one child talked about her abusing behaviour and even then not in depth. Because sexual abuse is often surrounded by secrecy and stigma, children are often unsure what they can talk about and with whom. We became clear that good practice requires that caregivers, at the time of admission, should always tell children both that they know about their past and that the children can talk about it at any time with them, if they wish to do so. Whilst this will not necessarily lead to an open discussion, it does lay the groundwork for opening up the issue. At the same time caregivers will need training and support to enable them to hear and contain the children's pain.

Children were more likely to talk about their past abuse or associated experiences when they had caregivers who were well engaged with them and when they were receiving or had received therapeutic help. Moreover, the best outcomes in terms of behavioural gains were for those young people who were helped to explore their difficult experiences and feelings *both* in a therapeutic relationship *and* in their everyday lives in care. Where young people were unable to talk about past experiences in their placements, therapeutic intervention could actually lead to an escalation of behaviour problems. Some of the most worrying cases were those where sexually abused young people had no therapeutic input and low levels of engagement by their caregivers. They did not talk about the experiences in their backgrounds and had never had the opportunity to come to terms with their past.

DISAGGREGATION: THE MANAGEMENT AND PLACEMENT NEEDS OF DIFFERENT GROUPS OF CHILDREN

Among the sexually abused and abusing young people distinct subgroups of children emerged with particular management and placement needs. The first of these was that of sexually abusing children.

Child Abusers

As already described, most of the child abusers were boys, the majority had disturbed behaviour and a considerable proportion (41%) had mild to moderate learning difficulties. The majority went into foster care with experienced carers and most of the remainder entered specialist residential placements, including secure provision. Since in over half of the cases the caregivers had not been informed about the young people's abusing

behaviour, and even when information was given it was sometimes minimised, it was impossible for caregivers to prepare adequately to reduce
the risks of a repeat of this behaviour.

Of the 22 young people in our follow-up study who sexually abused
others, 17 did so in substitute care. During the index placement, seven
young people abused other children, four in foster care and three in
residential placements. One other young person sexually abused another
child from foster care in a later placement.

The management of abusers while in placement generally consisted of
tight supervision and monitoring of the child's activities but, with one
exception, there was no work which focused on the abusing behaviour
itself. Nonetheless we found examples of good practice with children
who abuse. These suggest that effective management requires a combination of close supervision, assistance in developing more appropriate interpersonal boundaries and therapeutic intervention. Interventions need
to address past and present sources of distress for the children as well as
their current needs for education and recreational activities. In general,
more directness with the young people about their abusing behaviour
would have been helpful.

The experienced caregivers who looked after the young abusers were
well engaged with them and provided good care. Short-term outcomes for
this group were therefore fairly good, that is their behaviour improved and
their major needs were adequately met. However, little work was provided
on the extensive problems in their backgrounds. Moreover, because of the
lack of therapeutic intervention to address their abusing behaviour there
were very real risks that their abusing behaviour would re-emerge after
discharge from care. Indeed, their caregivers viewed the future for some of
them with considerable trepidation. Their placements would have benefited from consultancy for the caregivers and greater involvement of child
and adolescent psychiatrists with a specialised knowledge of this area
(Department of Health, 1991; National Children's Home, 1992). It was clear
that young perpetrators for whom sex and aggression were linked required
specialist placements which could provide tight supervision and access to
therapeutic help. In view of the risks that the young abusers posed and the
possibility that direct work on their abusing behaviour could have had an
influence on the development of an abusing orientation, the lack of therapeutic intervention was a very worrying gap.

Sexually Abused Children

Almost two thirds of the children who were known only to have been
sexually abused had emotional and behavioural problems which fell into

the clinical or borderline range. In addition, as many as 71% of them rated themselves on the child depression inventory as having suicidal thoughts. Whilst not as behaviourally disturbed as the child abusers, they were nonetheless a very needy group. The patterns of placement for the abused young people were quite different from those for the child abusers. Two sub-groups in particular need to be distinguished. The first is that of adolescents who show sexualised behaviour and the second is that of young people who are involved in prostitution.

Young People Who Showed Sexualised Behaviour

Most of the sexually abused adolescent young people, unlike the child abusers, were placed in children's homes. The young people who evoked concern about their sexual behaviour or activity were predominantly girls. Similar behaviours did arise among boys, but the sexual double standard ensured that professionals focused on the behaviours of girls. Girls who offered themselves sexually to other residents, acted flirtatiously with caregivers and made indiscriminate sexual approaches to the boys and men whom they met raised the anxieties of residential and foster carers. Part of the difficulty appeared to be a lack of confidence in differentiating what was normal behaviour for adolescents and what was not. Part appeared to be the deep feelings raised in caregivers and other professionals by such unbridled sexuality. The sexualised behaviour of girls tended to alarm male caregivers, who were fearful of an allegation being made against them, and this led them to distance themselves from the girls and sometimes their management was punitive.

Inside the placements, most caregivers lacked ideas about how to deal with teenagers who sexualised physical contacts with them and with other young people, but whose backgrounds of neglect and rejection indicated a clear need for affection. Social work advice tended to suggest that these behaviours were a search for emotional support, but few suggestions were made about how to offer alternative nurture to such needy children when they tended to sexualise physical contact. We found that few links were made between these behaviours and the children's earlier experiences of sexual abuse and often of having lived in hyper-sexualised environments.

Outside the placements, caregivers were generally at a loss as to how to deal with teenage girls who were sexually indiscriminate or were involved in sexually exploitative relationships. In general, residential workers did not see their responsibility for the young people in their care as extending beyond the walls of the children's home. Even when they knew that children were going out to engage in high risk behaviour, they would not attempt to stop them, although they might counsel them to desist. If they did not return on time the police would routinely be called. When appropriate limits to these behaviours were not set this replicated the home situations of girls who had never been made safe. However, two children's homes and some of the foster carers had found effective ways to exercise such supervision. Some gave children lifts to their evening engagements, others intervened if relationships were made which looked likely to be harmful and some would go out to look for children who did not return home on time. Clearly such active attempts to monitor young people's behaviour when outside the placement are important, since some abused and over-sexualised children have little idea of how to keep themselves safe.

Over two thirds of these young people received therapeutic intervention to help them with their behavioural and emotional difficulties during the index placement. But because of the uncertainties about how to manage their behaviours their broader needs as vulnerable young people from deprived backgrounds were not well met in placements. Their school attendance was very poor and many had few if any leisure activities.

Four of the 22 girls in the study (almost one in five) became pregnant. Five girls alleged rape or sexual assault. This included two allegations by children in residential care of sexual assault by a resident or staff member and three instances of sexual assault on children whilst they were outside the placement. In all but one case the sexual risks to the young people were presented either by adults outside the placement or by other children, not by staff members (see also Sinclair and Gibbs, 1998).

Effective management was provided when caregivers made it clear that they would do what they could to make the young people safe and provided assistance in the development of stronger interpersonal boundaries. Work was also needed on what kind of touch from others was safe and acceptable and what was not and how to give and receive affection in non-sexualised ways. Many girls also needed basic practical information about how to minimise risks when out alone at night. At the same time needs for nurture had to be addressed, for example by simple bedtime routines in which the young people received positive attention. In addition, it was important that caregivers worked to protect the young person from family members or others who might try to involve them in exploitative sexual activities. Ideally, such work would be accompanied by active attempts to develop good school attendance patterns and leisure activities so that children had access to socially approved ways to gain self-esteem and mastery.

The outcomes for these young people were among the poorest of all the children in the study. Their needs were not well met and they continued to be at considerable risk. Ideas about good practice do exist, as our study shows. It is interesting that interventions which are routinely used with young people after sexual abuse is discovered, including counselling for abused children and teaching them about safe touching, were not provided for these young people. These ideas need to be translated into practice for young people who enter care some time after their abuse has come to light.

Young People Who Were Involved in Prostitution

The only group with poorer outcomes than those of the sexualised adolescents was that of young people who were involved in prostitution. One in five of the young people in the study, both boys and girls, had been involved in or were on the fringes of prostitution during their placements, while absconding or after discharge from care. Three of these children procured other residents from their placements for the purposes of prostitution. Young people who worked the streets were extremely difficult to contain in any care placement, partly because they persistently absconded and partly because caregivers had little success in altering their behaviour. Their behaviours were resistant to change because of the lure of the money and because of the reinforcement provided by their networks of pimps and clients.

There was a real scarcity of ideas about ways to engage and contain these young people apart from incarceration in secure units, and almost no examples of effective practice. Nonetheless, it was clear that a rapid response was required when such behaviour came to light, in order to try to influence the child's choice of associates before the behaviour became entrenched and before too many other children had been drawn in. Careful recording of all the young people's activities and absconding was important, as was a log of all the contacts which staff observed between the young people and their adult associates. Such information needed to be co-ordinated with that held by the police and strategies developed with them aimed at containing the young people. Geographical distance from the child's networks appeared to be an important ingredient of good placements as were active efforts to involve the young person in a suitable school placement and in activities which might provide an alternative source of esteem as well as involvement with a positive peer group. In addition, the children required work on the problems underlying their behaviour. The attachment of a specialist resource worker for each young person involved in prostitution, who would try to maintain contact and offer support and continuity wherever the young person moved, might provide one way forward.

Given these findings it was not surprising that the overall outcomes for the children engaged in prostitution were the worst of all the groups of young people in the study. Their needs were not met, their behaviours did not change and they continued to be at high sexual risk. Moreover, when compared with others, this group of young people had the worst impact on other residents. This highlights a pressing need for the development of practice ideas about engaging and assisting looked after children who become involved in prostitution.

OVERALL OUTCOMES

In spite of the greater difficulties in their backgrounds the overall short-term outcomes for the abusing young people were considerably better than for the children who had only suffered sexual abuse. Indeed, three times as many of the child abusers had good outcomes as compared with the abused young people. The sexual behaviour of the abusers was better managed and their needs better met than was the case with the victimised children. These better outcomes appeared to be linked with the placements provided for the abusers. As we have seen, child abusers were predominantly in foster homes or specialist residential care with caregivers who were well engaged with them and where their difficulties were well recognised. However, their longer-term outcomes were likely to be more problematic. With so little work on their abusing behaviour there was a real risk that some would continue to abuse other children, once away from their supervised placements.

In comparison with the child abusers the young people who had only been sexually abused were not as well managed. Their sexual behaviour was less well dealt with, their caregivers were less strongly engaged with them and, perhaps in consequence, fewer than one in five had their main needs well met. On a more positive note, slightly more of the abused young people (61%) than the abusers (50%) received therapeutic intervention of some sort during the index placement and similar proportions talked about the abuse during the course of the placement (45%).

When the overall outcomes for the sexually abused young people were disaggregated we found that they were poor for over half of the adolescents showing sexualised behaviour and three quarters of the young people who were involved in prostitution.

UNMET NEEDS

In general, sexual abuse in the children's past was either the subject of intense focus by professionals or it got lost and forgotten. It was understandably difficult for practitioners to see the whole child and to view their experience of sexual abuse as one of a number of adversities in their backgrounds. Partly connected with this, caregivers tended to respond to the behaviours which children presented to them rather than to consider their needs based on a full consideration of the child's history. Moreover, opportunities to link the behaviours shown by the children with events from their past were often not taken, so that behaviours were sometimes dealt with in a superficial manner without a deeper understanding being reached.

There were a number of other areas in which children could have been better served while they were being looked after. In particular, more attention could profitably have been paid to the young people's educational needs. Some residential homes and most foster carers gave priority to education and as a result of their efforts children were found school places and given support in the early stages of a return to school. Indeed, such efforts transformed the attendance of at least three children in foster care who had previously enjoyed an unblemished record of non-attendance. However, there were also children's homes where non-attendance at school was accepted as the norm and newly arrived young people quickly established patterns of non-attendance (see also Berridge and Brodie, 1998). Demarcation disputes about whether caregivers or social workers were responsible for finding school places were not uncommon, yet the social workers who prevented caregivers from taking a more active role were usually the practitioners who were inactive on this front. The environments in the homes did not always encourage learning and two fifths of the young people who were still at school said that they possessed no books.

Our research has shown the particular educational disadvantage faced by looked after sexually abused and abusing children, whose attendance and behaviour at school has often been very poor and who may be subject to bullying and gossip about their backgrounds. More work was required to start to remedy this. In addition, young people whose histories include exploitative sexual contacts have a particular need for normal peer relationships and activities in which they can achieve, and schools have the potential to provide these healthy experiences. Research has demonstrated the importance of the contacts made at school in extending the life chances of children from deprived backgrounds (Quinton and Rutter, 1988). Moreover, at the most basic level, children who are in school are generally safe during their time there and are not out on the streets and potentially at risk during the day.

Another area in which more could have been done for these children was in encouraging them to become involved in recreational activities. Residential and foster homes were variable in their attention to this but some appeared to do little to widen children's interests and activities. We found that only two fifths of the young people in our interview sample

(42%) took part in any sports yet more than two fifths said that they would have liked to join a club or learn a new skill.

When children are being looked after social workers sometimes withdraw from active involvement and assume that their needs are being met within the placement. We rated as many as 60% of the social workers as having low engagement with the children, as not attempting to form a relationship with them and rarely meeting the child except at review meetings. In addition, little work was conducted with the children's families. At the other end of the spectrum, some social workers were very important to the young people and worked closely with the caregivers in ensuring that the children's needs were met. Some of the best practice found in the study occurred when good social work backed up committed and purposeful work by the caregivers.

In addition, little priority was given to providing information about sexual relationships and contraceptive advice and it was clear that the children in our sample were very poorly informed about these issues whilst frequently highly sexually active. This is particularly important when we realise that the scores on the locus of control measure showed that the young people in the study believed that events in their lives were more out of their control than do others of their age. If young people are to be able to make choices about their sexuality and about conception the passive approach to sex education adopted by local authorities will need to be rethought. It might be that developments in this area would be assisted by the employment of specialist workers who undertake part of the work and act as consultants and trainers.

IMPLICATIONS FOR POLICY AND PLANNING

Effective work by social workers and caregivers needs to be underpinned by unequivocal policy guidelines and well co-ordinated inter-agency planning. It is evident from the foregoing discussion that social services departments need to develop clear policies about the priority to be given to passing on information about young people's backgrounds of sexual abuse and sexually abusing behaviour at the point of placement. Indeed, our finding that incidents of sexual abuse by young people are rarely formally investigated or conferenced leading to potential minimisation and denial by young abusers, also suggests that policy on the management of such incidents needs to be reviewed. In addition, social service departments together with health and education services, need to develop unambiguous policy statements about where the responsibility for the sexual education of the young people in their care lies, including clear guidelines about who will deliver the appropriate information. It was evident from our study that this was often an area of great confusion for both caregivers and social workers. If caregivers are to be given the responsibility for this sensitive area of work then they need to be offered appropriate training and support.

Joint planning needs to address the shortfalls identified in the provision of education, particularly for sexually abused and abusing young people looked after in residential settings. Our research suggests that educational difficulties for this group of children had often been apparent at a much younger age. Social service and education departments need to work closely together to find constructive ways of managing early patterns of disruptive behaviour and non-school attendance in order to pre-empt more serious later problems, as well as addressing those later difficulties when they arise.

In addition to the deficits identified in planning for the young people's educational needs, gaps in provision of services were also evident in relation to arrangements for therapeutic help for both sexually abused and abusing young people. As discussed earlier, fewer than half of the sexually abused young people and only one of the young abusers had ever received help with the consequences of the abuse or the origins of their abusing behaviour, despite the high levels of disturbed behaviour in both groups. Current thinking is that all sexually abused and abusing children need at least a thorough assessment of their need for such specialist therapeutic help. It would be helpful if social services and health departments developed joint strategies which ensured that such assessments were routinely undertaken at the point of entry into care and subsequent placement. Joint planning is also essential in order to ensure that the requisite therapeutic resources are available. The inadequacy of the therapeutic services offered to the young abusers in the study clearly needs particular attention.

In addition to the provision of sufficient good quality therapeutic provision there is a need for the development of training and support for caregivers and residential workers to help them to provide the necessary well-informed, accepting and protective emotional environments in which therapeutic gains can be consolidated.

DIFFERENCES IN THE QUALITY OF CARE PROVIDED IN RESIDENTIAL AND FOSTER CARE

Whilst most of the young abusers were placed in foster care the preferred placement for those who had committed aggressive sexual assaults was in a specialised residential setting. Similarly, although two thirds of the sexually abused young people were placed in residential care, the other third entered a foster home. It will be recalled that our residential care category covered a variety of placements from ordinary children's homes to secure units and specialist provision.

The young people in residential care in our study had higher total behavioural and emotional problem scores on the measures used than those in foster care. Significantly more of them were clinically depressed and had low self-esteem scores when compared with those in foster care. The children in residential care also had more somatic complaints and suicidal ideation than their counterparts in foster homes. On the Looking After Children Assessment and Action records more than half of the young people in residential care admitted to having deliberately injured themselves as compared to over a third of those in foster homes.

It appears then that in a number of ways the residential care sector was dealing with some of the more difficult adolescents in our study. In addition, the average age at the time of interview of the children in residential care was a little higher than the average for those in foster settings. What then were the differences in the quality of care provided for the young people in residential and foster care?

Using the Looking After Children schedules to compare the care offered to children in the two sectors, a higher quality of care was recorded in more areas for those young people in foster care than for those in residential homes. Nonetheless, in some areas children's homes did better than foster placements. The children in residential care had less good health care, engaged in more behaviours which put their health at risk such as smoking and taking drugs, got on less well with other young people in the placement, were less well attached to their caregivers, received less praise and physical affection from them and less often received effective treatment for their emotional and behavioural problems. On the other hand the young people who were fostered were less involved in sports and clubs, more often had insufficient knowledge about their past and more often lacked adequate contact with their birth families (Berridge, 1997). These differences in what was provided in the two sectors were reflected in the somewhat better outcomes for children in foster as compared with residential care. The behaviour of more children in foster as opposed to residential care improved during the index placement, their sexual behaviour was better managed and more of them had their principal needs met. Moreover, slightly more of the caregivers in foster care were well engaged with the children when compared with those in residential settings.

These findings about the dimensions of outcome were reinforced by evidence about the overall outcomes of the children in the study. More of the children in foster homes (32%) than residential care (19%) had good overall outcomes and half as many had poor outcomes (21% as compared to 43%). The children's own views of their placements were very much in line with these findings.

The generally poorer outcomes achieved by the residential sector when compared with foster care have to be seen in the context of the higher levels of disturbance of the young people entering residential care. Nonetheless, there were examples of excellent practice in a number of the children's homes in our study, when staff were committed to helping particular young people and worked imaginatively with the fieldworker to achieve their aims.

THE NEEDS OF THE RESIDENTIAL WORKERS AND FOSTER CARERS

Overall, about half of both the foster carers and the residential workers reported that they were experiencing considerable stress in looking after the young people in the study. Managing young people's unpredictable and aggressive behaviour and self-harm, the emotional burden of dealing with very sexualised behaviour and fears that allegations would be made against them were all causes of stress. Over half of the foster carers felt that their needs for support from social services departments were not being met and this was true for a third of residential workers. Given the extent of the young people's disturbance and the trauma in their lives there was a clear need for better training for their caregivers, increased levels of support and regular supervision for residential workers. It was surprising that regular consultancy to the caregivers by outside specialists was so rarely provided (see also Berridge and Brodie, 1998) yet this is a means by which practice could readily be improved and more support supplied at a low cost to local authorities. Without such training and support the job for caregivers who were attempting to give the young people a secure base and keep them and other children safe from harm was a very difficult and sometimes overwhelming one.

Our findings suggest that the poor outcomes for some of the looked after young people, particularly the adolescents showing sexualised behaviour, most of whom were girls, and the young people who were involved in prostitution, stem, in part, from the lack of practice ideas and frameworks to help them. There is an urgent need for priority to be given both to the development of practice ideas in these areas and to the establishment of improved systems of training, consultancy and support for the caregivers who are charged with the responsibility of caring for these disadvantaged and needy young people.

Overall, the research highlights the need for greater sophistication in our approach to young people who live away from their families in public care. They are not all the same. The backgrounds of sexually abused and abusing children are significantly more disrupted and disadvantaged than non-abused young people but this is not reflected in their care and management. From the sexually abused and/or abusing children distinct sub-groups are identifiable. These could provide a basis for the development of more differentiated policy and practice to meet the particular needs of each group. Given the pain and exploitation in their backgrounds these children deserve no less

REFERENCES

Achenbach T.M. (1991a) *Manual for the Child Behavior Checklist/4–18 and 1991 Profile*, Burlington VT, University of Vermont Department of Psychiatry.

Achenbach, T.M. (1991b) *Manual for the Youth Self-Report and 1991 Profile*, Burlington VT, University of Vermont Department of Psychiatry.

Aldgate J. and Tunstill J. (1995) *Making Sense of Section 17. Implementing Services for Children in Need within the 1989 Children Act*, London, HMSO.

Barker M. and Morgan R. (1993) *Sex Offenders: A Framework for the Evaluation of Community-Based Treatment*, Report for the Home Office, Faculty of Law, University of Bristol.

Barnardo's (1996) *Streets and Lanes Annual Report, April 1995–March 1996*, Ilford, Barnardo's.

Barrett D. (ed.) (1997a) *Child Prostitution in Britain: Dilemmas and Responses*, London, The Children's Society.

Barrett D. (1997b) 'Conclusion: Where from here?', in Barrett D. (ed.) *Child Prostitution in Britain: Dilemmas and Responses*, London, The Children's Society.

Bebbington A. and Miles J. (1989) The Background of Children who Enter Local Authority Care, *British Journal of Social Work*, 19(5), 349–368.

Becker J.V. (1990) Treating adolescent sex offenders, *Professional Psychology: Research and Practice*, 21(5), 362–365.

Becker J.V., Kaplan M.S., Tenke C.E. and Tartaglini A. (1991) 'The incidence of depressive symptomatology in juvenile sex offenders with a history of abuse', *Child Abuse and Neglect*, 15, 531–536.

Beitchmann J.H., Zucker K.J., Hood J.E., DaCosta G.A. and Akman D. (1991) 'A review of the short-term effects of child sexual abuse', *Child Abuse and Neglect*, 15, 537–556.

Beitchmann J.H., Zucker K.J., Hood J.E., DaCosta G.A., Akman D. and Cassavia E. (1992) 'A review of the long-term effects of child sexual abuse', *Child Abuse and Neglect*, 16, 101–118.

Berridge D. (1997) *Foster Care: A Research Review*, London, Stationery Office.

Berridge D. and Brodie I. (1998) *Children's Homes Revisited*, London, Jessica Kingsley.

Berridge D. and Cleaver H. (1987) *Foster Home Breakdown*, Oxford, Blackwell.

Biehal N., Clayden J., Stein M. and Wade J. (1992) *Prepared for Living? A survey of young people leaving the care of three local authorities*, London, National Children's Bureau.

Bremner J. and Hillin A. (1994) *Sexuality, Young People and Care*, Lyme Regis, Russell House Publishing.

Brown A. (1993) 'Caution assessments for adolescent sexual offenders: Shropshire Adolescent Sexual Offenders Programme', *Nota News*, (March), 24–36.

Burch M. (1991) 'A foster carer's view', in Batty D. (ed) *Sexually Abused Children: Making their placements work*, London, British Agencies for Adoption and Fostering.

Burgess A. and Holmstrom L. (1978) 'Accessory-to-sex: pressure, sex and secrecy', in Burgess A. W. (ed) *Sexual Assault of Children and Adolescents*, Lexington Books, D.C. Heath.

Cavanagh C. (1992) 'Children and young people in out-of-home care: Treating and preventing individual, programmatic and systems abuse', *Children Australia*, 17 (2), 17–25.

Cavanagh Johnson T. (1993) 'Sexual behaviours: A continuum', in Gil E. and Cavanagh Johnson T. (eds) *Sexualized Children. Assessment and Treatment of Sexualized Children and Children Who Molest*, USA, Launch Press

Cawson P. (1987) 'The sexist social worker? Some gender issues in social work practice with adolescent girls', *Practice*, 1, 39–52.

Children's Legal Centre (1992) *Working with Young People, Legal Responsibilities and Liability*, Children's Legal Centre, Colchester, University of Essex.

Conte J. and Schuerman J. (1987) 'The effects of sexual abuse on children: A multidimensional view', *Journal of Interpersonal Violence*, 2, 380–390.

Conte J.R. and Schuerman J.R. (1987) 'Factors associated with an increased impact of child sexual abuse', *Child Abuse and Neglect*, 11, 201–211.

Creighton S.J. (1992) *Child Abuse Trends in England and Wales 1988–1990*, London, NSPCC.

Davis E., McKay B., McStae L., Pringle K. and Scott S. (1991) 'Fostering young people who have been sexually abused', in Batty D. (ed) *Sexually Abused Children: Making their placements work*, London, British Agencies for Adoption and Fostering.

Davis N. (1978) 'Prostitution: identity, career and legal economic enterprise', in Henslin J. and Sagarin E. (eds) *The Sociology of Sex*, New York, Schocken Books.

Department of Health (1988) *Protecting Children: A Guide for Social Workers Undertaking a Comprehensive Assessment*, London, HMSO.

Department of Health (1991) *The Children Act 1989 Guidance and Regulations, Volume 3 Family Placements*, and *Volume 4 Residential Care*, London, HMSO.

Department of Health (1992a) *Children and HIV, Guidance for Local Authorities*, London, HMSO.

Department of Health (1992b) *The Health of the Nation*, London, HMSO.

Department of Health (1992c) *Choosing with Care. The Report of the Committee of Inquiry into the Selection, Development and Management of Staff in Children's Homes*, London, HMSO.

Department of Health (1994) *The Child, the Court and the Video. A study of the implementation of the Memorandum of Good Practice on video interviewing of child witnesses*, Social Services Inspectorate, London, HMSO.

Department of Health (1995) *Child Protection. Messages from Research*, London, HMSO.

Devine C. and Tate I. (1991) 'An introductory training course for foster carers' in Batty D. (ed), *Sexually Abused Children: Making their placements work*, London, British Agencies for Adoption and Fostering.

Elgar M. and Head A. (1997) *From Court Process to Care Plan: An empirical study of the placement of sexually abused children.* Wolfson College, Oxford, Centre for Socio-Legal Studies.

Evans D. (1989/90) 'Section 28: Law, myth and paradox', *Critical Social Policy*, 27, 73–95.

Fanshel D., Finch S.J. and Grundy J.F. (1990) *Foster Children in a Life Course Perspective*, New York, Columbia University Press.

Farmer E. and Owen M. (1995) *Child Protection Practice: Private Risks and Public Remedies*, London, HMSO.

Farmer E. and Parker R. (1991), *Trials and Tribulations: Returning Children from Local Authority Care to their Families*, London, HMSO.

Finkelhor D. (1986) *A Sourcebook on Child Sexual Abuse*, London, Sage.

Fisher M., Marsh P., Phillips D. with Sainsbury E. (1986) *In and Out of Care: The Experiences of Children, Parents and Social Workers*, London, Batsford.

Fitzgerald J. (1991) 'Working with children who have been sexually abused', in Batty D. (ed) *Sexually Abused Children: Making their placements work*, London, British Agencies for Adoption and Fostering.

Ford N. (1991) *The Socio-Sexual Lifestyles of Young People in the South West of England*, Bristol, South Western Regional Health Authority/Institute of Population Studies.

Friedrich W.N. (1988) 'Behavior problems in sexually abused children: an adaptional perspective', in Wyatt G. E. and Powell G. J. (eds) *Lasting Effects of Child Sexual Abuse*, Beverley Hills, Sage.

Friedrich W. (1993) 'Sexual behavior in sexually abused children', *Violence Update*, 3(5), 1–11.

Friedrich W.N., Grambsch P., Broughton D., Kuiper J. and Beilke R. L. (1991) 'Normative sexual behavior in children', *Pediatrics*, 88, 456–464.

Friedrich W.N., Grambsch P., Damon L., Hewitt S.K., Koverola C., Lang R.A., Wolfe V. and Broughton D. (1992) 'Child Sexual Behavior Inventory: normative and clinical contrasts', *Psychological Assessment*, 4, 303–311

George V. (1970) *Foster Care: Theory and practice*, London, Routledge and Kegan Paul.

Ghate D. and Spencer L. (1995) *The Prevalence of Child Sexual Abuse in Britain: A feasibility study for a large-scale national survey of the general population*, London, HMSO.

Gibbons J., Conroy S. and Bell C. (1995) *Operating the Child Protection System*, London, HMSO.

Goldberg, D. (1978) *Manual of the General Health Questionnaire*, Windsor UK, NFER Nelson.

Grimshaw R. with Berridge D. (1994) *Educating Disruptive Children: Placement and progress in residential special schools for pupils with emotional and behavioural difficulties*, London, National Children's Bureau.

Grocke M. (1991) 'Family attitudes towards children's sexuality', in Batty D. (ed) *Sexually Abused Children: Making their placements work*, London, British Agencies for Adoption and Fostering.

Harter S. (1985) *The Self-Perception Profile for Children*, Denver, CO, University of Denver.

Harter S. (1987) *The Self-Perception Profile for Adolescents*, Denver, CO, University of Denver.

Head A. (1993) Letter to the Editor on separation of siblings after sexual abuse within the family, *Adoption and Fostering*, 17 (3), 7.

Hicks C. and Nixon S. (1989) 'Allegations of child abuse: foster carers as victims', *Foster Care*, June 1989, 14–15.

Hindle D. (1995) 'Thinking about siblings who are fostered', *Adoption and Fostering*, 19 (1), 14–20.

Hollows A. (1991) 'Children as abusers: where are we starting from?' in Hollows A. and Armstrong H. (eds) *Children and Young People as Abusers*, London, National Children's Bureau.

Holmes T.H. and Rahe R.H. (1967) 'The Social Re-adjustment Rating Scale', *Journal of Psychsomatic Research*, 11, 213–218.

Home Office, Department of Health, Department of Education and Science, Welsh Office (1991) *Working Together Under the Children Act 1989. A guide to arrangements for inter-agency co-operation for the protection of children from abuse*, London, HMSO.

Hoorwitz A.N. (1983) 'Guidelines for treating father–daughter incest', *Social Casework*, November, 515–524.

Hudson A. (1989) '"Troublesome Girls.' Towards alternative definitions and policies"', in Cain M. (ed) *Growing Up Good: Policing the behaviour of girls in Europe*, London, Sage.

Hymel S., Bowker A. and Woody E. (1993) 'Aggressive versus withdrawn unpopular children: Variations in peer and self-perceptions in multiple dimensions', *Child Development*, 64, 879–896.

James J. and Meyerding J. (1977) 'Early sexual experience as a factor in prostitution', *Archives of Sexual Behaviour*, 7, 31–42.

Jesson J. (1993) 'Understanding adolescent female prostitution: A literature review', *British Journal of Social Work*, 23 (5), 517–530.

Jones E. and Parkinson P. (1995) 'Child sexual abuse, access and the wishes of children', *International Journal of Law and the Family*, 9 (1), 54–85.

Kelly L. (1988) *Surviving Sexual Violence*, Cambridge, Polity Press.

Kendall-Tackett K.A., Meyer Williams L. and Finkelhor D. (1993) 'Impact of sexual abuse on children: A review and synthesis of recent empirical studies', *Psychological Bulletin*, 113 (1), 164–180.

Kirkwood A. (1993) *The Leicestershire Inquiry 1992. The Report of an Inquiry into Aspects of the Management of Children's Homes in Leicestershire Between 1973 and 1986*, Leicestershire County Council.

Kjeldsen M. (1991) *Outreach Work with Young Men involved in the 'Rent Scene' of Central London 1988/1989*, Ilford, Streetwise Youth, Barnardo's.

Kosonen M. (1994) 'Sibling relationships for children in the care system', *Adoption and Fostering*, 18 (3), 30–35.

Kovacs M. (1982) *The Children's Depression Inventory: A self-rated depression scale for school-aged youngsters*, Pittsburgh PA, University of Pittsburgh.

Kovacs, M. and Beck, A.T. (1977), 'An empirical clinical approach towards a definition of childhood depression', in Schulterbrandt, J. G. and Raskin, A. (eds) *Depression in Children: Diagnosis, treatment and conceptual models*, New York, Raven.

Lambert R., Bullock R. and Millham S. (1975) *The Chance of a Lifetime? A Study of Boarding Education*, London, Weidenfeld and Nicolson.

Lambert R. with Millham S. (1968) *The Hothouse Society*, London, Weidenfeld and Nicolson.

Lee M. and O'Brien R. (1995) *The Game's Up. Redefining Child Prostitution*, London, The Children's Society.

Lees S. (1986) *Losing Out: Sexuality and adolescent girls*, London, Hutchinson Education.

Levy A. and Kahan B. (1991) *The Pindown Experience and the Protection of Children. The Report of the Staffordshire Child Care Inquiry 1990*, Staffordshire County Council.

Lie G. and McMurtry S.L. (1991) 'Foster care for sexually abused children: A comparative study', *Child Abuse and Neglect*, 15 (1/2), 111–121.

Livingstone Smith S. and Howard J.A. (1994) 'The impact of previous sexual abuse on children's adjustment in adoptive placement', *Social Work*, 39 (5), 491–501.

Lowe M. I. and Verity P. (1989) 'The right to dignity, fairness and compassion', *Foster Care*, 57, 14–15.

Lowman J. (1987) 'Taking young prostitutes seriously', *Canadian Review of Sociology and Anthropology*, 24 (1), 99–116.

Macaskill C. (1991) *Adopting or Fostering a Sexually Abused Child*, London, Batsford.

Martin G. (1993) 'Foster care: the protection and training of carers' children', *Child Abuse Review*, 2 (1), 15–22.

McFadden E. J. (1986) *Fostering the Child who has been Sexually Abused*, Michigan Department of Social Services and Institute for the Study of Children and Families, Ypsilanti MI, Eastern Michigan University.

McFadden E.J. (1987) 'The sexually abused child in specialised foster care', Paper presented at the First North American Conference on Treatment Foster Care, Minneapolis, Minnesota, USA.

McFadden E.J. and Ryan P. (1986) 'Characteristics of the vulnerable child', Paper presented at the Sixth International Conference on Child Abuse and Neglect, Sydney, Australia.

McFadden E.J. and Stovall B. (1984) 'Child sexual abuse in family foster care', *Preventing Abuse in Foster Care*, Ypsilanti MI, Eastern Michigan University.

McFadden E.J., Ziefert M. and Stovall B. (1984) *Preventing Abuse in Family Foster Care*, Instructor's Manual, Institute for the Study of Children and Families, Ypsilanti, MI, Eastern Michigan University.

Millham S., Bullock R. and Cherrett P. (1975) *After Grace – Teeth*, Brighton, Human Context Books.

Monck E. and New M. (1996), *Report of a Study of Sexually Abused Children and Adolescents, and of Young Perpetrators of Sexual Abuse Who Were Treated in Voluntary Agency Community Facilities*, London, HMSO.

Morrison T. (1992) 'Discussion group: adolescent sexual offenders: prosecution or diversion?', *Nota News*, (December), 38–40.

Morrison T. (1994) 'Context, constraints and considerations for practice', in Morrison T., Erooga M. and Beckett R. C. (eds) *Sexual Offending against Children. Assessment and Treatment of Male Abusers*, London, Routledge.

Morrison T., Erooga M. and Beckett R.C. (1994) *Sexual Offending against Children. Assessment and Treatment of Male Abusers*, London, Routledge.

National Children's Home (1992) *The Report of the Committee of Enquiry into Children and Young People who Sexually Abuse Other Children*, London, National Children's Home.

National Foster Care Association (1988), *Policy and Practice Guidelines No.1: Agency Procedures for Handling Complaints Against Foster Carers*, London, National Foster Care Association.

National Foster Care Association (1993) 'Fostering a Child who has been Sexually Abused', *Signposts in Foster Care*, London, National Foster Care Association.

National Foster Care Association (1994) *Safe Caring*, London, National Foster Care Association.

Nixon S. and Hicks C. (1989), 'Unsubstantiated Accusations of Abuse: A Survey of Foster Carers' Experiences', unpublished report.

Nobbs K. and Jones B. (1989) 'Tread with care: Fostering sexually abused children', *After Abuse. Papers on Caring and Planning for a Child who has been Sexually Abused*, London, British Agencies for Adoption and Fostering.

Nowicki S. and Strickland B. R. (1973) 'A Locus of Control Scale for Children', *Journal of Consulting and Clinical Psychology*, 40 (1), 148–154

Nunno M.A. and, Motz J.K. (1988) 'The development of an effective response to the abuse of children in out-of-home care', *Child Abuse and Neglect*, 12 (4), 521–528.

Nunno M. and Rindfleisch N. (1991) 'The abuse of children in out of home care', *Children and Society*, 5 (4), 295–305.

O'Callaghan D. and Print B. (1994) 'Adolescent sex abusers: research, assessment and treatment', in Morrison T., Erooga M. and Beckett R. C. (eds) *Sexual Offending against Children: Assessment and treatment of male abusers*, London, Routledge.

O'Neill M., Goode N. and Hopkins K. (1995) 'Juvenile prostitution: the experience of young women in residential care', *Childright*, No.113, 14–16.

Packman J. and Hall C. (1998) *From Care to Accommodation: Support, Protection and Control in Child Care Services*, London, The Stationery Office.

Parker R. (1966) *Decision in Child Care*, London, Allen and Unwin.

Parker R.A. (1990) *Away from Home. A Short History of Provision for Separated Children*, Barnardo's Practice Paper, Ilford, Barnardo's.

Parker R., Ward H., Jackson S., Aldgate J. and Wedge P. (eds) (1991) *Looking After Children. Assessing Outcomes in Child Care*, London, HMSO.

Parkin, W. (1989) 'Private experiences in the public domain: sexuality and residential care organisations', in Hearn J., Sheppard D., Tancred-Sheriff P. and Burrell G. (eds) *The Sexuality of Organisation*, London and Newbury Park CA, Sage.

Part D. (1993) 'Fostering as seen by the carers' children', *Adoption and Fostering*, 17, (1), 26–31.

Quinton D., Rushton A., Dance C. and Mayes D. (forthcoming) *Joining New Families: Adoption and Fostering in Middle Childhood*, Chichester, Wiley.

Quinton D. and Rutter M. (1988) *Parenting Breakdown. The Making and Breaking of Inter-generational Links*, Aldershot, Avebury.

Rickford R. (1992) 'Endangered species', *Community Care*, 24 (5), 12.

Roberts J. (1989) 'Fostering the sexually abused child', *After Abuse. Papers on Caring and Planning for a Child who has been Sexually Abused*, London, British Agencies for Adoption and Fostering.

Rosenberg, M. (1965), *Society and the Adolescent Self-Image*, Princeton NJ, Princeton University Press.

Rosenthal J.A., Motz J.K., Edmonson D.A. and Groze, V. (1991) 'A descriptive study of abuse and neglect in out-of-home placement', *Child Abuse and Neglect*, 15 (3), 249–260.

Ryan P., McFadden E. and Weicek M.A. (1992) 'An analysis of maltreatment in family foster care in the United States', Presentation to the Ninth International Congress on Child Abuse and Neglect, Chicago, August 31.

Ryan P., McFadden E.J. and Wiencek P. (1986), *Analyzing Abuse in Family Foster Care*, Final Report to the National Center on Child Abuse and Neglect, Ypsilanti, Michigan, Eastern Michigan University.

Ryburn M. (1994) *Open Adoption: Research, theory and practice*, Aldershot, Avebury.

Schofield M. (1968) *The Sexual Behaviour of Young People*, Harmondsworth, Penguin.

Scottish Office (1995) *Guidance for Residential Workers Caring for Young People who have been Sexually Abused and Those who Abuse Others*, Caring for Scotland's Children, The Centre for Residential Child Care, Glasgow.

Secretary of State for Social Services (1988) *Report of the Inquiry into Child Abuse in Cleveland 1987*, Cm. 412, London, HMSO.

Sharland E., Seal H., Croucher M., Aldgate J. and Jones D. (1996) *Professional Intervention in Child Sexual Abuse*, London, HMSO.

Shaw I. and Butler I. (1998) 'Understanding Young People and Prostitution: A Foundation for Practice?', *British Journal of Social Work*, 28, 177–196.

Shaw I., Butler I., Crowley A. and Patel G.(1996) *Paying the Price? Young People and Prostitution*, School of Social and Administrative Studies, University of Wales, Cardiff.

Silbert M.H. and Pines A.M. (1981) 'Sexual abuse as an antecedent to prostitution', *Child Abuse and Neglect*, 5, 407–411.

Sinclair I. and Gibbs I. (1998) *Children's Homes: A Study in Diversity*, Chichester, Wiley.

Skuse D., Bentovim A., Hodges J., Stevenson J., Andreou C., Lanyado M., Williams B., New M. and McMillan D. (1996) 'The influence of early experience of sexual abuse on the formation of sexual preferences during adolescence', Report to the Department of Health, London, Behavioural Sciences Unit, Institute of Child Health.

Smith G. (1989) 'Personal and professional issues in child sexual abuse', *After Abuse. Papers on Caring and Planning for a Child who has been Sexually Abused*, London, British Agencies for Adoption and Fostering.

Smith G. (1995a) *The Protectors' Handbook. Reducing the Risk of Child Sexual Abuse and Helping Children Recover*, London, The Women's Press.

Smith G. (1995b) 'Do children have the right to leave their pasts behind them? Contact with children who have been abused', in Argent H. (ed) *See You Soon: Contact with looked after children*, London, British Agencies for Adoption and Fostering.

Smith G. (1996) 'Brotherly love: Ambiguities of peer abuse', Paper presented to the Learning to Change Conference, Barnardo's, March 1996.

Smith M. and Bentovim A. (1994) 'Sexual abuse', in Rutter M., Taylor E. and Hersov L. (eds) *Child and Adolescent Psychiatry: Modern approaches*, Oxford, Blackwell.

Stein M., Rees G. and Frost N. (1994) *Running the Risk: Young People on the Streets of Britain Today*, London, The Children's Society.

Trasler G. (1960) *In Place of Parents*, London, Routledge and Kegan Paul.

Triseliotis J. (1989) 'Foster care outcomes – a review of key research findings', *Adoption and Fostering*, 15 (3), 5–26.

Utting Sir William (1991) *Children in the Public Care. A Review of Residential Child Care*, Social Services Inspectorate, London, HMSO.

Utting Sir William (1997) *People Like Us: The report of the review of the safeguards for children living away from home*, Department of Health and the Welsh Office, London, Stationery Office.

Verity P. and Nixon S. (1995) 'Allegations against foster families', *Foster Care*, October 1995, 13–16 and January 1996, 11–14.

Vizard E., Monck E. and Misch P. (1995) 'Child and adolescent sex abuse perpetrators: A review of the research literature', *Journal of Child Psychology and Psychiatry*, 36 (5), 731–756

Vizard E., Wynick S., Hawkes C., Woods J. and Jenkins J. (1996) 'Juvenile sexual offenders. Assessment issues', *British Journal of Psychiatry*, 168, 259–262.

Walsh J. A. (1981) 'Risk factors, superior adaptive capacity and characteristics of the foster home as predictors of maintenance of foster placement', University of Montana, paper presented at Western Psychological Association, LA, USA, April 1981.

Ward H. (ed) (1995) *Looking After Children: Research into practice*, London, HMSO.

Westcott H.L. (1991) *Institutional Abuse of Children – From Research to Policy: A Review*, Policy, Practice, Research Series, London, NSPCC.

Westcott H. and Clement M. (1992) *NSPCC Experience of Child Abuse in Residential Care and Educational Placements: Results of a Survey*, London, NSPCC.

Whitaker D., Archer L. and Hicks L. (1998) *Working in Children's Homes: Challenges and complexities*, Chichester, Wiley.

Whitaker D.S., Cook J., Dunne C. and Rocliffe S. (1984) *The Experience of Residential Care from the Perspectives of Children, Parents and Caregivers*, Final Report to the SSRC, Department of Social Policy and Social Work, University of York.

Widom C.S. and Ames M.A. (1994) 'Criminal consequences of childhood sexual victimisation', *Child Abuse and Neglect* 18 (4), 303–318.

Williams G. and McCreadie J. (1992) *Ty Mawr Community Home Inquiry*, Gwent County Council.

Wyatt G.E. and Peters S.D. (1986) 'Issues in the definition of child sexual abuse', *Child Abuse and Neglect*, 10, 231–240.

INDEX

Related titles of interest from Wiley...

From Hearing to Healing
Working with the Aftermath of Child Sexual Abuse, 2nd Edition
Anne Bannister
Published in association with the NSPCC
0-471-98298-9   216pp   1998   Paperback

Making Sense of the Children Act
Third Edition
Nicholas Allen
0-471-97831-0   304pp   1998   Paperback

Women Who Sexually Abuse Children
From Research to Clinical Practice
Jacqui Saradjian in association with Helga Hanks
Wiley Series in Child Care & Protection
0-471-96072-1   336pp   1996   Paperback

The Emotionally Abused and Neglected Child
Identification, Assessment and Intervention
Dorota Iwaniec
Wiley Series in Child Care & Protection
0-471-95579-5   222pp   1995   Paperback

Cycles of Child Maltreatment
Facts, Fallacies and Interventions
Ann Buchanan
Wiley Series in Child Care & Protection
0-471-95889-1   328pp   1996   Paperback

 ## Child Abuse Review
ISSN: 0952-9136

 ## Children & Society
Published in association with the National Children's Bureau
ISSN: 0951-0605